AGAINST THE GRAIN

Eugene "Mercury" Morris

with Steve Fiffer

McGRAW-HILL BOOK COMPANY

New York St. Louis San Francisco Auckland
Bogotá Hamburg London Madrid Mexico Milan
Montreal New Delhi Panama Paris São Paulo
Singapore Sydney Tokyo Toronto

I have attempted to repeat conversations as they actually occurred. As a result, readers might want to take note that some
language in the book might be objectionable. I have also
changed the names of a few individuals to protect their iden-
tities.

1 2 3 4 5 6 7 8 9 DOC DOC 8 9 2 1 0 9 8

ISBN 0-07-043195-7

Morris, Eugene.
    Against the grain / Eugene Morris with Steve Fiffer.
      p. cm.
    ISBN 0-07-043195-7
    1. Morris, Eugene. 2. Football players—United States—
Biography. 3. Football players—United States—Drug use—Case
studies. 4. Cocaine habit—United States—Case studies. I. Fiffer,
Steve. II. Title.
GV939.M64A3 1988   796.332'092'4—dc19
    [B]   87-36631
                                                  CIP

Book design by Kathryn Parise

For my grandparents Mary and Flun Smith
and my parents, Jacquline and George Morris—
by loving me you taught me how to love.

I miss you all.

ACKNOWLEDGMENTS

As the title of this book suggests, I have for as long as I can remember gone *against the grain*. These acknowledgments are in keeping with that. I wish to acknowledge not only the people who helped me with this book, but also the people who helped me get to the place in my life where I could even think about writing a book.

In this latter category are my parents and grandparents, to whom the book is dedicated. In addition, there is my wonderful wife, Bobbie, who under the most difficult circumstances kept our family together and thriving and was a constant source of strength for me. She still is. My children, too, deserve recognition; Maceo, Duke, Tiffany, and our newborn twins, Elliott and Jarrett, have been a source of joy and pride.

I have had a number of coaches in my life—some on the football field, some off. They have all been important. The lessons I learned in athletics from Jack Gerber, Al Shriver, Charlie Avallone, Joe Kerbel, and Don Shula were just as applicable to life outside athletics. The spiritual and emotional guidance I received from Pastor Nick Schubert, Chaplain Joe Hunt, Dr. Clarence Crier, and Russ Buckhalt was equally significant in other areas of my life. The many friends I have made in football, in prison, and in my travels have also helped to bring me to where I am today.

A special thanks must go to Ron Strauss, my attorney and friend. His loyalty and persistence, as well as his skill, are a major reason why I am no longer sitting in a prison cell.

Ron helped in reviewing certain chapters of this book, as did my manager and friend, Blair Hull. It is a rare manager who can suc-

ACKNOWLEDGMENTS

cessfully wear the hat of literary critic, but Blair does it well. She contributed greatly to the material which follows. Sharon Fiffer has also provided input. Thanks, too, to our editor, Tom Quinn. Finally, I wish to acknowledge my co-author, Steve Fiffer, who was perhaps the only person capable of helping me tell my story.

Eugene Morris
South Miami, Florida

CONTENTS

INTRODUCTION

When I was about fifteen months into my mandatory fifteen-year prison sentence at Dade Correctional Institute in southern Florida, I was moved from one room to another. (I called the living quarters "rooms"; others called them "cells.") There was something special about this new room. It had a view.

My old room had looked in on the prison compound. This new room looked *out*. I had a wonderful, wide-angle-lens view of a huge field that ran in front of the institution.

It's hard to convey how important a view is. If you're facing inside, you begin to focus on being there, on being inside. If you're facing outside, then your thoughts can be outside, your dreams can be unlimited.

Looking out my window, I saw that the field—it must have been 150 acres—had been cleared. There was a cluster of trees, but otherwise it was just empty, level ground. Why is it like this? I asked myself. Easy. If somebody escapes, there's cover from the trees, but then there's all that open space. The cops will be able to get the dogs and surround anyone out there.

I was wrong. The level ground was actually a cornfield. It just happened to be in between planting seasons when I got my room. Soon, however, the next cycle began. One day I looked out my window and saw that there was a great deal of activity. Migrant workers were clearing the land of weeds. It seemed such a huge task. How are these people going to do it? I wondered. But by the next day, the field was cleared. I was mesmerized. I watched every day. The planting began, and after the planting came the growth.

I am a man who once got his kicks out of driving cars 150 miles per hour on Interstate 95. I had never taken the opportunity to slow down long enough to watch anything. Now, it became a daily adventure to watch the cornfield progress. The corn plants began to poke up through the soil. They got taller and taller until the field had become a sea of green. Flowing green. When a breeze would blow across that vast space, you could see the ripples turn into a flow. It looked like someone was fanning the whole field, purposefully fanning it to create so many different shades of green. It didn't take me too long to draw a comparison between my life and the life of the cornfield. There were a lot of weeds in my life that had to be cleared out before I could grow, too.

Since the weather was so warm, the field went through three planting cycles a year. As Christmas 1984 came, I told myself, I love watching the corn grow, but I don't want to be here to see it next Christmas. I knew that might be a reality. Unless the Florida Supreme Court overturned my conviction for cocaine trafficking, I would be spending every Christmas until 1997 behind bars. Picture that.

The field was only 50 or 60 yards away in distance, but maybe as many as thirteen years away in time. I can't even go from right here to right there, I thought. It was a depressing notion. My two boys, Maceo and Duke, would be grown by then; my little girl, Tiffany, would be 16. My mother had died shortly after I had been sentenced; who knew if my father would still be alive. And what about the burden on my wife, Bobbie?

I quickly dismissed this unpleasant scene from my mind. It just wasn't possible. I had been raised to believe in the American system of justice, and, despite some pretty devastating setbacks, I continued to believe in the system. After all, I reminded myself, I have the greatest weapon on my side—the truth.

This is not to say that I had not made some very bad mistakes of my own. I had, and for these I took (and continue to take) full responsibility. But I simply did not believe that I was guilty of the crimes for which I had been charged and convicted. Justice will eventually prevail, I kept repeating.

While I ended up spending Christmas of 1985 in prison, my faith in the system was finally rewarded a few months later when the

Florida Supreme Court overturned my conviction and ordered a new trial. This was what I had wanted so badly for the three and a half years that I'd been incarcerated: a chance to present all relevant evidence and vindicate myself in a fair trial before a jury of my peers—something I had not received the first time around.

This may sound hard to believe, but this need for vindication was every bit as important to me as my freedom. I guess I couldn't be totally free until I had unloosed myself from the bondage of the charges.

In dreaming of the day when the conviction would be overturned, I had considered the various courses of action which would be open to me. I could have my day in court again or, in all likelihood, I could cut a deal with the Dade County State Attorney's office—probably plead guilty to a lesser charge and have the time already served in prison count as my sentence. This latter approach had its benefits. I could emerge from prison without the risk of another trial and another conviction, then go home and make up for the three and a half years spent away from my wife and kids.

I had had the opportunity to make a deal with the State Attorney ever since I had been arrested. Like Dorothy in *The Wizard of Oz*, all I had to do was the equivalent of click my heels three times and I could get home. But I had always resisted such deals. I wasn't guilty, and I had to vindicate myself for my parents.

My parents. I felt I had let them down so badly—not just with the conviction but with my life-style in general. I had been so selfish during those years when I should have been giving back to them what they had given to me. They had been behind me from the day I was first arrested. But I knew I had disappointed them. A verdict of "not guilty"—a demonstration that I may have been guilty of bad judgment but not the crimes for which I had been charged—would be the first step in starting over.

While my mother was now gone—she died of cancer at age 51 a week after I was sentenced—I felt I could at least do something for my father. And then, less than a week after the conviction was overturned, my father was gone, too—dead of cancer at age 54.

We wear many hats over a lifetime. With my father's death, I took off the hat marked, "Son," and replaced it with one marked, "Head of the Family." My responsibility was now solely to Bobbie and my children. It was time to move forward. Without pleading guilty to any charges, I was able to enter a plea of convenience and leave prison. In effect the state of Florida and I agreed to stop fighting each other.

Moving forward does not mean forgetting where you have been. The best thing I can do for my parents (and my children) is look outward instead of inward and share my experiences—the bad ones as well as the good ones—with the world, particularly the young. That is why I have written this book, and that is why I spend a tremendous amount of time traveling around the country talking to students, community and business leaders, government officials, and others.

I feel blessed to have been given this second chance and feel strongly about using it to good advantage. I can think of no greater compliment than: "He made a difference." I hope my story will make a difference.

CHAPTER 1

HALFTIME

Like most people in Miami, the prisoners at Dade County Jail love football, and when the Dolphins take the field, the other activities—the diceplaying, the winemaking, the fighting—stop while everyone gathers around the radio. Actually, the distance between the jail and the Orange Bowl (where the team played until it moved to a new arena, Joe Robbie Stadium, in 1987) is only about 1000 yards, so close that you can hear the roar of the crowd and the echo of the stadium loudspeakers through the open windows in cell block 5.

On Sunday, November 7, 1982, those loudspeakers announced the return of the 1972 Dolphins, one of the greatest teams in the history of football—undefeated in all seventeen games played that year, the winner of Super Bowl VII, a team that with very few changes in personnel also went on to win Super Bowl VIII. Almost everyone from the squad had come back to commemorate that championship season. "Bob Griese, Earl Morrall, Paul Warfield, Larry Csonka, Jim Kiick, Larry Little," the voice on the loudspeaker blared, and the stars trotted out, "...Nick Buoniconti, Manny Fernandez, Garo Yepremian...Coach Don Shula."

Over the summer, I had received an invitation to the festivities and had every intention of going; I'd left a hospital bed to attend a similar event a few years earlier. But I confess, until almost every other prisoner in my cell called my attention to it, I'd forgotten that this was the day of the tenth reunion of the team for which I started at running back, gained 1000 yards, and was named All-Pro. All I knew was that this was my second full day behind bars and that it was proving a lot harder to get out of this jam than anything I'd ever encountered in the Orange Bowl or anywhere else.

To put it mildly, in between the time I'd received that reunion invitation and the reunion itself, things had not worked out quite as I expected. On August 18, I'd been busted by the Dade County authorities for cocaine trafficking, and on November 5, despite my well-documented defense that I had been set up or, in legal terms, entrapped, a jury had convicted me of four of the six counts that had been brought against me.

So I wasn't particularly interested in listening to the game or re-living what now seemed like the ancient past; my mind was on one thing: getting out of this jackpot. But one by one the other prisoners in cell 5A3 kept coming up to me:

"Hey, Merc, I listened to the whole thing and the Dolphins talked about every player, but they never mentioned your name."

"Say, man, it's like you never even existed."

I wasn't too surprised. I hadn't received any offers of assistance, any communications at all from the team in the days since the bust. My relations with owner Joe Robbie, of whom I wasn't particularly fond, and Shula, whose coaching ability I had always respected, had been strained for some time. Moreover, the climate of the times was not right for hearing from the front office. This was 1982, a few years before the wave of stories about the widespread use of cocaine in football, baseball, basketball, and every other major sport, and a few years before the tragic deaths of Lenny Bias and Donny Rogers opened a lot of people's eyes to the reality that athletes are human and vulnerable like everyone else and that the sports world is nothing more than a microcosm of the real world. The climate wasn't right for hearing from players either. I'd heard from only one of my teammates, the All-Pro guard Larry Little, who had been a long-time friend.

I couldn't be angry at such silent treatment. I'm a great believer in accountability. I and nobody else was the one responsible for my predicament. It was *my* habit that had gotten so bad that at the time of the arrest I was in danger of losing my family, friends, house, and other possessions (I'd already lost my self-esteem and my business). While I had not been dealing or trafficking in cocaine—the principal charges for which I'd been arrested—I had been a heavy user in recent years. Never as a pro, but frequently after I retired in 1976.

Although I wasn't surprised or angry that my current troubles were enough to erase me from the history of the Dolphins, I was hurt. But I wasn't going to let *anybody* know that, particularly the guys in my cell, most of whom seemed to have tremendous respect for me, and the guards, most of whom seemed to enjoy giving me grief whenever the opportunity presented itself. "I don't give a damn about any reunion," I told anyone who asked. I wasn't the kind of guy who wore my heart on the outside of my shirt. Yet, I secretly hoped that some of my teammates would come see me after the game.

One did. Paul Warfield, the classy Hall-of-Famer, who was the best wide receiver I ever saw play the game. While we had our share of wild men on the Dolphins, Paul was just about as straight as they come. (Until recently, he served as Director of Player Relations for the Cleveland Browns—that means he helped players with their lives off the field—a great idea that, unfortunately, didn't exist when we played.) And here he was at Dade County.

Paul was my very first visitor *period*. My wife, Bobbie, and my kids—6-month-old daughter, Tiffany, and 11-year-old sons, Maceo and Duke—had not been allowed to see me because the day for family visits had not yet arrived.

The steps that were necessary just to get from my cell to see Paul or my family or any other visitors will give you some idea of what it's like to lose your freedom. First, I had to go through the rolling bar doors from the cell I shared with about thirty other prisoners to a tiny attached compartment. Once I was in that compartment, the guards closed the doors to the cell behind me. This prevented other prisoners from rushing out at the same time. Then, the guards stood me on a spot near a door which led to the outside and, like on *Star Trek*, "beamed me up," or more accurately, out. After passing through the door, I was led down a hallway and placed in another cell.

This cell is about the size of a small closet. Its drab walls are covered with the graffiti and idle doodlings of visits past. A window divides the room in half. Loved ones and visitors must stand on one side of the window; inmates must stand on the other side. Apparently, communication was once accomplished by telephone. You can see where a phone was pulled out of the wall.

Now you just talk through the window. In the window there is a steel grate. Neither cleanliness or the facilitation of conversation is a high priority of the jailkeepers. The grate is clogged with the soot and dust from years and years of visits, making it difficult to speak or hear; you have to bend over, cock your neck and talk, then stop and listen carefully while the person across from you does the same thing.

Paul was very encouraging. "Well, Merc, I don't know what you've done," he said, "but you've got my support and I want you to hang in there the best you can."

I think that's when it really hit me. My conviction carried with it a minimum mandatory sentence of fifteen years. Sentencing was set for January 20, just two months away. Unless my post-trial motions proved successful or unless I agreed to "play ball" with the Dade County State Attorney, there was a good chance that I would be hanging in there until that same Dolphins team was holding its quarter-century reunion. I tried to hold back the tears. I'd been telling myself all day that I wasn't going to let this reunion thing get to me. The last thing in the world I wanted to do was cry in front of Paul, a former teammate. But there was nothing I could do. I broke down and wept.

If I hadn't felt so strongly that I'd been unjustly convicted, the conditions in my cell alone might have been enough to persuade me to cut a deal with the State Attorney. When most people think of a cell, they think of two guys sharing a room behind bars. That's prison, not jail. There were thirty of us in a 50- by 20-foot space designed for twenty. We were all Black, and half our number were awaiting trial, sentencing, or shipment to prison on murder charges.

In the cell there were ten double bunk beds, one toilet, a shower, and a small day room with a television set. I think that by the time Paul came to see me I had a bed. The first night I slept on the floor because the bunks—metal slabs topped by thin, worn, stinking mattresses—were all taken. Who cares about where an inmate sleeps? Or how? Or if?

Someone had torn a sheet in half and put it up around the john. You take your privacy wherever you can get it. The sheet couldn't hide the smell. "Hey, that's no electric chair... yet! Mash that button, man."

I wasn't kidding when I said that winemaking was a popular pastime. You had to be impressed by the creativity of the would-be Gallo Brothers. They made their stuff out of fruit—orange juice and plums were especially popular—or anything else they could get their hands on. I knew some guys who made it out of Lysol. Lysol! And

4

then they drank it. Of course, they got drunk. That led to visits from the guards, which led to shakedowns where we all got taken out of the cell while the guards searched for the "buck." They acted so surprised. As if you couldn't smell that stuff a mile away.

As you might guess, this environment does not lend itself to peace or quiet. The guys in jail reminded me a little of the guys in the locker room—with one big exception. Prisoners find it more necessary to constantly prove their prowess than football players do. Fights broke out pretty often. And despite the fact that most of the guys wanted to get along with me, there were always a few troublemakers who wanted to see if they could mix it up with Mercury Morris.

For a long time I was ready, almost eager to meet these challenges. I had been my whole life. If you threatened me, crossed me, treated me unfair in any way, you were going to hear about it for sure and maybe even feel it. I don't care if you were a Texas punk who called me "nigger"; a Don Shula who didn't give me enough playing time; or a prison guard who felt the need to remind me that I wasn't wearing number 22 anymore. I saw life as one big, never-ending contest of "bull in the ring."

Bull in the ring is a brutal, but common, football drill designed to toughen you up physically and psychologically. I first "played" it at about age 9 in the Pop Warner League, and it was a part of our routine on my junior high school, high school, and college teams, too. We didn't do it in the pros because there was too great a chance that someone would get hurt. It goes something like this: All eleven guys on the team are assigned a secret number. When the coach calls your number, you become the "bull" and you have to get in the middle of the "ring," a circle formed by your teammates. One at a time, the coach then calls out the numbers of the guys surrounding the bull. Their job is simple: take the bull out. If you're the bull, you don't know where the next attacker is coming from. You just know that everyone is out to get you, you can never let your guard down, and that it's better to make the first move and meet the attacker head on before he can build up enough steam to knock you on your ass, which is the object of the game. This may or may not make you a better football player. But when you're not wearing your uniform and you see yourself as the bull and the rest of the world as the ring, trouble is never too far away.

While I was tempted to oblige any prisoner or guard who wanted to prove his manhood by taking out Mercury Morris, I learned very

5

quickly from a fellow prisoner, Lonnie McDuffie, to ignore these jerks. Lonnie, whose brother's death at the hands of the Miami police in 1980 had triggered the Liberty City riots, told me: "Hey, man, as long as they don't put their hands on you, let them say whatever they want." He went on to explain that the troublemakers were usually the guys who already had a truckload of time to serve and that the only kicks they got was by trying to trip up someone else.

Of course, I had a truckload of time staring me in the face, too. But at this point, I was still thinking that I'd be out and back with Bobbie and the kids real soon. I was beginning to find faith in God— a journey that would take several years to complete—and I figured He would straighten things out. I believed one of two earthly things would happen: either the motions filed by my lawyer Ron Strauss would be granted and a new trial would be ordered, or if that failed we'd immediately take our case to the Florida District Court of Appeals and get a quick and favorable ruling. I would come to find out that the criminal justice system oftens acts criminally slow and isn't always just.

The blind faith in the legal system that I had at this point, the faith I'd had since the day I had been busted, was one of the reasons I wasn't interested in the overtures of the State Attorney. This faith was not in the people running the system, but in the capital "S" System itself. Don't get me wrong. I knew the constitutional safeguards hadn't been written for me, but at the same time I knew they were available for me to use. And that was just what I was going to do. I may have been guilty of bad judgment, of stupidity, but I knew I wasn't guilty of the charges against me. I knew I'd been set up. The bottom line was that I knew I was telling the truth.

On the wall behind the judge who presided over my case was a giant inscription written in gold letters: "We who labor here seek only the truth." That inscription, coupled with the fact that the official courthouse cafeteria featured large pictures of me and teammates Griese and Csonka, had convinced me I would receive a fair trial. I hadn't. But sooner or later, I still believed, truth and justice would prevail. Thus, the offer of a reduced sentence in exchange for a guilty plea and cooperation in targeting others involved with cocaine, particularly other former National Football League players, was not attractive to me. I would never name names. That's not my style or my responsibility. Besides, by going that route I was not only admitting guilt, but also waiving any right to appeal. That was something I would never waive. I had to have a forum where I could show how the State had abused its power and entrapped me. I'd let many people down in the years since my retirement. Now, I had to vindicate myself for my parents and for Bobbie and the kids.

I'm a great fan of old movies and old television shows. One of my favorite television series when I was growing up was called *I Led Three Lives*. In it Richard Carlson played Herb Philbrick, a mild-mannered fellow who everyone thought was a spy for the Russians but was really a double agent working for the United States. Philbrick's three lives were so confusing, even to himself, that there was only one way he could keep track of what he was supposed to do, where he was supposed to be, *who* he was. This was by talking to himself: "Well, it's 6 o'clock now, I'm supposed to be in this park, meeting this guy," he'd mumble.

In prison, I found myself following the same procedure for the same reason—survival. And one of the things I'd mumble to myself was the facts of my case as I saw them and wanted the court and the world to see them. "Well, man," I'd begin, tucking my chin into my neck and kind of looking around like a spy who doesn't want to be overheard, "here it is: your former gardener told you he was gonna get even with you because you owed him money for yard work, told another guy that he was gonna set you up with the police, and he did. He made up a story and told the authorities that you had all this cocaine at your house and were dealing it. They didn't believe him, had no reason to believe him—this was a guy who was out on probation after having bitten off the ear of some guy—but they went ahead and set you up anyway. Without getting a warrant they put a bug on him and told him to tell you he had someone named Joe who wanted to buy two kilos of coke from you. And you, messed up as you were because you were freebasing your brains out, thinking maybe you could score a little money so you could continue your habit or maybe even pay the mortgage you were so far behind on, you strung him along even though you didn't have any coke to deal, had never dealt it. Five times in one day you met with this Joe, who was really an undercover agent. He showed you the 120 grand he was willing to pay for the stuff. All you had to do was deliver, but you didn't. Because you couldn't. And when you told him you could put him in touch with a supplier, he wasn't interested, said he only wanted to deal with you.

"Joe told his bosses at the State Attorney's office that he didn't think you had any coke, didn't even have access to two kilos. But they didn't stop. They called you the next day and you met again. Again you didn't deliver, even though they had all that money ready and waiting. And then, finally, on the next day, they called you again and you told them to come over to the house and you had your buddy Eddie Kulins there and a supplier named Vince Cord, who'd brought half a kilo of cocaine. It wasn't your coke and you were only gonna get $500, *that's right $500*, chump, for your role in this scam.

"Cord told you to carry the cocaine from his car to the buyers, and when you started to hand it over, that's when the bust went down. You tried to throw the coke in the canal behind your house. (You were so messed up that you weren't thinking that this would save your ass as much as you were thinking that later when this all blew over you'd go back and get it and smoke it up.) But they retrieved it. Then they put you in handcuffs and tore up your house looking for more coke and anything else they could take out and show the press that you were a real Cocaine Cowboy. Oh yeah, the camera crews were outside waiting; they'd been waiting for the last *three days*.

"And what did the cops find? 'Weapons,' they said proudly to the television people. Weapons: an antique goose gun, a rusted out carbine given to your kid by his great grandfather, and an old .22-caliber rifle which also belonged to your kid. Didn't seem to matter that they were so old they could never fire and that there weren't any shells in the house. They found a loaded .45, too. But they found it outside in the trunk of Cord's car.

"And don't forget the cash. $124,000 to show that Mercury Morris was into the big time. Only trouble was this wasn't your money. It was the 'buy' money they'd brought along—even though the deal was for less than $30,000—and they took it out of their own car *after* the bust. Remember, you sat there in your house as they counted it out and put it in a shoebox, wishing it was yours so you could pay the mortgage or the phone company or any of the other bills you owed because your freebasing had ruined your business and left you broke.

"And then they paraded you and the money and the weapons before the cameras. You watched it yourself on the news that night...." I'd pause to catch my breath. "This is what happened and what you're up against, Philbrick."

After I went through *what* had happened, I'd start asking myself *why* it happened. Why such an effort to get me? I mean the State Attorney's office had even gone so far as to bake a cake with my old Dolphins number 22 on it. "They've been waiting for three days to eat this," someone in the criminal justice system told me after I was arrested.

I know my life-style while I was with the Dolphins had rubbed some people the wrong way. I had really enjoyed being a cocky son-ofabitch. I drove fast cars. I dated the prettiest women I could find. And I always said what was on my mind:

- That if Shula had played me in Super Bowl VI we'd have beaten the Cowboys

- That I should be starting in the backfield with Csonka because I was better than Kiick

- That a state of de facto segregation existed in the Dolphins' locker room.

But was that enough for the State to go through such an elaborate scheme? Some people have suggested that I was so important because my arrest would send a message to traffickers (and the public, too) that the state of Florida—which had recently been embarrassed by a *60 Minutes* television segment on drug dealing gone wild—had a new, tough law imposing minimum mandatory sentences. A lengthy article titled, "The Railroading of Mercury Morris," in the May 1983 issue of *Miami/South Florida* magazine, suggested, "The chance to nab Mercury Morris seemed to give them (prosecutors in Florida) the publicity they needed." Friends and well-wishers kept telling me, "They needed to make an example of you." To which I replied, "An example of *what?*"

If my friends were right, then it's pretty ironic, because for years I thought the fact that I was Mercury Morris, football superstar, actually protected me from certain injustices in the world rather than exposed me to them. Indeed, I think one of the major reasons I succeeded in athletics was because I believed prowess on the field could be translated into prowess in the real world. Let me give you an example.

I grew up in Ben Avon, Pennsylvania, a little borough on the outskirts of Pittsburgh. When I was a kid, I was subjected to a small amount of racial prejudice and I was certainly aware of the racism that existed in some parts of society. But for the most part I didn't personally encounter anything particularly traumatic. Then, in 1965, I went to West Texas State University in Canyon, Texas, on a football scholarship. It's sometimes hard to recall the racial climate in those days, but to put things in perspective, remember this: at the time I left for college, the powerhouse Southeast Conference, which in recent years has given the NFL so many Black stars, didn't have any Black players at all, had never had one, and the equally prestigious Southwest Conference only had one; Houston's Jerry Levias. Actually, there were only a handful of Blacks enrolled in these schools period.

One night in February, 1966, five of us—all from Pennsylvania, three Whites and two Blacks—went to a James Brown concert in Lubbock, Texas. On our drive home, we stopped at a restaurant in Plainview. There, a young Mexican waitress met us at the door and asked if we were members of a basketball team. We said, "No." Then, were we members of a band? Again we shook our heads. Well, were we members of any team? "No." In that event, she explained, the Whites could sit here, but "the coloreds" would have to sit in a different area. It was the first time I had really ever experienced segregation, except in the movies. That it was at the hands of a Mexican woman—even though she was obviously just stating the policy of the White owners—made it all the more ridiculous. As I remember, my White buddies were just as upset as I was. Needless to say, we left.

But I didn't forget the lesson. If I'd been a member of a team that night, I would have been perceived and treated differently. For the rest of my freshman year, I hardly had any social life at all. When the weekend rolled around and everybody else would take off for nearby Amarillo to have a good time, I could be found in the basement of Stafford Hall pumping iron. Man, I was obsessed. I hit the weights three times a day, six days a week. Because I now knew the way the game was played. If I could become a hero on the gridiron then I'd be entitled to certain "rights" and "privileges" that I might not ordinarily receive. So I got stronger, broke all sorts of college records, became an All-American, was drafted into the NFL, made All-Pro, and played on back-to-back Super Bowl championship teams. And you know what? For the most part I was treated differently. Better. The "isms" that existed because of the color-I-was-not were relaxed because of the athlete I was.

"And now," (again I'm muttering to myself like Herb Philbrick) "now the fact that you were all those things is what landed you in this cell, made them set you up. You gotta figure a way to get out of this, man."

That way was by convincing an appeals court, that, among other things, (1) the State had illegally obtained certain evidence and the trial judge had been mistaken in allowing the jury to hear that evidence, and (2) that I had not been permitted to present the jury with evidence that would have allowed me to have prevailed in my defense that I should be found not guilty because I had been entrapped.

Entrapment. I didn't know anything about that term before August 18, 1982, but now I consider myself somewhat of an expert. I've probably read more cases about it than a lot of lawyers. Basically, if a defendant can prove he was entrapped—that he was not predisposed to commit the crime in question and instead the "criminal design" originated with the government—then a not guilty verdict is in order. If a defendant wants to adopt this defense, he must admit that he conducted himself in the manner described by the prosecution, but then argue that this doesn't matter because it was the State's conduct which led to the commission of the crimes in question. The reasoning is that the State has no right to test the limits of an individual's vulnerability if that individual hasn't initially demonstrated a disposition to commit a crime. Although the case law in Florida state court where I was being tried made it more difficult to prevail with this defense than in other states or in federal court, the way I was nabbed seemed to be a classic case of entrapment, and this was the defense Strauss and I decided to take.

Of course, we thought we'd be allowed to present the jury all of the damaging evidence which would prove how I had not been predisposed and how the State's conduct had led me to the events of August 18. But we weren't. We were not permitted to offer the testimony of a man named Eugene Gotbaum, who was ready to testify that the gardener-turned-informant had boasted that he was going to set me up for the police in a drug deal. Our judge, Ellen Morphonios Gable, nicknamed by the press "Maximum Ellen" because of her stiff sentences, wouldn't let Gotbaum take the stand because she didn't think his testimony was relevant. Strauss and I were confident that the District Court of Appeals would rule Judge Gable had been wrong and that the conviction would be overturned.

If it sounds like I was thinking pretty clearly while I was sitting in the cell, it's because I *was* thinking clearly. Cocaine, which makes it impossible to think clearly, wasn't even an issue at this time. Although I had, as I'll describe later, used the drug a few times after the bust and there were opportunities to get it in jail (an inmate once offered me some in the jail's law library!), once I was convicted I wasn't interested. It may have been the most important thing in my life before then, but it wasn't now—getting out and making a new life with Bobbie and the kids was. I realized I had to be sharp and alert and devote all my energy toward that goal. So I quit. It wasn't a difficult decision, and it wasn't a difficult task. It was fourth and one again and the clock was running. But this wasn't a game. My family, my freedom, and my life were on the line. And that's what I'd fight for. My days with cocaine were over.

That may sound hard to believe. But when faced with a do-or-die situation, the human spirit is capable of miraculous things. Picture the mother who's able to lift the car up because her kid is pinned underneath it. Under certain circumstances we can perform things that we might have thought were impossible.

As I've already indicated, I wasn't interested in the way out that the State Attorney had offered before and during the trial and would continue to offer even after I was convicted—a reduced sentence in return for my cooperation. Why would the government want to make a deal with me *after* they'd already won a conviction? I didn't know. Maybe they thought they'd lose the case on appeal. Maybe they thought I could deliver them some people who were even better known than I was. Whatever the reason, in mid-January of 1983, just a few days before sentencing, a very strange turn of events occurred.

I was to be sentenced on January 20. On January 17, I was sitting in my cell when I was informed that Martin Dardis, an investigative reporter for *Sports Illustrated,* wanted to visit with me. I had met Dardis before in the offices of Ron Strauss. Dardis had been the reporter who helped break the *Sports Illustrated* story in 1982 in which former Dolphin Don Reese talked about his own cocaine habit and the widespread use of the drug in the NFL. Before working for the magazine, Dardis had worked for the State Attorney's office in southern Florida.

During the two months since I'd been convicted, I'd met with various members of the press. But on this day, since Strauss was out of town, he had left instructions that nobody could see me unless he was present. Nevertheless, Dardis prefaced his talk by stating that he had just come across the catwalk where the court and prosecutor's offices were located and that "everyone" had given him permission to talk with me. He had brought an associate, a man named Phil Edgecomb, whose title was something like special investigator for the magazine. It was my understanding that Edgecomb, too, had been an investigator with the State Attorney in Florida and now was a private investigator. Edgecomb was Black, and it's my guess that Dardis was thinking that because there was a Black dude in the room with me now, I'd feel at ease and maybe spill my guts out. That's what they wanted me to do. (*Picture that!*)

Their pitch went something like this: It was going to take two and a half or three years for my appeal to be heard and decided. And even then there was no guarantee that I would win it. In the meantime it was gonna be tough on me and my family. On the other hand, they could give me the opportunity to get out on the street almost immediately. As I recall, they said that in return for my cooperation, they would give me $25,000 right away and a grand total of $100,000; that they would get my sentence reduced to conspiracy; get me a stay of sentence; and get me out on bond. All I had to do now was nod my head "Yes" in response to five names that they were going to mention. Later, after they'd got me out, I could come to New York for a more extensive interview. The names in question were former Dolphin players who were alleged to have had something to do with drugs and gambling in the early 1970s. Dardis and Edgecomb recited the five names to me.

"Drugs and gambling. In what respect?" I asked.

Initially they indicated that they had heard these players had shaved points in return for drugs (later they indicated that the players were suspected of giving information to gamblers in return for drugs). Apparently Dardis couldn't substantiate these rumors and he wanted me to provide him with the necessary information.

So here we were. I'd continually refused to name any names for the State Attorney and now these guys, with what they claimed was the permission of the State, were telling me that they could negate all the legal proceedings I'd been through *if* I would only help them get out a story. The Philbrick in me starting thinking, "Hold it. How can these guys come over here and offer you something that God can't even offer you right now: your freedom? And if what you did was as terrible as the State told the jury and the public, how could it consent to your release in return for talking to a magazine?"

Even if I had known anything regarding Dardis's wild ass story about drugs, I would never have given anyone any names. But I didn't believe the story. Still don't. I firmly believe that no such thing ever went on with the Dolphins when I was there. I know nothing went on in 1972, one of the years that *Sports Illustrated* was particularly interested in. Hey, we were winners on that team. 17–0. No other team has ever had a season like that. I know of NFL players who used cocaine. But never during a season and absolutely never in connection with the scenario Dardis had just laid out.

Although I had no interest in cooperating with Dardis and Edgecomb, I was real interested in finding out what they were up to. So, as is my style, I strung them along. "I don't know anything about those guys you mentioned," I said. "But I seem to remember something from those days. Let me think about it."

So they left and came back the next day, January 18. Again they told me they could help me, but only if I could give them specific information. Names. Places. Deals. Finally, I said, "These are all Black players you mentioned. I don't have any information about them." I paused and then told a little (white) lie. "I can give you the names of some White players from the Chiefs. You see I know this guy who knows a guy who said he heard these guys were doing this and that." I was playing with them. I knew what they were doing. They were trying to use me as the vehicle for establishing the credibility of a bullshit story. If I confirmed the rumors and got my freedom for doing so, then they could say that the story had to be true. "Say, how is it a magazine can come in and do something my lawyer couldn't do—get me out?" I asked. Dardis said something about having good connections with the State Attorney's office because he had once worked there. End of conversation. But before they left, Dardis gave me his card. After writing down his telephone credit card number on the back of the card, he told me that I should feel free to use it to make any calls. I know what he was thinking: that I'd use the card to call some of the guys whom he'd mentioned and that when he got his phone bill he'd have a record of the calls (*like I came down with yesterday's rain*).

Dardis and Edgecomb came back the next day, January 19. But I told Russ Buckhalt, the jail's assistant director of social services, that I had no desire to talk to them. Before they left they asked Russ if I'd give them back Dardis's card. I did, of course, but it's not like I couldn't have written down the number and used it. When Strauss came back and I told him that Dardis and Edgecomb had come to see me without his authorization, he about hit the ceiling.

(I know *Sports Illustrated* denies this version of the story. The magazine's managing editor Mark Mulvoy told the writer who wrote "The Railroading of Mercury Morris" that his investigators had spoken with me, but only to seek corroboration of material they had already dug up. Mulvoy claimed that his investigators never offered me a nickel. But I'll stand by my story and say, "Horseshit!")

I think the State Attorney's office was surprised by my continuing refusal to accept any deals for a reduced sentence. After all, I was facing, in the language of the statute, "a minimum of 15 calendar years, day for day, without parole." But to me it didn't seem fair that I should serve any time. Pleading guilty seemed like saying, "I'm sorry," to someone who has just stepped on your hand. Maybe it's my sports background, but I've always thought it is important to play by the rules. When I played football, I never got mad if an opponent tried to knock my head off, *as long as we were in bounds.* But if he hit me on the sidelines or after I'd crossed into the end zone that was a different matter. That's against the rules. (I'd usually respond by throwing the ball in the offender's face. Defensive players get really pissed off when you do that to them!)

I felt now as if the State had blindsided me while I was out of bounds. I wasn't trying to escape responsibility for the downward spiral my life had taken since my retirement. I knew it would take a good many years to straighten out that mess. My conviction had nothing to do with that; it had to do with specific acts, specific charges.

The jails are full of people who feel they've been treated unjustly but have finally caved in to authority. I call this the "Toby syndrome," and I wasn't going to have any part of it. Time and again— when I was arrested, when I was on trial, when I was in prison—I knew I was up against people who thought they had me by the nuts and could get me to do whatever they wanted. And then I'd flash back to the televised version of *Roots*, where they strapped this kid named Kunta Kinte up on a wheel so they could show his people that anytime they wanted to they could break him. "Your name is Toby," they told him. "Not Kunta Kinte. We are going to strip you of your roots. You don't have any roots here. All you have is us telling you what to do." They kept asking him his name and he kept saying, "Kunta Kinte." And they kept whupping his ass, until finally after thirty or forty lashes, he said, "Toby."

Not me. I kept saying to myself, "You can give me three million lashes or three million years, but under no circumstances are you going to make me say my name is Toby when it's not."

"Merc," is what Judge Gable called me on January 20, two days after I turned down Dardis's and Edgecomb's deal, which apparently had the State Attorney's blessing. "Sorry, Merc," the judge said. And then she sentenced me to twenty years in prison, the fifteen year mandatory plus five more years just in case I were to hit a guard. She explained the bonus by saying something like, "I have to give the Department of Corrections an edge." *Like I was Al Capone or something.*

Because Florida permits the televising of trials, the cameras had been in the courtroom from Day 1. This sentencing hearing was also televised, and if you watch the tapes carefully, you'll see that "Merc" was less like Toby and more like the bull in the ring that day.

I stood before Judge Gable, my feet apart, arms behind my back, eyes forward, ready to take the bad news like a man. As the judge spoke, I inched over toward the table where the prosecutor George Yoss sat. I had caught Yoss in a lie during the trial. He had allowed a witness to falsely relate a conversation that took place shortly after my arrest, a conversation at which Yoss himself had been present. At that time someone in the State Attorney's office had asked me why I did it, and I had said, softly and sorrowfully, "I was just hoping to make a few bucks." At the trial, under Yoss's questioning, an investigator said my words were, "I did it for the money." Yoss asked him to repeat this. "**I did it for the money.**" Each time he said it in a forceful voice that conveyed not sorrow, but arrogance and greed. I felt the witness and Yoss were again hitting me out of bounds on this one. The jury was left with the impression that at the time of my arrest I wasn't confused or contrite about what had happened, but proud.

"Well, boy, I caught you," I said to Yoss. I knew I was baked anyway, and I felt I had to call him on this. I said it quietly, but my move toward his table was sufficient to bring the marshalls over to make sure I didn't do any damage. "If you had such a strong case, why'd you have to get that guy to lie like that? What kind of man are you?"

"I won," he said smugly.

I stared at him long and hard, and then I said, "No, pal. This is halftime. I know how the game is played now."

CHAPTER 2

THE HOLLOW

How does a reasonably intelligent man, a man with a wonderful wife and kids, a man who seems to have everything going for him, find himself facing fifteen years in prison without parole? In other words, how the hell did I get into this jackpot? Let's start at the very beginning.

I'm not exaggerating when I say that I grew up with my parents. They were each 15 years old when I was conceived, and 16 when I was born in Pittsburgh on January 5, 1947. My mother, Jackie, dropped out of high school after I arrived in the world. My father, George, remained in school. He also worked at an icehouse in nearby Sewickley. How many kids can remember when their father got his first car? I can. I was 4 and he was all of 20. Up to that time, he pedaled a bike with a big basket to work.

My parents were too young to raise me. They were always around to love me and lend a helping hand, but I was actually raised by my mom's mother and stepfather, Mary and James Flun Smith. Mom, Dad, and I lived with "Mama" and "Smitty" (that's what everyone called my grandparents, including me) in a small but comfortable two-story frame house on Spruce Street in the section of Ben Avon called the Hollow. Look carefully at a map of Pennsylvania and many of the neighboring states and you'll find plenty of hollows—Sleepy Hollow, Willow Hollow, and so on. These are valleys that are geographically lower than the surrounding terrain. Generally, they are also socioeconomically lower. Our Hollow was down by the Ohio River. It was inhabited by humble working-class people, most of whom were Black. Most of the twenty or so families that made up

17

our Hollow had lived there for generations, almost melting into one big, extended family. Everybody looked out for everybody else's kids. Every woman was "Aunt," regardless of whether you were really related to her.

The Hollow was about half a mile long. Above it was Powell's Hill. The middle-class folk lived part-way up the hill. The upper middle class lived still higher. Finally, up on top of the hill, there was the nicest section of town, Ben Avon Heights.

Blacks and Whites lived together quite harmoniously in Ben Avon. While the Heights was exclusively White, I had many friends that lived there and I was welcome in their homes. In fact, my earliest football memories are of the Heights. My best friend from the Hollow, Denny Edmunds, and I would trek up there for games of tackle—no equipment, of course—in the huge backyard of an elementary school classmate, Chip Garber.

Although I sometimes wished I had an estate like the Garbers' or their neighbors, I wasn't overly jealous. Our house on Spruce Street was a happy one. My parents were so young and had their hands so full—I was followed by three sisters and a brother—that Smitty and Mama provided the stability in our lives. Smitty, who was in his fifties when I was born, was the boss. Mama and everybody else were expected to do what he said, when he said it. "May," he'd tell my grandmother (it was always May, never Mary) "why don't you get up and get me something to eat now." They were married for well over 20 years and she dutifully obeyed him, until one morning when she simply refused. Smitty shook his head. "May," he said. "You about the sorriest woman I believe I ever saw in my whole life."

Smitty was a self-made man, a tough man who carried an ax under the front seat of his car. He had his own small trucking company. He had started out as a truck driver, but by the time I was born he had three dump trucks working for him. Two of the trucks hauled asphalt from an asphalt factory to crews building roads. The third truck removed and disposed of ashes from Pittsburgh's coal-burning schools.

My dad eventually quit the ice factory to work as a driver for Smitty, and when I was old enough, I went on the payroll, too. During the summer I'd get up with Smitty at 5 o'clock in the morning to get the truck he drove ready. It would still be dark when we left the house for the asphalt factory. I'd try to sleep on the way, but there is nothing more difficult than trying to fall asleep in a dump truck driving through Pittsburgh at 6 o'clock in the morning. It was a long day, driving back and forth from factory to road site. We'd break only for lunch. There was no such thing as "fast food" in those days; but even if there had been, Smitty wouldn't have wanted it. His lunch was a production—a strawberry preserves and butter sandwich or a pork chop and gravy sandwich. I'd carry chipped ham and cheese. We enjoyed each other's company.

Besides working on the truck, I shoveled ashes off the floors of the school cellars into ash cans, hoisted the cans up, and then dumped them into the truck. Sometimes there would be as many as ninety full cans in a cellar and another fifty cans worth of ashes on the floor. Getting rid of them was hard work and no fun, but soon I was driving trucks, too. I was only about 13 or 14, yet I knew what I was doing. I'd been driving since I was 12. I started out by "stealing" the trucks when Smitty was out. One day I'd stalled up the street and he'd caught me. He grabbed me by the collar and said, "I'm gonna tell you twice, hear. The first time and the last time. I don't want no nonsense. I'm tired of you doing that. You're going to learn how to drive that truck right." This was a typical reaction. Instead of whupping my ass, he'd turn my youthful mischief into something positive.

Driving and cars and *speed* have always been an important part of my life. I often remember dates and events by the kind of car somebody was driving at the time. With the money I earned working for Smitty, I bought a go-cart. Smitty had already given me a lawn-mower-engine-powered go-cart that could go about 35 miles per hour. That wasn't fast enough for me, so I saved $220 and bought a chain-saw-powered beauty that could go 60. I wasn't supposed to take it into the street, but I couldn't resist. I quickly became the terror of the Hollow.

Smitty wouldn't let me spend all my time behind the wheel. He didn't have all the smarts in the world, but he had a great deal of common sense. Although he only had a fourth-grade education, he was well aware of the world around him and he made sure I was, too.

"Gene, why don't you watch the news sometime, so you can find out what's going on in the world," he'd say.

He insisted I watch the evening news on television and read the daily newspaper rather than hang out on the corner. So instead of constantly tooling around on my go-cart or taking my rightful place in front of Isily's Dairy on Lincoln Avenue with Edmunds, Nato, Darryl, and the boys, I began to take an interest in what was going on in the world outside Ben Avon and the corner.

I can remember watching the civil rights marches of the early sixties on TV, seeing the peaceful demonstrators hosed down and beaten. I can remember reading about the little girls who lost their lives when their church was bombed in Birmingham, Alabama, and about Cheyney, Schwerner, and Goodman, who disappeared so mysteriously in Philadelphia, Mississippi. Those towns seemed far away from Pittsburgh geographically and politically. As I watched these events on television, they did not seem real. They were like something out of a movie, not a play. A play was something live, something that happened to you. A movie was something you watched, something that happened to others. Thus, when I saw the movie *To Kill a Mockingbird*, I thought what happened to the Black man, Tom Robinson, was sad and terrible, but I didn't relate it to my own experience.

Looking back, I can see that even when I was in a "play" myself, I believed or *chose* to believe that the story had nothing to do with me. When I was 13, I visited my cousins in Richmond, Virginia. My grandfather's brother Oliver owned a 900-acre tobacco farm there. He had so much land that a White man sharecropped some of it. One day I was playing with the sharecropper's daughter. She hit me. I hit her back. My cousins, all of whom were older than I was, couldn't believe it. "Don't you go hittin' no White girl," they told me.

"She whacked me first," I said. That seemed fair. It was certainly the rule in the neighborhood where I came from—if someone hit you, boy or girl, Black or White, you hit back— and I saw no reason to behave any other way.

A few days later we went to the local movie theater. I was amazed to find out that Blacks were not allowed to sit on the main floor. We were restricted to the balcony. "Man, you can't go down there," said one of my cousins. And I thought to myself, Here's a guy whose father owns a 900-acre farm and because of his color, he can't sit where he wants. How can this be? But I was detached, not involved, curious, not angry.

A final incident during that visit almost cost me my life. I was playing with my cousins when a cousin of theirs took my special Davy Crockett knife away from me. The culprit was a girl. I was so embarrassed that I had been "disarmed" by a female that I started to go home—not to my uncle's house, but to Pennsylvania! I was walking on the side of the road, destination Pittsburgh, when a big old 1940 Ford approached. There were a bunch of White kids in the car. All of a sudden, I heard a whoosh! and a thunk! I followed the sounds and saw a Coke bottle lying close by. I didn't think too much of it, figuring the kids had just wanted to get rid of the empty bottle and had tossed it. I continued my journey. In a little while, my uncle, who had been advised of my departure, caught up to me. I told him about the Coke bottle. "Gene, dammit," he said, "don't you ever walk along this road. Don't you ever leave the house. Don't you be caring about a knife. You better be caring about your life. There've been eight kids killed along this road by people throwing bottles and rocks." I could have been victim number nine, but I didn't take it personally. It was my cousins whom I saw as being forced to play by a strange set of rules, facing injustice, subject to bodily harm or death —not me. I was just a visitor passing through, observing, perhaps, but not experiencing segregation.

I was happy to get back home from that almost foreign land where Blacks had to worry about ducking bottles, pulling punches with White girls, and not sitting where they wanted to sit in the theater. There was a certain amount of what would have to be called racism in Pittsburgh, but again, I felt more the observer than victim. Here's an example.

Smitty made good money and would periodically buy a new car. He wanted nothing to do with time payments. He'd go down to the showroom carrying a big wad of cash, pick the model he wanted off the floor, and that was that. When I was about 11 or 12, I went with him to the local Buick dealership. It was right after work, and Smitty hadn't bothered to change. He was still pretty dirty, wearing heavy old shoes caked with asphalt, the kind of hat Indiana Jones wore in *Raiders of the Lost Ark,* and overalls. Tucked into a bib pocket in the overalls was about $7000.

We must have stood amongst the shiny new cars for fifteen minutes. No one acknowledged us. It didn't seem so much that they were refusing to wait on us, but that they didn't even see us, or at least didn't see us as customers. We might as well have been George and Marian Kirby in the old *Topper* series. Smitty looked at me. "Gene, what the hell is going on here?"

"I don't know."

But he refused to ask for service. "I come in here to buy a car," he told me. "I expect them to come up to me and ask me what do I want or can they help me." When they didn't, he took his $7000 and we walked out the door. "Those cocksuckers don't want to sell me a car, they can't get my money."

The next day he went and got dressed up. He put on his good bib overalls (his clean ones) and his clean Indiana Jones hat. He took an extra $1500 out of his trunk (he didn't like banks). With $8500 in his pocket now, he went to a Ford dealership. This time we got service. "Can I interest you in a Ford?" a salesman asked.

"No, you can't interest me in nothin'. I already know what I want."

"What's that?"

"I want that one there." And he pointed to a big black Lincoln with an all black interior. It was a house on wheels. The back window went down. The car was like a tank. It was beautiful. It was bad. It was black. And about fifteen minutes after he got there, it was his.

At the time that it happened, I didn't perceive the Topper treatment at the Buick dealership as happening because we were Black. I figured it was because Smitty was dirty and that we weren't considered important enough to wait on. Color never entered into my consciousness.

Color didn't enter into my consciousness when it came to my grandmother's work, either. She was a domestic. She lost more than a few jobs when her employers saw her dropped off in a Lincoln Continental, a car better than the ones they owned. When I was old enough to drive her, she'd make me let her off around the block from where she was working so as not to cause any trouble with the people she worked for. I guess I could have picked up from incidents like these that because I was Black I had to act different for White folks. But quite honestly, not only did I not act different, I didn't even pick up that I was *supposed* to act different.

If I were to sum up my response to such incidents, I'd say, "The bells were ringing, but not for me." Until the scene in the Texas diner, I was simply not a participant. I never felt that I had to play the game of life by a different set of rules from anybody else.

Why did I feel this way? Perhaps it was because of my success in athletics at such an early age. Perhaps by high school my success on the football field, the basketball court, and the baseball diamond had already created my own "Gardol," an invisible shield protecting me from the isms that confronted my working-class grandparents, my southern cousins, and most other Blacks.

The invisible shield took a few years to develop. My formal football career began when I joined the Pop Warner League at age 9. Denny Edmunds and I were teammates and stars. He played quarterback and I played running back, and as would be the case all the way through high school, we were the only Blacks on the roster.

Black quarterbacks are a rarity today. You can imagine how strange it was to have one in the 1950s. When Denny and I were in junior high, we got a visit from Al Shriver, who would be our varsity coach in high school. "Do the best you can, but don't try to be stars," he told us. Of course, hearing this, we tried our hardest to become stars. (This has always been the case with me. If a coach challenged me in any way, I don't care if it was Al Shriver or Don Shula, my first reaction was to shove it up his rear by excelling on the field. I think Shula knew this, and I suspect Shriver did, too. Years later I would learn that Shriver had been under intense pressure from certain parents to move Denny to another position and to keep both Denny and me in the background. I admire Coach Shriver for sticking with us despite the prevailing attitude that our place was in the back of the huddle as well as the back of the bus. He dutifully gave us the message—knowing and hoping we'd ignore it—and was somehow able to persuade those who weren't happy with the presence of Denny and me in the backfield that he had to go with the best players at each position. He had had Black players before, all of Edmund's brothers had been stars, but never a quarterback. I now see that this discrimination, if not racism, in my beloved Ben Avon had to be dealt with creatively.)

Although I could always run faster than everybody else and had great moves, I was far from a complete football player when I began to play. Blocking and tackling were not my fortes. In those days, I played defense, too, and I can remember a game in junior high in which I chased, caught up to, and then ran alongside an opposing ballcarrier for 65 yards. I was simply afraid to tackle him, thinking one of his feet might come up, hit me in the chin, and knock me out. On the Monday after that performance, my coach, Charlie Avallone, called me into his office. He sat me down, went to the blackboard, and wrote, YELLOW and NO GUTS in huge letters. Then he read me the riot act. "That move you pulled out there, that's

'cause you were scared," he said. "Those words on the blackboard—
that's you." From that day forward, I was just the opposite—intense
and fearless. I'd known Coach Avallone since the sixth grade, but
this was the beginning of a special relationship that would last for
years. He became my adviser, my sounding board, my mentor.

When I was in junior high, my parents separated. My mom was
a free spirit—hard to pin down, much less to tame—and I think it
got to be too much for my dad. And so they split. Our family of
seven—Mom, Dad, and five kids—had never lived on its own. We
had always lived under the roof and the rules of Smitty and Mama.
I had never perceived Jackie and George in the role of parents—
they were more like my older sister and brother.

Dad moved in with his mother in Sewickley. Mom moved to the
north side of Pittsburgh with my brother, Russell, and my sisters,
Valerie, Joyce, and Janice. (Ironically, the building they lived in was
later torn down to make room for Three Rivers Stadium, home of
the Steelers and Pirates, and the site of some of my better games
when I was with the Dolphins.)

Although my parents and brother and sisters moved, I stayed in
Ben Avon with Smitty and Mama. This seemed perfectly natural, for
they were the ones who had been raising me. This was home to me. I
loved my room. It was my private place, a place where I could be away
from everything and lose myself in the jazz of Miles Davis and Ahmad
Jamal, whose album *But Not for Me* was and still is a favorite. This
was a place where I could look out the window, block out the light
from the street, and just stare at the beautiful pine trees, and dream.

Smitty and Mama had always regarded me as something special—
in part, I think, because I was the first-born child of their daughter,
in part because I was a character. Smitty seemed to love having me
at his side, showing me the ways of the world. And there wasn't
anything Mama wouldn't do for me. Although my grandfather made
enough money to support us, my grandmother insisted on working.
There's a song by the Intruders called, "I'll Always Love My Mama."
The lyrics go something like this:

> *Sometimes I feel so bad when I think about the things I*
>   *used to do*
> *How mama used to clean somebody else's house just to buy*
>   *me a new pair of shoes*

She taught me little things like saying, "Hello," and "Thank
*   you, please."*
While scrubbing those floors on her bended knees
Talking about my Mama.

That's the way it was in the Smith household. I got more than
shoes. When it was time for me to have a bike, my grandparents got
me an English racer. When it was time for me to have a car, they
got me a 1956 Chevy.

I not only lived with Smitty and Mama, they became my legal
guardians.

"Mr. McGlocklin, I've just got to play football."

I was in the office of our junior high principal, scared to death,
tears in my eyes. I had just learned that in order to play interscho-
lastic sports, you had to live in the district in which your parents
lived. With my parents gone, I no longer met that criterion. Here I
was in the eighth grade, my football career apparently already over.
I guess I could have just accepted this and said, "Oh well, I can't
play, no college scholarship." But that wasn't my style. (It never has
been.) Scared as I was, I took matters into my own hands, learned
what the rules were, and figured out how to meet them.

"We'd like you to play for us, Eugene," Mr. McGlocklin said,
"but in order for that to happen, your grandparents would have to
become your legal guardians."

And they did.

I excelled in three sports at Avonworth High. In my first few years
there, I achieved as much recognition in basketball and baseball as I
did in football. I eventually captained our basketball team, making honorable mention All-State. I was also a good enough center fielder to
attract the attention of scouts from the Phillies and Orioles.

But football was my true love. I loved the challenge of using my
mind and my body to get from one point to another against tremendous odds or at least tremendous linemen. It was an exercise in individual creativity. At the same time, I loved the idea of a group of
individuals working together as a team toward a common goal. I
dreamed of a career in professional football (although if that failed,
I figured I could be happy driving a truck—not a dump truck, but a

25

fancy eighteen-wheeler, dressed up with enough lights so that you might mistake it for a Christmas tree).

I didn't set the gridiron on fire my first three years at Avonworth. In fact, I was kicked off the team a few times after getting into disagreements with Coach Shriver. These expulsions were always over some principle. If Coach Shriver insisted we do a drill which I considered ridiculous or dangerous, I'd question him, and if his rationale didn't satisfy me, I'd refuse to participate. For example, I was kicked off the team before the last game of my senior year. Up to this point, I'd had an excellent season despite missing the first two games because of a back injury. I had been very conscientious, pumping iron daily (I started at home by lifting a broken axle from one of Smitty's trucks, then progressed to the point where I was cutting out of study hall to go around the corner to the house of a friend who had a basement full of barbells. I eventually placed first in the Marine fitness exam taken by every high school senior in Pennsylvania, and finished second in our three-state region.) I'd broken all the school records, and in one game I had rushed for 285 yards on only five carries.

The drill I walked away from involved two teammates lining up about 15 yards apart and then running full steam at each other, trying to knock the shit out of each other. "Wait a minute, coach," I said. "This is the last game of the season. Why are we doing this?" He didn't answer. I decided to try the drill before trying to reason with him again. I got my ass rocked and I rocked my opponent's ass. I looked around. It was clear that everybody was getting beaten up by this exercise in futility. "This drill is crazy," I muttered under my breath.

Coach Shriver overheard me. "If you think it's crazy, you can hang up your stuff."

I left a trail of my uniform from the field to the locker room. Helmet first, then jersey, shoulder pads, left shoe, right shoe, and pants. By the time I got to the door, I was in my jock strap, and I threw that out toward the field.

Not missing a beat, I changed into my basketball gear in the locker room, then ran upstairs to the gym. The beginning of basketball practice overlapped with the end of the football season, and Coach Avallone was putting the varsity team, which I co-captained, through its drills. As far as I was concerned, I had made the right choice in leaving the field. Coach Avallone didn't think so. After I told him what had happened with Coach Shriver, he said, "You're going back down there, and you're going to apologize. You've got too much to lose by getting kicked off the team. You've got a chance for a scholarship if you hang in there." I admit: I not only respected Coach Avallone, I was afraid of him. He was a powerful figure in his late twenties.

Coach Avallone was right. He always was. (In some ways, he provided a fatherly wisdom I didn't always get at home.) I knew I had to go to college, not only to get an education and to play football, but to avoid being drafted and being sent to Vietnam, which was suddenly becoming a reality. I'd been watching the war in my living room every night, and I didn't like what I saw. It seemed to me we had enough problems in the United States without having to worry about the situation in a land halfway around the world where we didn't understand the people or their culture. So, I picked up my jock, swallowed my pride, and apologized to Coach Shriver.

By spring I'd received a few scholarship offers and had narrowed my choice to Florida A&M, which was an all-Black school, and West Texas State, which was integrated. If you're wondering where the recruiters from the big schools like the University of Florida and University of Texas were, remember, this was 1965 and their respective conferences were still lily-white. As for the big-time schools that were integrated, until my senior year I had done little to warrant national recognition, and then I'd missed the first two games. I think, too, that I simply wasn't the large, prototype running back most of them coveted. Still, I had received several feelers from schools around the country. For example, Syracuse, a traditional hotbed of running backs—Jim Brown, Ernie Davis, Floyd Little, Larry Csonka—was interested in me. But because the school already had enough backs for the coming year, the coaches wanted me to go to prep school and sharpen my running skills for a year before coming. I wasn't interested in this farm system arrangement. I wanted to get to college and play right away.

Two things, or more accurately, two individuals, led me to settle on West Texas State. First, my mentor, Coach Avallone. He firmly believed I could achieve greater recognition at an integrated school. And second, Joe Kerbel, the head coach at West Texas State.

Kerbel recruited me by accident. He had been interested in a defensive player from rival Coriopolis High. In looking at films of this player's game against us, however—it was the game I would have missed if I hadn't gone back and apologized to Coach Shriver—he noticed me. I was hard to miss. On our first play from scrimmage I ran 70 yards for a touchdown. There was a penalty against us on the play and the ball was brought back. No matter. On the next play, I ran 75 yards for a touchdown. Again, there was a penalty against us. No matter. On the next play, I ran 80 yards for a touchdown. No penalty.

Kerbel saw that film on a Thursday and was in Ben Avon the following Monday—not to see the guy from Coriopolis, but to see me. I didn't know he was coming until I was called out of English class and told he was there. Man, I was impressed. This coach had not only come all the way from Texas to recruit me, he actually had enough clout to get me out of English for an interview. That really sold me. This was the first guy to come and say, "Hey, man, I really want you."

Kerbel was a real character. He was about 5-foot-9, weighed over 325 pounds, and spoke with a drawl right out of *In the Heat of the Night*. "Now, I have one question I want to ask you about Eugene," he said to my grandparents (I was known as Eugene or Gene or "King Gene, the Running Machine," then). "Does the boy go to church regular?" My grandparents and I were impressed and nodded obediently. Little did we know that the first time he'd get me on a football field, he'd grab me by the throat and say, "Listen, boy, there's only one sonofabitch with brass balls around here, and you're looking at him." And later, "Listen, you little sonofabitch, it'll snow in Amarillo in July before you play football for me."

While my grandparents could truthfully answer Kerbel that I was a churchgoer, that didn't mean I always kept myself out of trouble. Like most kids, I had my share of fights. Some were over little things like someone knocking my hat off. That one, during my sophomore year at Avonworth, got me a brief suspension from school and the basketball team and a lecture from good old Coach Avallone, who told me that I was wasting my time as an athlete and student if I couldn't keep myself under control. But some fights were over larger things, somebody using the word "nigger," for example. (I wasn't totally oblivious to racial issues. There were occasional incidents of such name-calling, and for a long time that was the red flag that got my fists going. It took many years before I realized that it was the name-caller who had a problem and not me and that I should just walk away.)

Whether I was in trouble or in church, chances were that Denny Edmunds was right beside me. We were inseparable friends as well as teammates. Not only were we the only Blacks on the football, basketball, and baseball teams at Avonworth High, we were the only Blacks period in the class of 1965, except for my cousin Antoinette. (There were only about ten or fifteen Blacks in the entire school of 800.) Here's how the school newspaper characterized us: "Denny Edmunds, who cannot even pass a towel in the huddle without first handing it off to Gene Morris. . . . " And it was true. I remember once when we were on our way home from school, I had to stop and pee in the woods. When a little splashed on Denny's shoe, I thought he'd be angry. But he said, "That's okay. Now I get to pee on your pants leg." He only got upset when I refused. That's the way it was with our friendship. Everything was 50–50.

Denny was in on most of my pranks, like taking the bullets from my grandfather's pistol and dumping them in trash fires and listening to them explode like firecrackers. One day when we did it in the Edmunds' yard, a shell accidentally took off and went flying past Denny's brother, through a window, and into the house. End of caper.

Even if Denny wasn't really at the scene of an adventure, I could convince him that he had been. When I was 13 or 14, a bunch of us went into our neighbor Todd Simonz's garage and swiped some strawberries from the freezer. We forgot to close the freezer door, and by the time our deed had been discovered, several hundred dollars worth of meat was ruined. We got hauled before the local magistrate, who ordered us to pay for all the food that had been lost. It came to about $65 a prankster. Denny hadn't been involved, but I figured if I could persuade him that he had been, it would ease my financial burden.

"Well, Eugene, I just don't remember," he said.

"Oh, c'mon, you were there. We're always together."

"Well, maybe."

I finally let him off the hook.

The only serious trouble I had with the authorities came during my senior year. That was a rough period for me because our house on Spruce Street, the one in which I'd lived my whole life, burned down just five days before Christmas. I had been at a high school basketball tournament scouting the opposition with Coach Avallone when a policeman found me and told me our house was on fire. The policeman had said everything was under control, but when we got

there, it looked like Fort Apache. There was nothing left but a pair
of steps. My grandfather had refused to let the firefighters into our
home with their axes to tear up the house in order to stop the fire.
"Hey, you put that ax on my house, I got an ax in my car under my
seat I'm gonna put on you," he had told them.

Smitty was sitting in that same Lincoln Continental he had purchased seven years earlier. He was crying. The car was beginning to
show the effects of age, and so was Smitty. He had led a hard life.
He had forgotten to renew the insurance policy on the house. Nothing was insured. Nothing was saved. He had lost everything. He
was devastated. Here was a man who had always relied on his own
judgment, and he had made a terrible mistake. While Mama—who
was your typical persevering, strong Christian woman—took the disaster well, this was, I think, the beginning of the end for Smitty.

There was no talk of me going to live with my mom or dad.
Smitty, Mama, and I moved into a Black community center in the
neighborhood. We lived there for three months before finding a new
place to live about half a mile from the burned-down house. The
folks in the Hollow rallied around us, bringing food and clothing.
Coach Avallone was also terrific. He realized I was a proud young
man. He couldn't bear to see me in the old poorly fitting clothes I
had been given, so he took me shopping and bought me a whole
new wardrobe, including shoes. It was a beautiful gesture. He
couldn't have been making very much money as a gym teacher and
coach, yet here he was spending his hard-earned cash on me.

It was during this time of displacement that I had a few scrapes
with the police. First, a bunch of us got into a big fight at a lake in
nearby North Park with some punks from a rival high school. People were hitting each other with oars and it got pretty rough. The
only reason we didn't get into serious trouble was because the Chief
of Police of Bellevue, the town next to Ben Avon, was a nice guy
named Red Morcroft. He was a big football fan. His sons played the
game, and on weekends he was a referee in the NFL. He had followed my high school career and taken an interest in me. So when
the trouble started in North Park, he intervened with the North Park
police and saved my ass.

He saved me again in the summer of 1965. Shortly before I was
to leave for college, I ran into a kid I knew and some of his friends.
"Hey, man. How about doing us a favor," he said. "Ride us out to

Westview and we'll dump this car, 'cause we stole it. And we'll let you take the tires off of it."

Not exercising the best judgment, I said, "All right. If all I gotta do is follow you out there."

So we drove out to this wooded area and they jacked up the stolen car, which was a Buick Special, took off the tires, and put them on my car, which was a Chevy. It was a terrible match—small new tires on a big old car—but I drove around town for a couple of days with the new tires. One of my stops was a bowling alley that Chief Morcroft owned. I parked, went in, and thanked him for getting me off the hook earlier in the year.

"Think nothing of it, Eugene," he said. "I've known you for years. In fact, what I want you to do before you leave for Texas is take those tires off your car and deliver them to my office at the police station. Because the Westview Police had a warrant out for your arrest, but I told them to drop it because you were on your way to school and really didn't have nothin' to do with the theft. All right?"

I got those tires off in about eight seconds and had them to Morcroft's office in no time. I was so grateful, because although I didn't think I'd done anything too terrible, that was the first time I was involved in something that could have had serious repercussions.

So, as usual, I dodged another bullet. A pattern was developing. Whenever it looked like I was painted into a corner, either on the field or off, I managed to somehow wiggle my way out and move forward, usually with a smile on my face. If I couldn't do it by myself, there always seemed to be a helping hand from someone who had taken a special interest in me—Smitty, Mama, Coach Shriver, Coach Avallone, Red Morcroft.

Now I was off to college, in search of good times, good football, and another guardian angel.

CHAPTER 3

COLLEGE DAYS

Denny Edmunds and I said our good-byes in my Chevy. We drove through Ben Avon, the adjacent suburbs, and Pittsburgh itself. We talked about the fun we'd had in the past and shared our dreams about the future. We vowed to stay as close as we'd always been. He was off to Hiram Scott College in Nebraska to play basketball, and I was headed for West Texas State with a "full boat" (our slang for a scholarship) to play football.

My grandparents, parents, sisters, and brother saw me off from the airport. It was my first time on an airplane. My destination was Canyon, a town of about 8000 which sat in the middle of nowhere, some 17 miles from Amarillo.

Besides the university, the town is best known because it sits in the second largest canyon in the United States. Only the Grand Canyon is bigger. It's no wonder that my first impression of Texas was that it was flat, stark, and huge. The rolling green hills of Ben Avon were just a memory.

My second impression was that there was a tremendous amount of egotism in the air. In the stores you'd see combs and other knick-knacks that were 4 feet by 2½ feet with the legend, "Everything is big in Texas." That kind of sentiment was reflected not only with products but in almost every other area of life down there. Whatever the topic, Texans were certain that Texas was the best and the biggest.

West Texas State had about 7000 students. I had decided to study pre-law. If I didn't make it in football, I'd be an attorney, not a truck driver! I didn't last too long in the pre-law major. When Coach Kerbel heard about my plans, he said, "Look, get out of the damn law shit and get into something where you'll be at practice every day, or I'll send your ass to Wheelin', and I don't mean West Virginia."

That was vintage Kerbel. He was as colorful and salty as he was big. And he was Texas big! As short as he was, carrying so much weight in his belly, you could have fit his jock strap over a 55-gallon steel drum. Try to imagine Bum Phillips, the onetime Oilers and Saints coach. Then almost double him.

Although we had our moments, I respected him and liked him as much as any coach I ever had. Unlike most other coaches I had, I also feared him. You might think that with my bull-in-the-ring attitude that I would not do well with an ex-Marine captain who ran his team like he ran his troops. But I have always been willing to buckle down and give my all for coaches I've believed in and coaches that were fair. By fair, I mean that they applied the same set of rules and standards to everyone on the team.

"If you listen to me, you'll never be wrong," Kerbel would tell us. "I'll be the sonofabitch that's wrong. So don't be out here thinking, just be out here listening." (Don Shula was a great coach, but I learned more from Joe Kerbel than any coach I ever had.) The man was so brilliant that as a center for Oklahoma in the late 1940s, he had called the plays in the huddle rather than the quarterback! He was fair, too. He was the boss and he treated us all the same... like dogs. He never gave us anything like cars or cash. He certainly never pampered us. We had to work hard for everything. I think that's the major reason why his teams were always so good (we were one of the top-ranked independents, right behind Penn State, my senior year).

When I arrived at school, I heard a slew of Kerbel stories. My favorite involved the game in which Kerbel sent in a substitute for Russell Mundy, one of his better running backs, after Russell made a mistake. Russell didn't think he should come out of the game, so he sent his would-be replacement off the field. When Kerbel saw the sub on the sidelines, he asked him why he wasn't in the game.

"Well I'm a sonofabitch," Kerbel said. "He told you to come out, huh? I'm the one with the brass balls around here. I say who goes in and who comes out." Whereupon the coach stopped the game and sent the West Texas State campus police onto the field to "apprehend" Russell. The coach then made Russell stand by himself in a corner of the stadium down by the end zone for the remainder of the contest. Kerbel warned the rest of the team not to go near him.

"If I catch any of you talking to him, come Monday, I'll take your laundry check," the coach said. (We received $15 a week for laundry.)

The National Collegiate Athletic Association (NCAA) did not permit freshmen to play on the varsity team when I was in school, so I spent my first year practicing and traveling with the team without seeing any game action. (Smitty and Mama visited me that fall in Athens, Ohio, when our team played Ohio University. Smitty was so happy to see me—college was the first time we had ever been separated for any length of time—that he broke down and cried.)

I also spent freshman year adjusting to life in what sometimes seemed a foreign country. There weren't any Blacks living in Canyon, save the fifty or so of us enrolled at the university. Of this scant number, about half were on the football team. There hadn't been any Blacks in Canyon period until 1960 when Kerbel had come to the school. He was one of the first southern coaches to go looking for Black talent. I had been in a minority at Avonworth High, too. But the ambience had been dramatically different up north.

The scene at the diner after the James Brown concert was an eye-opener, but it was not an isolated incident. It was impossible to escape the fact that Blacks (usually referred to as "Negroes") were in many ways second-class citizens. Much of this was so ingrained in society that it had ceased to be malicious. For example, the punter on the team, a local boy, had a black horse which he had affectionately called "Nigger." There was that red flag again. When I confronted him, he seemed genuinely surprised. He'd never even considered that such a name might be inappropriate or offensive.

Although I spent most of my weekends pumping iron to make myself exempt from the social barriers, I did begin to date a fellow student toward the end of my freshman year. It had been suggested to us Black students that we refrain from dating White women. Guess who I started seeing? Her name was Theresa Herrington. Her family lived in Amarillo. She was White, and she was beautiful (she was Miss Amarillo and would later be runner-up in the Miss Texas pageant). I hadn't set out to find one of the prettiest White girls on campus, but I had found her. There was a certain satisfaction in rebelling against the advice of the administration.

We met as I was on my way to Stafford Hall. "How come I never see you on campus?" she asked me.

"Because there's nowhere to go."

34

"You can go to Amarillo."

"What's there?" I asked snidely.

"Well, the town is there."

"And dirt roads. I been on them."

I'm not sure how interracial dating is looked upon in Texas these days, but in 1966 it was not viewed very kindly. Theresa and I knew from the outset that we would have to keep our relationship as secret as possible. We usually drove her car to a lover's lane off campus. Once a policeman from Canyon shone his flashlight on us. Next thing I knew I was talking to a dean, who suggested that I shouldn't be messing with "those" White girls because they were "trash." His point seemed to be that any White girl who would date a Black man had to be trash. I ignored him.

Theresa never played *Guess Who's Coming to Dinner* with me and her parents. They found out about us during sophomore year. Theresa's Irish father had married a Mexican woman, but he did not have a soft spot in his heart for those of my color. He reacted by saying that he was going to come to a football game and shoot me when I was in the end zone. This didn't deter me from trying to cross the goal line, but it scared some of my teammates. For a while none of them would come over to congratulate me after I scored.

"Hey, no offense, man, but you know what's up. Her old man might miss you and get me."

Even my Black roommate, John Henry Favors, cautioned me to avoid Theresa. "I'm gonna tell you somethin', boy," he said. "You better watch what you doin' with Theresa. You notice John Henry don't never wear no necktie, 'cause he don't like nothing tight around his neck. You better think about that when those White folk catch you with her. That's her car. You still got your feet. You better get on them and get your ass away from there." I ignored John Henry, too.

College football teams hold a week of practice each spring. "If you don't play well in spring ball, I'm not gonna invite you back," Kerbel told me my freshman year. "'Cause this is like a party. If you want to get invited, you gotta play well."

I received my "invitation" to play my sophomore year, and it was then that I moved from observing Joe Kerbel to *experiencing* him. Kerbel was like the great Green Bay Packers' coach Vince Lombardi in that he stressed the fundamentals of the game. This was ideal for me, because if you are to become a complete player capable of competing for a starting job in the NFL, you must have those fundamentals to complement your natural abilities. Problem was, if you messed up on fundamentals in practice or, heaven forbid, in a game, Kerbel was Ming the Merciless. More than once after I had fumbled in a game he grabbed me by the neck of my jersey, pulled me over so that we were eye to eye, gigantic belly to belly, asked me why I'd fumbled, released me, and then punched me in the solar plexus, where you can't tighten up. I'd known it was coming; I was just happy when it was over. Try to imagine the late Woody Hayes, the former Ohio State coach, and then double his intensity.

"You drop one more ball, you run one more pattern wrong, and by god, I'm gonna tell you, the both of us are gonna have to go to the hospital, 'cause they're gonna have to get my foot out of your ass."

Kerbel was so intense and animated—stalking up and down the sidelines yelling at us, yelling at the opposition, yelling at the officials—that no matter what the weather, he was always sweating. We played games where the temperature was only 8 degrees and he'd be drenched in perspiration. Such sideline behavior didn't endear the coach to those in the stands. Most of our supporters disliked him because of the way he yelled at us. Opposing fans absolutely hated him. At some road games, we had orders to stand around Kerbel so that the fans couldn't reach him to do bodily harm.

I remember one road game my sophomore year in which the coach really drew the wrath of the home crowd. We were in Tempe, playing Arizona State. We were leading 21–20 with less than 10 seconds to go when ASU called a time-out and set up for a short field goal that would beat us. Kerbel marched up our sidelines, ordering us all to shout, "Miss it! Miss it!" We thought that was bush, so instead of yelling we sat there chanting the words softly. He got so mad, he started hitting players. So of course we started shouting.

"Louder you s-o-b's," Kerbel cried. So we started screaming. And sure enough the kick hit the crossbar and bounced back and we won the game.

"Damn, you s-o-b's did it!"

Usually the day after a game, Sunday, Kerbel would have us down to the practice field to do what he called "triple 3's": three times around the field, three 100-yard dashes (form running the first 50 yards and sprinting the last 50 yards); and three 100-yard dashes running backward. In light of our victory in Tempe and the fact that we had stayed there overnight and didn't get back to Canyon until 6 p.m. the next evening and it was already dark out, some of us were foolish enough to think that the drills might be suspended. But as our bus pulled into school, assistant coach Harris relayed a message from Coach Kerbel (who drove his own station wagon to games). We were to get our cars, drive them to the practice field, put them in a circle, and turn our lights on so we could do our triple 3's. Kerbel was waiting for us. "You didn't think I was gonna let you all slide by, did you?" he grinned. I went and got my car—a 1965 Dodge Coronet—like the rest of the guys.

Although Kerbel had no qualms about me driving my car to the practice field, he didn't like me driving anywhere else. He thought I was going to get myself in trouble. (He had my number off the field, too!) Once he ran into me when I was trying to leave campus. "Dammit," he said. "Every time you start this car up you think you're supposed to go to Dallas or Houston. Give me the keys." He wanted me to stay on campus, so just like that he gave my car to our quarterback, Hank Washington. If I wanted to go anywhere, Kerbel said, I could ride with Hank.

Hank was one of several interesting individuals on our team. He was a junior college transfer from California, 6-foot-4, 210 pounds. He was so strong that he could throw the ball from end zone to end zone. In one all-star game, I saw him throw a sidearm pass 70 yards as he was on his way down to the turf. In 1965 and 1966, he was among the top in the country in total yardage. Yet he wasn't even drafted. Apparently the world, or at least the NFL, wasn't quite ready for a Black quarterback. The New York Giants did sign Hank to what was then a sizable free agent's contract of about $40,000. But they stuck him on a farm club, the Westchester Bulls. Apparently the Giants thought that just in case the NFL ever did become ready for a Black signal caller, they'd have one in the fold. Hank, of course, was ready to call signals. He could have been a star. But they disqualified him because of the color-he-was-not.

Hank never got his chance. He played on the farm club for a few years, then died of cancer. He was still in his twenties.

In addition to Hank, I had the privilege of attending school and playing football with some fellows who put the John Belushi character in *Animal House* to shame. Kerbel had a knack for recruiting excellent players who for some reason, maybe color or character, didn't appeal to many of the other schools in the country. Loaded with outcasts, we were the Oakland Raiders of the college ranks. The Funk brothers (yes, Dory and Terry Funk), Stan Hansen, Bob Duncum, and Dusty Rhodes were good old country boys. (Dusty is now a famous professional wrestler who bills himself "The American Dream.") On weekends, Dusty and company adopted a unique form of the American dream. They had a few drinks, took out their guns, and started shooting at each other... with live ammunition! Our team was about half Black and half White, and for the most part everybody got along fine. I had a terrific relationship with these guys, but, valuing my life, I tried to stay as far away from them as possible on the weekends.

Some people forget that Duane Thomas and I were in the same backfield at West Texas. Duane, who went on to star with the Dallas Cowboys, was a year behind me and had to wait until his senior season, after I was gone, to gain national recognition. But he had an outstanding junior year when I had my record-breaking senior year. It was clear that the coach really liked him. Kerbel was always looking for excuses to put Duane in ahead of our other running back, Albie Owens. (Albie was my roommate—another Black from Pennsylvania—and an excellent runner in his own right. The battle between him and Duane for playing time in 1968 reminded me of the battle I had in Miami with Jim Kiick.)

Duane got away with more than most of us. I recall one practice where Kerbel was screaming even more than usual at everybody. He'd temporarily demoted me to the second team because I'd done something like line up one inch away from where I was supposed to be. Then he yelled at Duane for something equally minor. Duane got mad and started to walk off the field.

"You come back here," yelled Kerbel. But Duane kept walking. "Did you hear me, Duane?"

Duane, a man of few words, turned around. "Fuck you," he told the coach. It was the only time I saw Kerbel at a loss for words. "Well, er, well, fuck you, too," he stammered.

The next day at practice Kerbel announced, "Duane has something to say. He wants to tell everyone he's sorry, that something in his personal life was bothering him and he's sorry. Right, Duane?"

Duane said, "Right." And that was the extent of the apology. I thought, man if I'd have done that, my invitation would have been rescinded and I'd be on my way back to Ben Avon.

Duane was a truly gifted runner, but he gained more notoriety for giving the press the silent treatment at Super Bowl VI than he did for his superb performance in that game or anything else he ever did between the sidelines. There was always a great deal of speculation about why he acted like he did. Some people saw him as a Black militant; some thought he was mentally unstable; and some thought he was just plain crazy.

Duane was reclusive before he reached the NFL. I watched at West Texas State as he became more and more withdrawn. But don't confuse silence with ignorance. Duane was an intelligent young man. He was also a product of his environment and the times. He grew up in Dallas, where Blacks had long been considered and treated as inferior. Local football hero that he was, he couldn't even play in the Southwest Conference because of the color barrier. He went off to college at a time when Black pride and Black power were spreading, when some Blacks were expressing their frustration through riots and others were sending a message with raised fists at the 1968 Olympics. Duane chose to "express" himself through silence. He also experienced a great deal of personal tragedy. When we were in college, his parents died within a short time of one another.

If he hadn't been in the giant fishbowl of sports, few people would have given a second thought to his actions. But then again if he hadn't been in the fishbowl of sports there would have been no press for him to shun. I think the problem was that he let his psychological makeup off the football field carry over onto the field. It might have been better if he had talked. Writers are going to write about you regardless of how you feel about the press. You might as well try to exercise some control, and I figure the only way you can do that is by keeping the lines of communication open. Unless people can understand you, then they're going to misunderstand you. I remember when football great Jim Brown started "talking" for Duane. That was ridiculous; Duane could talk for himself. (I wouldn't be surprised if Duane sometimes wishes he'd given his own interpretation of himself and his actions in those days.)

Duane wasn't the only Black on campus affected by the times. I had never subscribed to the isms that were supposed to keep me and others of my race in place, and now other Blacks weren't subscribing either. The assassination of Martin Luther King, Jr., had a great deal to do with this. The death of this brilliant nonviolent man by violence begat more violence. I remember talking to my grandparents on the phone and listening as they described how tanks were rolling down Center Avenue (now named Martin Luther King Jr. Boulevard) in Pittsburgh. Across America, Blacks rioted. "Enough is enough," we finally said. We raised our fists. And for the first time, Whites began to fear us...and listen.

On campus, there were candlelight vigils, not riots, after Dr. King's death. But a new militancy, a new pride, was apparent. By this time, Blacks were beginning to come to previously all-White institutions, not just to play sports, but to get an education. The Black population at West Texas State had grown with nonathletes from urban centers like New York and Boston. There were demands for Black organizations, Black fraternities, and a Black student union. As was the case on most campuses, most of these demands were met.

This is not to say that West Texas State was in the forefront of the civil rights movement. Old beliefs, particularly those which perpetuate your own status, die hard. I kept hearing: "You have to understand it's gonna take time for me to get used to the fact that you're equal to me."

Each of us had our own way of dealing with such stupidity. Although I participated in many of the protests on the campus, I was not a political person. When I saw John Carlos and Tommy Smith defiantly raise their fists at the 1968 Summer Olympics, I was glad and proud. I felt a certain amount of prowess. Here was a positive display, not of power, but of independence. The powers that be wanted the runners to put their hands on their hearts during the national anthem, knowing well and good that the closest these men could get to the reality of what the anthem stood for was right there where they were. It virtually took winning an Olympic gold medal (or excelling on the football field) to gain respect and fair treatment. The runners raising their fists and the boycott of the games by Lew Alcindor (now Kareem Abdul Jabbar) and other Black basketball players changed the life of every Black athlete. Athletics was now a forum for making a larger statement.

While I was proud that these symbolic gestures had been made, this was not the way I would have chosen to express myself (not the way I did choose to express myself). Instead of making grand gestures, I believed (and still believe) in one-on-one confrontations. Wars are won by fighting a seemingly endless series of small battles. Thus, if somebody has a horse named Nigger, you call him on it. If somebody tells you to sit in a separate section of the diner, you overcome that situation personally. In other words, you learn to control your own destiny so that whatever obstacles are thrown in front of you, you don't even see them as obstacles. On the football field, my style was to make defenders react to me, not for me to react to defenders. Off the football field, my style was exactly the same. I sought *control.* Political statements were important, but I was more concerned in making sure no one screwed me or anybody else (for I was quick to stand up for my "brothers and sisters") as we tried to achieve our goals.

Tanks never rolled down the streets of Canyon, but I can remember one incident that precipitated the use of such words as "riot helmet" and "snipers." The Kappa Alpha fraternity had a longstanding tradition of staging a "The South Shall Rise Again" celebration each spring. Members would dress up in Confederate uniforms, mount horses, and ride to the university president's home to inform him the Kappa Alpha "regiment" was "seceding" from the university. Dr. King's death signaled an end to Blacks' passive acceptance of such traditions. My personal response was, "Yeah, the South will rise again, and *I'll* be leading it."

The collective response of West Texas State Blacks was to plan a counterdemonstration. On hearing this, many White students said, "Oh, no you don't. We'll stop you." On hearing this, the Blacks said, "Okay, bring it!" There was talk that some of the White folk in Canyon might lie in waiting for any "niggers" who were going to protest this hallowed tradition. But the end result was that the fraternity exercised its constitutional right to make a fool of itself and we exercised our constitutional right to protest their tasteless not-so-hidden message.

The Kappa Alphas often seemed more comfortable with the past. On another occasion, they started waving a huge Confederate flag in the stands at one of our basketball games. My fraternity, Kappa Alpha Psi, was sitting right in front of the flag-wavers. We didn't appreciate this either. A confrontation almost ensued. To its credit, the university administration made those nostalgic for the Confederacy refrain from demonstrating such longings in public.

Black power wasn't the only political issue when I was in college. There was Vietnam. Everybody was involved in this debate. The lottery system made sure of that. You knew that if you were only taking twelve hours of class that made you a part-time student and, therefore, eligible for the draft. During the spring of 1967, I found myself in exactly that position. I was taking a double major in communications and psychology. I had started the semester by taking fifteen hours, but, failing one course, I dropped it. That meant I only had twelve hours. I had to go to summer school to pick up the hour needed to reclassify me as a full-time student. Unfortunately that short span of time when I had been considered part time was enough for Uncle Sam to send me the letter so many in my generation dreaded. "Greetings..." it began.

I had grown up watching the war on television. The graphic tale of death and destruction measured in the nightly body count—which reminded me of baseball box scores: Yankees 4, Red Sox 3. Yankees 25, Viet Cong 1500—brought home the reality that this was not a John Wayne or Audie Murphy movie, that the bodies, both maimed and lifeless, belonged to the people who were watching at home. While I had tremendous respect and sympathy for the young men who were serving in this undeclared war, I strongly opposed our involvement in Vietnam. I saw no reason for us to try to impose our form of government on another nation, particularly through military means; I couldn't see myself shooting at somebody I didn't know for a reason I didn't have; and I did not want to die for a cause I didn't believe in. By the end of my freshman year, three guys I'd grown up with had already been killed, and I didn't want my name added to the list. I am willing to protect my family and my house with a gun. I'll even protect my neighbor's house. But I'm not going to go halfway around the world and start killing people because they don't think the way I think.

Many people from my era devoted much time and energy to avoiding the draft. I was no exception. After hearing from Selective Service, I filed for a 1SC, which deferred proceedings for another semester. Then I joined ROTC. Me in ROTC? I had a reason. I was hoping the same back injury which had caused me to miss part of my senior year football season in high school would cause me to flunk the Army physical. I knew I couldn't just walk in to any draft board and say, "I want a physical right away, because I think I'll flunk." At the same time, I knew that before joining ROTC, I had to take and pass a physical. Signing up for ROTC forced the issue.

I was sent to the induction center in Amarillo for my physical. It was a zoo. There were guys who had cut off their thumbs to avoid the Army. There were guys insisting they were homosexual, guys wearing brassieres, guys who literally defecated all over themselves.

I failed the physical at the center and was sent to another doctor in Amarillo. As luck would have it, he was the brother of our team doctor. He wrote down something to this effect: "This fine, young, strong Negro specimen is neither fit for ROTC nor any other military service because of a bad back in the lumbar region of L-4 and L-5." So I was out. The Army didn't want to take the chance that I'd aggravate my old injury and end up on the dole the rest of my life. My ROTC career had lasted all of twenty-four hours. Although I had hoped this would work, I was finally relieved to know they wouldn't take me. That fear and anger about somebody making me have to fight an unjust war was over for me at least, but not for some others. The war would permeate all our lives until long after it ended.

My fellow cadets had thought I'd been eager to join. "Glad to have you on board," they'd said. But I only had one purpose in mind—to fail the physical. Taking nothing away from those who served so valiantly, I was determined to be in B Company—be here when they leave; be here when they come back. I never looked at a gun or uniform. That night I put on a different uniform. Dressed in West Texas State maroon and white, I gained something like 175 yards on ten carries in a spring game.

My junior year marked the end of one era and the beginning of another. In 1967, Smitty died. He had been real sick with emphysema. Then he developed pneumonia on top of that. When I came home from school that summer, I put him in the hospital. He looked right through me and told a nurse, "I wish Gene could be here with me." He was so ill that he didn't even recognize me. I was devastated. Still, the doctor told us that Smitty would be fine. We believed him.

The next night we got a call from the hospital. Smitty had taken a turn for the worse. My grandmother was already on her way over there, and when she arrived at 7:15, he was dead. He was 77.

His death hurt me so bad. He was such a giant of a man. That night I tried to console my relatives, tried to comfort my grandmother. This was the first death I had experienced in my family. I knew that I was the one who would have to be the strength in the family now. After pretending to be strong for a while, I just couldn't take it. I walked all the way down the road to the Ohio River, down by the railroad tracks. I thought about killing myself. A train came by and I almost jumped in front of it. I remember screaming out as the train roared by. "God, why him? Why not me?" I couldn't have been more than a foot from it. It could have sucked me in.

I couldn't bear to go to the funeral. I wanted to keep the memories of Smitty that I had. So I went to the park and played basketball as if it were just another day and he was gone off to work. My grandfather had raised me, and I didn't want to see him for the last time in a casket.

While my twentieth year was devastating on the home front, it was just the opposite on the football field. At long last I gained national recognition for my ability to run with the football. I rushed for 1274 yards, leading the nation until the final game, when a fellow named O.J. Simpson sneaked past me. This marked the beginning of a personal rivalry—more in my mind than his, I suspect—that was to last for the next decade.

Before 1967, O.J. had been as obscure as I had been, waiting in the wings at a California junior college for the chance to enter the University of Southern California. Running behind an incomparable line in an offense designed to highlight his talents, at a school in the national spotlight, the USC tailback was almost assured of making All-American and had a head start in the race for the Heisman Trophy, which is given to the outstanding collegiate player. "Juice," as O.J. was nicknamed, was a terrific runner, and I did not begrudge him his success our junior year when he was a first-team All-American and I was honorable mention. But I did envy the fact that he got so much more attention than I did. That, of course, was the difference between going to USC in the glamorous Pac 8 Conference (now the Pac 10) and independent West Texas State.

Juice's USC team was 10–1 in 1967 and went on to play in the Rose Bowl in Pasadena. Our team went 8–3 and earned a trip to the Junior Rose Bowl, also held in Pasadena, but with much less fanfare. While we were in California, I got a note from Juice. Enclosed was his autograph, which, he said, he thought I might like to have. Who does this guy think he is? I thought. I don't have anybody's autograph, and he's sending me his?

In 1968, our running battle intensified. I set a number of NCAA records, including most yards in a single game (340); most yards in a single season (1571); and most yards in a three-year career (3388). I almost didn't achieve the last two records. Entering our final game, I needed to rush for 112 yards to break each of them. We were playing Colorado State at their home in Fort Collins. It was a wet, snowy day in December, and the going was tough.

On one particular play there was an offsides whistled, but we continued with the play and threw a pass which Colorado State intercepted and then fumbled. In the middle of all this chaos, I ended up on the ground with a Colorado State lineman and we got into a wrestling match. The referee came over. "Number 99, number 22 , you're out," he said. He wrote down our numbers and ejected both of us from the game. I wasn't one to keep track of personal records during a game, but I knew I hadn't broken the all-time mark yet.

I trotted over to the sideline and told my replacement Curly Watters, "You better go in. I just got tossed out."

"Oh, shit," Curly said. "You told coach yet?"

"You crazy?" I wasn't anxious for a shot to the solar plexus.

At this moment, Kerbel came over to me. "What the hell are you doing here?" he asked.

"They kicked me out."

Kerbel grabbed me by the collar. "You sonofabitch. *I'll* tell you when you get thrown out of a game. Get your ass back in there."

So I went back in. I fully expected to be thrown right back out, and as soon as we broke the huddle, the Colorado State defense started screaming that I'd been ejected along with their own number 99. The officials called time-out and held a conference which must have lasted five minutes. Finally, they motioned for the Colorado State guy to come back. It turned out that in the midst of all the confusion, the referee had written down the wrong numbers. He had written "99 white" and "22 green," whereas it was just the opposite. Because of this technicality, I was allowed to stay in the game, and number 99 was also allowed to return. Our team was behind at the time, but I caught a pass for about a 50-yard gain and we rallied to win. It took me 35 carries (the same it had taken to gain 340 yards earlier in the season), but I got my 112 yards (exactly) to set the record.

The all-time rushing record lasted two years before it was broken by Don McCauley. The single-season mark lasted only one week. Juice broke it in his final game. Juice also won the Heisman. Although I thought I was the best player in the nation that year, I hadn't expect to win. But I was disappointed that I finished a distant ninth in the balloting. I know what the voters thought: Because Morris goes to such a small school, his records don't mean that much.

My response was and is: I believe whatever you do, you should be measured by what you accomplish, by your ability, not where you come from. Unfortunately, the media focus year after year on the big glamour schools like USC, Notre Dame, and Michigan. Take a look at the NFL, and you'll see that as many people come from the West Texas States and Gramblings of collegiate football as come from the so-called big-time schools. My senior year nine players from our team were drafted. That was the second highest total of any school. If what I did was so easy, there should have been a lot of people breaking those records. But some had stood for seventeen years until I broke them, and I was the only one to hold the single-game, season, and career rushing records at the same time. I knew what I'd done, and I was damn proud of myself.

I did achieve some recognition. I moved up to first-team All-American on some lists and I was the feature of a big spread in the October 1968 *Life* magazine. It was this *Life* article which solidified the image of me as "Mercury" Morris. In 1966, a local sportswriter described my running style as "mercurial" and this led to the nickname. Did I like it? Not particularly. I wanted to be known for my ability, not my nickname, but I really didn't have much say in the matter; that's what people started calling me.

When *Life* came down to Canyon, they played up the Mercury bit, putting wings on my feet and helmet for the photo session. Then they stood me in uniform on top of a big fiberglass buffalo that stood outside our stadium, the Buffalo Bowl. Nine feet above the ground, decked out like the Greek god of speed, I was supposed to be elusive, invincible, superhuman. What I was was scared! I've never enjoyed heights. Here I was one full story above terra firma.

Several of my teammates seemed excited about the possibility of sneaking into a picture or two, but Kerbel nipped that in the bud before the photographer arrived. "Some people from New York are coming down to take some pictures of Eugene," he explained to the entire team. Then he spoke to the second stringers: "I don't want any of you driftwood sonsofbitches hanging around him. I want only first team ballplayers. If I catch any of you hanging around him, I'll take your laundry check."

Kerbel didn't put himself in the "driftwood" category. At one point, the coach called me over. I stood by his side for five minutes waiting for him to say something as the photographer clicked away. Never saying a word, Kerbel finally dismissed me. Obviously, he had hoped to get in a photograph. His ploy worked. When the magazine came out, there was indeed a photo of Kerbel and Morris. It was fitting that we weren't the only two in the photograph. Standing behind us, captured with the coach for eternity, were a couple of the driftwood sonsofbitches that he had warned to stay away.

The end of my final college football season did not mark the end of my relationship with Kerbel. Shortly after the last game, a prank I was playing backfired...literally. I had been attempting to throw a cherry bomb from the window of a dormitory bathroom so that it would explode in a courtyard outside the dorm's television room where about fifty students were watching the movie *The Great Escape*. Because of a faulty fuse, I suddenly found myself holding a cherry bomb that was going to explode significantly ahead of schedule. I hadn't had time to properly lift up the screen of the bathroom window. I tried to force the cherry bomb out the window, but it hit the screen and bounced back into the tiny bathroom. It rolled across the floor, landed in the urinal, and then: BOOM!

The urinal exploded. The bathroom filled with smoke. My intended victims came running toward the bathroom door. Thinking quickly, I took the offensive. By the time everyone arrived, I had dropped my trousers halfway down to suggest I'd been sitting on the toilet. "What sonofabitch threw this thing in here at me?" I screamed. "I'm gonna kill that sonofabitch if I find him." I looked and sounded like a madman. The dorm head kept trying to calm me down, but I wouldn't stop.

The damage to the urinal was $380. The bombing remained a mystery for about three weeks. Then I was called to the dean's office. "We've been investigating the situation," the dean told me. "We've come to the conclusion that the only person who possibly could have done it was you."

Again, I attacked. "*What?* Are you out of your mind? Don't you realize I could have been blinded. I've got a pro career ahead of me and somebody comes in and ruins it just like that, and you want to say it's me?" I reached into my pocket. "I'll tell you this: you can take this student card 'cause I don't want to be here anymore."

"Now hold on," the dean said. "We didn't say you actually did it. We're just saying our investigation showed..."

"What *are* you saying?"

"That it's gonna cost everyone in that dorm $1.20 to fix that urinal."

"Are you saying you want me to pay for it?" I acted as if I were outraged. "Who was gonna pay for my funeral if it killed me?"

"Take it easy."

Kerbel knew I'd done it. He called me in and said: "Look at me. Just as sure as I'm a s-o-b, I know that you're the one. Hear? 'Cause I know you. Remember, I'm the one who came up and got you from Pittsburgh. I'm not gonna say nothin' 'cause that's not my business over there, *you're* my business. But you better watch your ass or you're gonna get your ass in trouble. They've already told me they don't want you on campus, so you're gonna have to move off campus." I did...gladly.

The NFL draft was in February of 1969. I was certain that I'd be drafted in the first round, and pretty sure that the Dallas Cowboys would be the team to pick me. I already had found an agent. Or rather he found me. First thing he did, long before the draft, was buy me a double-breasted coat and a pair of alligator shoes. (Actually, I bought them. He advanced me the money, then took it out of my signing bonus.) He also took me to Super Bowl III, held that January in Miami. This was the game in which Shula's Baltimore Colts were upset by Joe Namath and the Jets.

This wining and dining of potential clients by agents was commonplace and rivaled the recruiting at some colleges. Some of my teammates were jealous. After an All-Star game in Tampa, my friend AZ went out and bought a pair of fake alligator shoes (they were "pleather"—plastic and leather). "Look man, we're tight, we're friends," he told me. "Don't you tell nobody that these aren't the real thing."

As expected, Juice was the first player selected. He was on his way to the lowly Buffalo Bills. When the Cowboys got their first chance, they chose Calvin Hill, an almost unknown running back from Yale.

The first round passed. I was highly disappointed no one had selected me. I thought the criterion was to be able to gain yards and score touchdowns, and that my record spoke for itself. Then, the second round passed. Man, what's happening? I wondered. It wasn't until the third round that the Dolphins picked me. Fifty-five players preceded me. How could that be?

Only later did I realize that the prototype NFL running back was a Paul Hornung type, 6-foot-2, 215 pounds. At 5-foot-10, 180 pounds, I didn't fit the stereotype. There was no place for a "little" guy like me, the story went. Backs needed to do so many things that required strength. "Well, I have the strength," I argued.

"Yes, but you don't have the size."

No pun intended, it was Catch 22.

Shortly after the draft, I received news that a girl I had been dating for a short time was pregnant and expecting our child in the fall. Her name was Kay. She was a stewardess based in Miami. I had met her at a party after an All-Star game in the winter (several months after I had broken up with Theresa) and we had begun a long-distance relationship.

I had always said that I had no intention of marrying until my days in the NFL were over. I didn't want to be tied down, didn't want the responsibility of a family. I wanted to be able to devote all my energies to succeeding on the football field (and maybe a little energy to enjoying the fast life of an NFL bachelor!). Now, here I was before my career had even begun with a critical decision to make. Kay and I barely knew each other. I barely knew myself. If she hadn't been pregnant, we wouldn't even have considered marriage. But I did the White, er right, thing and married her. After I finished school (a full 47 credits short; there was little pressure for us athletes to get a degree), we settled in together in Miami.

I had to return to Texas during the summer to clear up one rather large loose end. In February, not too long after the draft, I had run into trouble off campus. I was at Gene Morrison's Shamrock Station in Canyon gassing up the new Corvette I'd bought after signing with the Dolphins. Also at the station were three old Black dudes in an old 1949 Pontiac. They had their hood up and smoke was pouring out of the radiator. A car full of high school kids drove by, and I heard those words, "Hey, nigger." I figured the kids were yelling at the three old men—my status as football hero made me immune to such attacks—but it didn't matter. In essence, they were yelling at me.

I controlled myself. Might as well let them go, I thought. I'm going into town. But then the car came back and the kids yelled at the men again. Wait a minute. I can't let this go now. The men don't deserve that. I don't deserve that. The war will be won, not by dramatic gestures, but by fighting one battle at a time. I took off after the kids in the Corvette. I caught up with them and then like Broderick Crawford in *Highway Patrol,* I pulled them over to the curb. I got out of my car.

One of the kids recognized me. "Oh, Mr. Morris. I'm sorry. I didn't know it was you."

"I've got no problem with you guys, but if you want a problem you'll have it. Get out of your car." I said.

"Oh, Mr. Morris."

I slapped him three or four times à la Joe Kerbel. Then I let him go. "Hey, I don't ever want to hear or see you again."

The next morning I was arrested for aggravated assault and battery, a felony. The police took me to jail. I bonded out. There was a big to-do in the press. The kid who brought charges against me claimed he had said, "Hey, Mercury." I said that wasn't so and took a lie detector test, which I passed. The felony charges were eventually dropped, but then the kid had his mother sue me for $25,000 in civil court.

I knew I was up against it. Here I was. The kid's a minor. He lives in Amarillo. I'm a Black. I live in Pittsburgh. I drive a Corvette. I'm a football star, on my way to the pros. I'm known to date White women, a mortal sin in White folk's eyes. The judge, the jury, the lawyers are all White. In fact there's only one other Black besides me in the courthouse and he's cleaning up. I'm wearing a pinstriped suit, probably looking like a Black Al Capone.

My lawyer put the kid's mother on the witness stand. "How do you feel about Blacks, about Negroes?" he asked.

"Well, 'niggers' is as good a word to refer to them as anything else," she answered.

Again, I controlled myself.

My lawyer, who had been referred to me by my agent, was totally incompetent. He knew it and had enlisted the aid of an old, retired Texas Supreme Court justice. The old man would lean over his shoulder, coaching him and telling him what to say. It looked ridiculous. Meanwhile, the kid's lawyer was a regular Hamilton Burger, running circles around us. We broke for lunch. My lawyer could see how depressed I was. "Don't worry, son," he said, putting his arm halfway around my shoulder, "we've defended niggers before, and we're gonna get you off."

I left town right then. I went straight to the airport. "I'll call you and you can tell me how it comes out," I told my lawyer.

Initially, the jury split 11 to 1 in favor of awarding the full $25,000 to the kid. They finally agreed on $2500. I never paid it. And for a long time, I never returned to Texas unless I absolutely had to. It was an unpleasant way to end my college career. I stood up for what was right—but right to whom? It just seemed to get me into a lot of trouble.

Looking back, I'm not particularly proud of some of my actions. The bull-in-the-ring attitude rarely served me well off the football field. I could have turned the other cheek and never chased those kids. It would have made things a lot easier for me and everyone else. But, I was 22 years old and my experience up to that point had led me to believe I could do anything... from rushing for more yards than anybody in history to stamping out racial injustice. To understand me—to understand anyone from Joe Kerbel to Duane Thomas to these kids to my lawyers—you must be aware of time and place. The kids were reflecting where they were; I was reflecting where I was—in the deep south, 1969. We make progress in this world when your "where" and my "where" come closer together.

CHAPTER 4

THE APPRENTICESHIP, 1969–1971

As disappointed as I was at being drafted in the third round, I liked the idea of going to Miami. I liked the idea of playing in a warm climate, and the Dolphins, an expansion team born in 1966, seemed to be heading in the right direction. The team had improved in each of its first three seasons, beginning with a 3–11 record, then moving to 4–10, and then in 1968, a record of 5–8–1. The Dolphins' Director of Player Personnel, Joe Thomas, was highly regarded, and he had started to put together a fine team, making Bob Griese, the unflappable All-American quarterback from Purdue, his first round pick in 1967, and Larry Csonka, the bruising running back from Syracuse, the first pick in 1968.

There was one more reason that I liked Miami. O.J. Simpson had been drafted by Buffalo. The Bills had been in existence since 1960 and had enjoyed glory during the early years of the upstart American Football League, but the franchise had fallen on hard times, winning one less game than the Dolphins in 1968. So in my continuing rivalry with Juice, I saw an opportunity for us to finally duel on common ground, playing on teams that were of equal ability.

While our teams were equal, our contracts were not. Juice stayed away from preseason camp, holding out until he received a huge salary. On the other hand, I signed a three-year contract which consisted of a $17,000 signing bonus and $19,500 salary the first year, $21,500 in year 2, and $23,500 in year 3; there were also incentive clauses which could earn me a little more money if I won, say, the conference kickoff return championship.

The Dolphins preseason camp began in July. One of my first official duties was attending and speaking at a local boosters' breakfast. At the gathering our coach, George Wilson, told the group he had high hopes that the 1969 Dolphins could win half our games and improve to 7–7. When it was my turn to speak, I took issue with him and said: "Did I just hear him say that it's okay to lose seven games? Well, that's not okay with me. I'm here because I want to go 14–0. If we lose the first game, I want to go 13–1, and if we lose the second I want to go 12–2. But I certainly want to do better than 7–7."

Those remarks didn't stand too well with Wilson, and about this time Joe Thomas told the press something like, "You have to watch Mercury. He's as quick with his tongue as he is with his feet."

I enjoyed public speaking and, for the most part, talking to the press. And the press and the public seemed to enjoy listening to me. Your stereotype football player, certainly your stereotype Black football player, is generally not viewed as particularly articulate. The response to me was: here's a guy that can articulate, a football player that can talk, and he's Black, too. The fact that I spoke my mind made me even better copy. Soon I was doing a column called "Diary of a Rookie" for a local paper.

My entry dated July 30, 1969, caused a bit of a stir. It carried the headline "De Facto Segregation in Dolphin Camp," and read in part:

> There's a sticky situation here at the Dolphins' camp. I've been doing my best to get rid of it. There's a de facto segregation being practiced here and it's as much my Black brothers fault as anyone else's. The first day in camp I noticed it right away.
>
> In the dining hall there'd be a table with nothing but Blacks sitting there, all whites at another table, etc. There aren't any signs on the tables saying anyone has to sit at any specific table, but it always ends up the same way....
>
> One day I walked into the shower and saw all the Black fellas crowded into one area, and the whites off to another side. I said, "Oh, no, we can't have this stuff." So I moved them all about, mixing them up, you know. I want us to be a team. All that dirty water rolls down one drain.

I didn't mention in the article that the White guys were standing under the nozzle where the water was coming out like Niagara Falls, while the Black guys were willing to accept this little trickle. Not me.

In addition to the Black-White division in camp, there was the split between rookies and veterans. Some of this was fun, some not so funny (to me). I didn't like veterans cutting in front of me in the food line, just because they'd been around longer, and I'd say so. That protocol was okay in the taping room, but not in the cafeteria.

Not surprisingly, some of the veterans didn't appreciate such behavior or my behavior at the party when each rookie had to get up and sing. The purpose of this exercise was for the rookies to make fools of themselves. But if you didn't sing, the veterans threw you in the small lake outside of our training complex with delight. I sang all right. Three Temptations' songs. That was two too many, and by the end, I had the veterans begging me to stop. I avoided the lake that day, but the older guys eventually decided I was a little too much of a smart ass and tossed me in a few days later.

The worst part of the rookie ritual was the annual rookie party. We had to chew tobacco, then drink warm beer and chase it down with pineapple wine. I got sick before I got drunk. I can remember crawling on my knees from the bar to the Atlantic Ocean to throw up. I've never been as ill. Worse, each time you got sick, the veterans would say, "Now he's got room for more again." And start the cycle over.

I was happy when the season began, and happier after I got my hands on the ball for the first time. Of course, I wanted to be starting in the backfield, but my rookie status and the stigma relating to my size were working against me. Wilson had designated Csonka and the hard-nosed halfback Jim Kiick as his principal ballcarriers. I was penciled in as kickoff and punt returner. (Over at Buffalo, Juice was also running back kicks. His contract dispute set him back several days and then, believe it or not, he lost some more time when the Bills couldn't find a helmet to fit his unusually large head!)

My career began in fairy-tale fashion. Our first game of the season was against the Cincinnati Bengals. The Bengals scored first and then kicked off. I caught the ball 5 yards deep in our end zone— although I didn't know where I was at the time. I just knew that this was my first game and I was taking off. I think a lot of guys must have thought I was going to down the ball in the end zone, but I just started hauling ass. I came up the middle, then broke out to the left and went straight down the field for 105 yards. Our bench was on the opposite side of the field, and after I got into the end zone, I ran another 100 yards over there, where teammates, Black and White, rookie and veteran, mobbed me. The run was a team record and the second longest return in NFL history.

I thought it was going to be that way every week. I thought that I'd be able to break away on every kickoff and punt I returned. I didn't. I had some successes and some failures. My most notable failure came in a game against the Patriots when I caught a punt on our 8-yard line, got bumped back to the 4 by my up blocker, and then, not knowing where I was, backed up five more yards to get some running room. By then it was too late. I was tackled in the end zone for a safety. This time my teammates weren't so friendly. "What the hell you doing, rookie?" they yelled. We had been winning 16–0. The safety made the score 16–2. We ended up losing 38–23. After the game I saw Coach Wilson on television saying, "As far as I'm concerned, Mercury Morris lost the game for us because he pulled a high school move." I thought, We lost 38–23. How can he blame me for the game? Then I realized that his job was on the line and he had to say something.

I didn't like running punts back that much. It's a dangerous job which requires a lot of skill. While eleven big, fast, hungry special teams' players charge down the field intent on burying you, you must catch a ball that seems to hang interminably in the air, determine where you are and where you have to go. It took me a while to get accustomed to it.

My best effort that year was against the Chiefs, who would go on to win Super Bowl IV a few months later. We played them on a cold, rainy day in Kansas City. When we went out for pregame practice, Hank Stram, the Chiefs' coach, saw me and said, "Hey, Willie." Willie West had played cornerback for Miami the year before and had worn the number I now wore—22.

I pointed to my jersey and said, "Hey, my name's not West. Look at my name back here."

"Okay," Stram said.

"I'm going to make you remember that," I said.

I returned six punts for over 160 yards. On my best return, I caught the ball on our 4-yard line, went into the end zone 9 yards deep, and brought the ball out 57 yards. When I went 9 yards deep,

I raised some eyebrows, but I figured getting caught 1-yard deep in the end zone and 9 yards deep is the same thing, and nine yards gave me more maneuverability. The moral is: if you're gonna take a chance, take the whole chance. In that game, I also scored a touchdown on a 7-yard run, one of the rare rushing touchdowns which the Chiefs gave up all season.

I only rushed the ball twenty-two other times that entire year. That was disappointing, as was our record of 3–10–1. For the first time in its four-year history, the team had not improved.

My rookie year as a husband was even less successful than my rookie year as a Dolphin. It's hard enough for two adults to make a marriage based on mutual love and respect work. Kay and I were two kids who had shared a mutual physical attraction. We had also shared the desire to legitimize the result of that attraction, but that was about it. We weren't ready for each other or marriage.

Our shotgun union was shaky from the beginning. This was OJT (on-the-job training) for me. I didn't really know what being married and being a father meant. For one of the few times in my life, I felt that I hadn't been able to control my destiny. I had planned not to marry until after my career was over. Yet, never even having carried the football one time in the NFL, I found myself with not only a wife, but with a child on the way. The on-the-field and off-the-field distractions of being a high-profile NFL player did not help matters. Coach Wilson demanded my time during the day, and I wanted to spend much of my free time being free—carousing with teammates.

In November, Kay bore Eugene Morris, Jr. Our apartment complex did not allow children. I sent Kay home to her family in Columbus, Ohio. We never got back together. (For many years, Kay felt a great amount of animosity toward me—much of it warranted. She eventually remarried. I have seen Eugene, Jr., periodically, but not as much in recent years as I would like. I plan to remedy that situation.)

Kay wasn't the only fixture from my rookie year missing as I entered my second season. Owner Joe Robbie had fired Wilson and brought in Don Shula, who had been so successful with the Baltimore Colts. It was a brilliant move. Shula was a superb coach, and the Miami Dolphins turnaround began immediately.

The nucleus for a championship team was already in place when Shula arrived, but he quickly added the missing pieces and, equally important, he completely changed the attitude from one of complacency to hunger. You weren't going to hear Shula or anyone else on the Dolphins say a 7–7 season was the goal, even if that was realistic.

In 1970 alone, Shula and Joe Thomas either drafted or traded for such stalwarts as Paul Warfield, Jake Scott, Marv Fleming, Bob Kuechenberg, Tim Foley, Curtis Johnson, Mike Kolen, Doug Swift, Jim Mandich, Hubie Ginn, and Garo Yepremian. All played a major role in the eventual success of the franchise—be it on defense, the offensive line, or in the kicking game—but Warfield and Scott were pivotal. Coming to Miami after five years with an established and highly professional organization like the Cleveland Browns, Paul was a wonderful role model, not to mention a complete football player. He had the best jumping and timing ability of any receiver I've ever seen. He is remembered for his smooth-as-silk moves, but he was also an excellent blocker. Paul was not an inciter, but he led by example. Jake, on the other hand, was a holler guy. A good ole country boy who came to the team from the University of Georgia via the Canadian Football League, he added spunk and savvy to the defensive backfield and a lot of fun to the team's off-the-field comings and goings.

The preseason strike of 1970 set Shula's rebuilding program back a few weeks, but it was apparent from the beginning that the somewhat casual practice atmosphere which had prevailed under his predecessor was history. Coaches are thought to be tough if they hold two long practices a day. Shula ordered four such sessions a day. Although, like everyone else on the team, I didn't relish four-a-days, I was delighted that we had such a committed leader. Unfortunately, I was injured on the very first day of practice.

The strike ended after fourteen days, and everybody went straight to camp. I remember the events of our first day of practice quite clearly. We were running sprints and drills, and it was getting darker and darker. Then the next thing we knew, it was nighttime and we were still practicing—with no lights. One of our linebackers ran into me, putting his knee into my thigh. The team doctor took a look at the thigh and said I'd be okay in a day or two. I went up to the team meeting after practice. The thigh started to swell. It hurt so much I was actually crying. The swelling continued, and my thigh became hard as a rock because it was hemorrhaging inside. It was bleeding so hard, it seemed like it was about to burst. The next morning I was in surgery.

The procedure the doctor used was a new one at the time, called aspiration. Up until 1970, the normal procedure was to cut open the thigh, cut open the muscle, milk the bad blood out, stitch up the leg, and tell the player to go home for the season. Aspiration allowed the doctors to put holes about the size of a straw in my leg and drain the blood through small tubes. The hope was that I'd be able to return to play in a couple of months.

When I woke up from surgery, I saw the bandage on my leg. Whew, that's over, I thought. But next thing I knew it was back to the operating room to remove the tubes from my thigh and stitch me up. For some reason which I still don't understand (and to this day it still angers me), the doctor refused to give me an anesthetic, either general or local. He took the bandage off, put me on the table, and a nurse said, "Here, take these two fingers and hold onto them."

That was my anesthetic as, only one day after the initial operation, they removed seventeen tubes that were set into my leg almost all the way to the bone and then stitched me up. No novocaine, no nothing. Lying there, I felt like I was in the old west. "Doctor, please," I said. I was sweating like a pig. "You gotta do something." Then, never having felt such intense pain, I threw up.

I started to cry. The doctor was calm. "You'll have to stop moving," he said. "Each time you move I have to go back in there." The seventeen stitches required going in and out thirty-four times. The doctor missed once, so it was in and out thirty-five excruciatingly painful times. The needle was thick because the meat of my thigh was deep. I passed out after the last stitch.

A few days later, the Dolphins left Miami for Jacksonville to play their first exhibition game against the Steelers. The team doctor went with them, and when the hospital released me that same day, I learned he hadn't left any instructions for me.

I didn't know what to do. I felt abandoned. So I did what any sane human being would do. I called another doctor, a gentleman affiliated with the University of Miami. He looked at my thigh, told me to keep it elevated, to keep a pressure bandage on it, and he prescribed some medication.

When I came back to camp and mentioned to Shula that I'd seen another doctor, he hit the roof and told me I was never to do that again without consulting him or someone else first. "But you were gone," I said. "How could I consult anyone?" Shula got even madder.

I was pissed off and hurt. They'd left me alone with no instructions and I'd tried to do what's right, and now the head coach was jumping on me because (I figured) my actions made the team's actions look bad. I've done plenty of things in my life to earn a dressing down, but this didn't seem like one of them. So from the start, Shula and I did not get off on the right foot so to speak.

It was about ten weeks before I could practice again. On my first day back in pads, I noticed something about Nick Buoniconti, our excellent veteran linebacker. Nick, who had come to the team in 1969 from the Patriots, seemed to be hitting some of our backs harder than others as they ran through the line. Some of the other defenders seemed to be following his lead. Thus when a Csonka or Kiick would run, Nick and the others might hit him, but not that hard. But when, say, a Hubie Ginn, another of our backs, ran, Nick and company would try to knock his head off. Nick and I would go on to become fairly good friends, but I didn't like this one bit. Here we go again, I thought. What the hell is this? This is practice. You want to warm up like that on somebody, then warm up like that on everybody. Don't pick and choose. 'Cause you ain't picking me.

Sure enough, I came through the line and Nick whacked me à la Ginn, rather than in the Csonka or Kiick manner. And sure enough, I turned around and threw the ball and hit him in the face. I'd been out for two and a half months. I hadn't been back for ten minutes, and I'm already getting ready to fight. Teammates were holding both of us back. I said, "You want to rock me in practice, that's fine. But do it to everybody."

We left our animosity on the practice field. That's the way it's done. But I'd sent a message. I wasn't going to take any of that shit. I wasn't demanding special treatment. All I wanted was the same treatment as everybody else.

The 1970 season was a bad news and good news one. The bad news was that my injury limited my opportunity to help the team. I didn't carry the ball until our fifth game of the season and rushed but sixty times all year for 409 yards. Still, I averaged 6.8 yards a carry, the best average in the NFL for backs carrying the ball over fifty times. The good news was that under the new Shula regime, the team did an about face, moving from 3–10–1 in 1969 to 10–4. We made the playoffs for the first time in the club's history. Over in Buffalo, Juice Simpson gained a disappointing 488 yards and the Bills finished 3–10–1.

Our success was tempered by the fact that Mama died in the middle of the season. Her death hurt me. She had been the quiet, but omnipresent, backbone of our family. Shula had a rule that you could only leave the team to attend the funeral of your mother or father. I lied and told him my mother had died. I didn't like doing it, but in a way Mama was my mother. She had raised me. I wanted to say good-bye properly.

Life goes on. Not too long after Mama died, I became a father for the second time. Maceo was born February 16, 1971. His mother, Dorothy, was a stewardess whom I had met at the swimming pool in my apartment complex shortly after Kay left. After dating for a short while, we moved in together in the spring of 1970. We felt no need to get married after we found out Dorothy was pregnant or after Maceo was born. This was hardly unusual. The early 1970s were a time of free love and rebellion against establishment traditions like marriage.

I was still far from being the perfect mate. I still didn't know what a strong two-way relationship entailed. I still believed in the old double standard: The man should have the freedom to go out and do what he pleases, but "Woman, I better not catch you messing around."

Despite this lack of maturity, I tried very hard to be a good father. It wasn't easy. When Maceo was 8 months old, Dorothy left to pursue a career as a Playboy Bunny. I couldn't understand how she could do this, but I'm sure there were things that I did that she couldn't understand either. Our family would never have been mistaken for *Ozzie and Harriet* or *Leave It to Beaver* before Dorothy left, but I hadn't expected to be playing *Bachelor Father*, either. (What goes around, comes around. I had left Kay in the same position.)

Dorothy's timing was rotten. It was the middle of the 1971 season. I arranged for a neighbor to care for Maceo. I would drop him off before practice and pick him up on my way home. The only silver lining in this cloud was that Dorothy's absence (she eventually came back) brought Maceo and me close together.

Despite these distractions, I had a fine 1971 season. More important, so did the team. We won the division title, the AFC championship, and earned a trip to the Super Bowl—a phenomenal achievement for a franchise that had only been in existence for six years.

I had hoped to see more action at running back, but a preseason ankle injury and Shula's infatuation with the backfield tandem of

Csonka and Kiick, aka "Butch Cassidy and the Sundance Kid," limited my playing time. So in this, my third season, I was still primarily a kickoff and punt returner. I ended up leading the conference in kickoff return average that year (28.2) and ran back one 94 yards for a touchdown against New England. I even made the Pro Bowl as the AFC's kickoff return specialist. I saw Juice there, but he was just a spectator, having gained 742 yards while the Bills went 1–13. "What are you doing here, man?" he teased me from the sidelines. "Gimme a break," I said.

I was pleased and proud of my accomplishments, but I was also frustrated. I thought I should be running the ball more and periodically made those feelings known to the coaching staff and the press.

There is no doubt that Csonka and Kiick, two meat-and-potatoes runners who were the best of friends, made for a potent combination. They were hard working and they were successful. In 1971, Csonka gained 1051 yards, while Kiick gained 738 and picked up another 338 on forty receptions. Their play was instrumental in leading us to the Super Bowl that season.

Kiick was a better blocker and receiver than I was, and could throw the halfback option pass better than I could, but I believed that I could bring a dimension to our game that he could not—speed, the breakaway threat, and the ability to run the ball outside. I was, as the events of 1972 and 1973 proved, correct. But for a long time I was perceived as a villain, the man who would dare to break up Butch and Sundance.

I think Jim would be the first to agree that none of this was personal. We got along just fine. I respected him and his abilities and always made that clear to anyone who asked. But I also respected my own abilities and truly believed I should be getting my hands on the ball more frequently. As it was, I only carried the ball 57 times for 315 yards that year, a 5.5 yards per carry average, and scored one rushing touchdown. Most of those carries came during two games Kiick missed due to injury, and I carried only once in three postseason games.

While it's hard to quarrel with the team's success that season, I felt we could have been better if I had been better utilized. To me the proof of the pudding was Super Bowl VI, in which we were humiliated by the Dallas Cowboys 24–3. The game was more of a rout than the score indicates. We were the first team in Super Bowl history not to score a touchdown, and we gained only 80 yards rushing and three rushing first downs under Shula's conservative up-the-middle game plan. My old teammate Duane Thomas alone gained 95 yards rushing on 19 carries for the Cowboys. I never rushed the ball once.

I didn't disguise my feelings about this turn of events. I knew that if I was out there, I could be turning the corner and opening up our offense. As the game progressed, so did my frustration. In the fourth quarter, the Cowboys, already leading 21–3, tried a fake field goal. This was the straw that broke the camel's back. Our offense was being embarrassed; I wasn't being used; Duane was having a great game; and now the Cowboys were sending the message that they weren't satisfied just winning the game; they wanted to bury us. I took all of this personally. How could we come this far and lose? I erupted on the sidelines, kicking over the tables which held our drinks and telephones. But it was after the game that I *really* let my feelings be known. I second-guessed Shula in front of the media. (Why did I do that? I ask myself fifteen years later!)

I was sitting in front of my locker, arms crossed, my frustration evident. A reporter came up and I told him that we would have won the game if I would have played, that my outside speed was ideally suited to beat the Cowboys' defense, which was strongest inside because of the presence of tackles Bob Lilly and Jethro Pugh and middle linebacker Lee Roy Jordan. "But I never got a chance," I said. "The only time I got off the bench was for the kickoffs and the national anthem." The odd thing was that in preparing for the game, we had been practicing sweeps all week, and I'd been the one running them. Then, come game time, Shula never used the sweeps or me. (Did I really think we'd have won if I'd played? At the time, I probably did. Looking back now, I'm not so sure we would have won, but we'd have done a lot better.)

It didn't take Shula long to learn I'd said something. He came out of the shower with that wet-head look of his and found me. We were among the few left in the locker room. It was like a scene from *The Gunfight at OK Corral.* He said something like, "If I find you've said anything, you've had it."

"Fine," I said.

We were both mad. Shula, I imagine, because for the second time in the last four years, he'd lost a Super Bowl (the first was the Joe Namath–led New York Jets' monumental upset of Shula's Colts in 1969), and me because I didn't get a chance to help us win.

The next day he was quoted in the press as saying, "I know he's disappointed and wanted to play more. But we got here with Kiick and Csonka.... I can understand an athlete being disappointed because he wants to play. It shouldn't be any other way. But if he has a complaint, he should come to me first." He did acknowledge that we had known we had to run outside to beat Dallas, but said he wanted Kiick in the backfield because he was a good blocker and could set up Csonka's runs.

The confrontation after the game and the tremendous amount of publicity it generated was Step One in convincing Shula to give me a shot at making the starting lineup in 1972. Step Two came a week later at the Pro Bowl. (This was my first, and I took a certain satisfaction in having made it before O.J., who had not yet hit his stride in the pros.) I fully expected to be used only as a kick returner, but with injuries nagging Csonka and the other AFC backs, Cleveland's Leroy Kelly and Denver's Floyd Little, our AFC coach, Don McCafferty, played me in the backfield, too. I had a good game, running back three kicks for 93 yards (including the opening kick of the second half for 61 yards) and carrying the ball seven times for 55 yards. We won 26–13, and as I recall, after the game both McCafferty and Dallas's coach Tom Landry had high praise for my play and wondered openly why I wasn't seeing more playing time in Miami. Their comments would make it even harder for Shula to ignore the situation.

Being the great coach he was, I don't think Shula really wanted to ignore me. He wanted to win as badly as I did. Before the 1972 season began, he told me he was going to give me my shot to play. I didn't expect him to give me a second chance if I failed. I'd shot my mouth off. Now the ball was in my hands. The apprenticeship was over.

CHAPTER 5

GLORY YEARS, 1972–1973

All the pieces were in place for 1972 to be the year of the Miami Dolphins. Our team had tremendous talent. We were still a young squad, but we were maturing rapidly and had veterans like Nick Buoniconti and Paul Warfield in key spots. We had playoff experience and, humiliating as it was, Super Bowl experience, too. Maybe most important, we had a closeness, a togetherness that could get us over any hurdle. We were one of the few teams I have ever been on where there was no rivalry between the offense and defense. Everyone pulled for each other, including me and Jim Kiick.

We had our cliques, but they never deteriorated into the disruptive forces I've seen them become on other teams. Ours were more humorous than anything else. I belonged to the "180 Club." We discriminated only on the basis of weight. Membership was open to anyone who weighed 180 pounds or more, but less than 200 pounds. (I was up to about 190 pounds at the time.) As you might guess, our constituency was largely running backs, wide receivers, and defensive backs. Our opposite number was the "250 Club." Sole requirement for membership here was weighing at least an eighth of a ton. Defensive linemen, offensive linemen, and small trucks only need apply. There was also the Redneck Club. These were your good old beer-drinkers. Jake Scott was the leader of this group.

Despite our different backgrounds, Jake and I were birds of a feather. It was always quite a battle between the two of us to see who would be fined the most over the course of a season by Shula.

One year Jake got a big jump on me in this department because he defied the coach and went skiing during the season. We had ten days between a Thursday game and a Monday night game, and Jake just headed for the slopes of Colorado. He was kind enough to send a "Snowed in!" telegram. Mad as Shula was, it was obvious he loved Jake, and if there was any group the coach seemed to hang out with, it was the Rednecks.

Finally, there were the Rowdy Boys. Who's the most rowdy? The guys who play defense, of course. The members of this group, Nick Buoniconti among them, could be identified by their weekly haircuts. As it was not popular (in some quarters) to have curly hair, these guys would make sure their hair was as straight as possible. Once a week they'd come to the practice field from the barbershop with hairdos looking like Dion and the Belmonts or Bobby Rydell. Problem was the minute they put their helmets on, the hairdos disintegrated.

To some extent the de facto segregation that I had noted three years earlier still existed, but it was merely a reflection of the times, nothing malicious. I considered the White guys as well as the Black guys as friends. Attempts to overcome any racial differences were often funny. For example, the club provided combs, haircream, and other toiletries and grooming aids in the locker room for $5 dues per week. In 1971, Shula took it upon himself to bring in a variety of products for the Blacks on the team. All of a sudden, in addition to Brylcreem and straight combs, there was Afro Sheen and Afro picks. It was a nice, if a bit awkward, gesture. A few weeks later Shula approached Larry Csonka. "How did the Afro Sheen go over?" the coach asked sincerely.

"Ask them," Csonka responded. "What the heck are you asking me for? I'm Hungarian like you are!"

The bittersweet bottom line is that the well-intentioned Shula didn't feel comfortable enough then to ask the "non-Hungarians" on the team. (Obviously, he has since gained in character. Having a Black center, Dwight Stephenson, today is an honest move. I wish all coaches were as open-minded.)

As practice began, there were very few question marks about personnel. The defense was set. Dubbed the "No-Names," it featured Buoniconti in the middle with outside linebackers Doug Swift and Mike Kolen. Manny Fernandez, Bill Stanfill, Vern Den Herder, and Bob Heinz were on the line, and Scott, Dick Anderson, Curtis

Johnson, and Lloyd Mumphord were in the secondary. On offense, Shula had acquired Marlin Briscoe, a fine wide receiver from Buffalo, during the off-season, and he would split time with Howard Twilley in the spot opposite Warfield. Marv Fleming and Jim Mandich would again be our tight ends. The offensive line was as good as any in football, a running back's dream. Jim Langer (a future Hall-of-Famer) would be taking over at center. He would be flanked at guard by the skilled Bob Kuechenberg and my good friend, the perennial All-Pro, Larry "Chicken" Little. Our tackles were Norm Evans and Wayne Moore.

Bob Griese, who had been named All-Pro in 1971, would again be our signal caller. Bob wasn't as flashy as some quarterbacks, but he was bright and the perfect person to run Shula's balanced offense. In looking over the cliques outlined above, I find it hard to place Bob with any particular group. That's fine. Unless your quarterback is a Sonny Jurgensen type who can run the show after a night that would put the Rowdys or Rednecks to shame, you'd just as soon have him going home each night with a can of film under his arm, which is exactly what Bob did. He took his business seriously. He was a fine tactician. And he commanded our respect on the field.

Bob was always under control. I can remember the first time I heard him swear. It was in 1972, my fourth year. He had just come into a playoff game for Earl Morrall after being injured much of the year. We were buzzing in the huddle, talking it up, and he said, "Shut up, damn it." Everything got real quiet. Holy cow, I thought, Griese actually cursed.

Morrall, Bob's backup, was in his seventeenth season, having gained notoriety as Johnny Unitas's replacement at Baltimore under Shula in the late 1960s. In 1968, when Unitas had been injured, Morrall had stepped into the starting lineup and led the Colts to the Super Bowl. His performance had earned him recognition as the league's most valuable player. History would repeat itself in 1972. In game 5, Bob suffered a dislocated ankle against San Diego. With Earl in, the offense hardly lost a beat.

It was a real treat for me to play with Earl. As a kid in 1960, I had sneaked into games at old Pitt Stadium to watch the Steelers. And who was the quarterback? Earl Morrall. Now all of a sudden we were playing together in the same backfield. Earl was just like Bob. They both acted like old men. The only difference was that

Earl really was old. I liked playing with him. He gave me the ball a lot, maybe more than Bob would have.

This brings us to the running back position. It was here that the only real question mark for 1972 existed. Fullback was set with the All-Pro Csonka. But the starting halfback spot was up in the air. Would it be Kiick or Morris?

I worked hard to make sure it would be me. But before I began my intense off-season training routine, I went to California to act in a movie called *The Black Six*. While there was never any pretense that this was going to be a quality production, I signed on for several reasons. I love movies, and the idea of actually being in one appealed to me. The idea of being in Hollywood and getting the star treatment appealed to me still more. And the idea of making some money while having what promised to be a lot of fun appealed to me most of all.

I was supposed to be paid $20,000 plus a small percentage of the profits. That was a lot of money. (People sometimes forget that the NFL salaries in the early 1970s were nothing like the salaries paid today. In 1972, I signed my second contract with the Dolphins. The terms: one year, $30,000. In 1987, the New York Giants each received about $60,000 for winning the Super Bowl; the Denver Broncos received about $45,000 for losing. When we lost to the Cowboys we received $7500, while the Cowboys earned $15,000 for their win. Furthermore, endorsements, particularly for Black players, were very difficult to come by.)

While *The Black Six* was conceived at a time when civil rights groups were lobbying for more Blacks in the film industry, it did little to advance the cause. The producer was White, as was the director and all the key off-screen personnel. Yes, the Black six were Black! But we were all carpetbaggers, not professional actors who had paid their dues and deserved a vehicle to showcase their skills. Our sextet was composed of the 49ers' Gene Washington, the Steelers' Mean Joe Greene, the Lions' Lem Barney, the Chiefs' Willie Lanier, the Vikings' Carl Eller, and me.

The plot of the movie was straightforward. Washington played a Vietnam veteran who had returned to the States only to learn that his brother was in trouble in the south. The rest of us played Gene's Vietnam buddies, who set out across country on motorcycle to straighten things out. The Black six were, in effect, a poor man's

Magnificent Seven or Black man's *Easy Rider*. As might be expected, along the way the Black six encountered numerous obstacles, among them hostile motorcycle gangs (led by the Oakland Raiders' Ben Davidson) and prejudiced officers of the law. The final scene involved an armed battle with some despicable southern policemen.

We were told that we were selected from all the Black players in the NFL because we fit particular roles in the script. Surprise! I was cast as a troublemaker. I lived up to my advance billing. Along with Eller and Barney, I was a thorn in the producer's side from day one (Lanier, Greene, and Washington seemed happy just to be in the movie and didn't want to make waves). Our first confrontation concerned "the star treatment." We weren't getting it, but felt we deserved it. So a couple of days after we arrived, Carl, Lem, and I piled our suitcases onto a bed and (much to the dismay of Willie, Joe, and Gene) told the producer we were leaving unless some changes were made immediately. "This is Hollywood," we said. "We want limousines. We want broads. We want parties."

The producer was flustered. Like so many nonathletes do, he tried to talk to us in football terms. He was so nervous he muffed his lines. "It's important we develop a good *gam plane*," he said. We hadn't actually packed the suitcases. They were empty. But our scam worked and we did begin to get the star treatment.

There was a more serious problem: the script. We hadn't seen the complete version (written by a White man) before we'd signed on. When we did see it, we didn't like it. Although it was clear that the Black six stood for truth, justice, and the American way, we didn't get to win in the end. The producer advised us that it would be too controversial, too radical, if we actually prevailed. (Remember this was 1972. California was still reeling from Angela Davis, the Soledad Brothers, and the Black Panthers.) "You mean the Black six are going down just like the Indians used to in all the films I ever saw?" I asked. The producer nodded.

Again, Carl, Lem, and I threatened to leave. "We're out of here unless you can assure us the movie will end in a positive fashion," I said. "If you're gonna kill us, you can get six niggers off the street and do that. We've got hundreds of thousands of kids who watch us play football every week. I'm not gonna have them coming up to me in every city saying, 'Hey, Mercury Morris, you got killed in *The Black Six*. What happened, man?'" We also couldn't understand, why when the Black six fought back against the White hundreds, we only wrecked property, never our enemy. If a shopkeeper gave us trouble, we tore up his store, not him. "How come we destroy furniture and the White guys kill people?" we kept asking.

We were wearing out the producer by now. He agreed to make some script changes. Not leaving anything to chance, Eller took matters into his own hands and constantly rewrote his own lines. As he was 6-foot-8, 230 pounds, and the producer was 5-foot-8, 130 pounds, Eller's revisions were always accepted.

We were extremely creative in figuring out ways to bother the producer. One night we went to the bar where those playing the motorcycle gang in the movie hung out. Actually, the role as gang members was not what they call a "stretch," or a difficult adjustment, for these actors. In real life, they actually were motorcycle gang members. Finding them already a bit inebriated, we manufactured a story, telling them that we had learned they were being paid less than they should be for their appearances. They got so angry that they kept the bar open all night, running up a tab well into the thousands of dollars, and insisting that the bill be sent to the producer.

By the time we reached the end of the filming, the producer had had enough of us and we had had enough of him. The movie's ending still hadn't been resolved. One of the final scenes involved an armed battle between us and our racist enemies. We were supposed to throw flares at them. Instead, Lem threw his flares at the producer and his entourage. For this and other indiscretions, we were fired on the next to last day of shooting. "Due to your failure to respond to work calls, your constant harassment of the producer and your total disruption of the set, you are hereby relieved...."

We were relieved—relieved to be out of there. The ending was shot without us. The movie, still available for video rental, concludes with a firestorm. Do the Black six die? That's left up in the air. The message is : Beware honky, the Black six may just return. Needless to say, there was never a sequel.

After the filming was over, I returned to Miami and began training for what I knew would be my most important season. I had always lifted weights during the off-season. Nautilus training was brand new at this time, having only recently been developed by Arthur Jones in Florida. I started on the machines and found they greatly improved my size and strength. (Eventually I could bench press more than anybody on the team—420 pounds.)

I had a great exhibition season. I stayed free of injury and led the team in rushing while averaging something like 7 yards per carry. The press described me as, "a man on a mission," a man possessed, and I was. I realized that if I was to beat out Kiick, I couldn't just do as well as he did. It was like challenging for the heavyweight championship. You have to really beat the champ.

My excellent preseason, climaxed by a 100-yard rushing performance in the final exhibition game against the Washington Redskins, guaranteed that I'd see much more playing time than in previous years. But I didn't start every game. Kiick and I alternated. I didn't particularly like this—I thought I'd earned the starting role—but I understood that Shula was appeasing Kiick, who had been and would continue to be so valuable. The important thing was that Shula was giving me the opportunity to play.

I quickly realized that the guy who was doing the job would be the one to play. This echoed Shula's Super Bowl VI comments that he was going with Csonka and Kiick because they got us there. I didn't have any complaints with this philosophy in 1972; I just wanted Shula to adhere to it. If I was doing the job, I wanted to stay in the game.

As the season progressed, I was doing the job and therefore played more and more. Sometimes Kiick started and then I'd come in on the second play of the game. As the game wore on, I'd usually be in on first-and-10 situations and I knew if I picked up my yards, I wouldn't have to come to the sidelines. I also knew that if it was third and 11, I had to gain 12 yards if I wanted to stay in. And so it became customary for me to do this. The press sometimes reported that Kiick and I and even Csonka and I were at each other's throats. That was horseshit! Csonka was a good man about making the transition. He and Kiick were best friends, a clique unto themselves, and the Butch Cassidy and Sundance Kid routine was getting them a lot of notoriety. Larry could have refused to cooperate for the sake of Kiick and put Shula in a difficult position. But for the sake of the team, Larry went along with the move to give me more playing time.

Kiick, always the fierce competitor, was understandably reluctant to see his playing time cut. Periodically, he'd be quoted as saying something like, "I need to play more if I'm going to get better." Then I'd turn around and say, "The more I play the better I get."

That was true. It wasn't until the seventh game of the year that I had my first 100-yard rushing day. That marked the beginning of a strong last half of the season. For the year I had exactly 1000 yards on 190 carries. (As always seemed to happen with me, this total was surrounded in controversy. After the final game, the records showed that I had 993 yards, but a review of game films revealed that I had not been credited for an additional 7 yards.) Csonka ended up with 1117 yards, and thus we became the first members of the same backfield to gain 1000 yards each in a single season in the history of football (and it was a fourteen-game schedule, instead of today's sixteen-game season).

Csonka was just about the most punishing runner I have ever seen. He seemed to relish making contact with a defender or, as usually was the case, several defenders who would try to bring him down as his big legs kept on churning. (I still enjoy watching the highlight films of his runs.) It's apparent that most defenders wanted no part of him one on one. I remember one play in a game against St. Louis in 1972 where it took nine men to bring him down.

Csonka was a great practical joker. Once he put a baby alligator in Shula's shower. The speed the coach showed in escaping the creature would have qualified him for a spot in our defensive backfield.

On another occasion, Larry went one on one against Howard Cosell. We were playing a Monday night game in Cleveland in 1973, and ABC made the fatal mistake of putting Cosell in our hotel, on our floor. Even worse, Howard was in the room next to me and across from Kiick and Csonka. We were making some noise in the hallway when Cosell's door opened. Howard must have taken his toupee off and then tried to put it back on. It was hanging crooked on his head. He was wearing one of those old sleeveless H-shirts. "What's going on here?" he said. "Let's keep this noise down."

Next thing we knew, Csonka had reached over, grabbed the toupee off Howard's head, and tossed it down the hallway. "Boy, that'll teach him," Larry said.

I think one reason Csonka didn't resist my entry into the backfield was that it took some of the pressure off him. Because I possessed the ability to get outside quickly and was always considered a breakaway threat, teams could no longer key on him as they had. If an opponent stacked up in the middle in anticipation of one of Csonka's patented blasts, Griese or Morrall could turn me loose outside. Before my arrival, teams were scared of Csonka; now they had to be scared of Csonka and me.

My running style can be described just like most everything I've done in life: against the grain. Running seems instinctual, not calculated. But it's really a combination of the two. My philosophy was to play in reactionary terms like in touch football. That way I had a jump on my opponents: if they couldn't touch me, they obviously couldn't tackle me. I had certain moves that Shula would call "dancing." He'd say, "Quit dancing around in the hole." But I wasn't dancing; these were calculated moves. Watch the films of my runs. I'm usually coming around the corner and there are two guys—linebacker and safety or cornerback and safety—and they have the angle on me. But if I stop, they have to stop. And when I start, they have to start. But now I'm by them. So I've turned a situation in which it seems like I'm trapped into an escape because the defenders have followed their own instincts. If they see I have the ability to cut back inside, then they're instinctively going to make that move inside. And when they commit themselves, I'm gone.

I tried to turn every carry into an end run. Up the middle and then out to the sidelines. The sideline then becomes my ally because nobody's gonna come from the sideline to hit me. I only have the people on the other side of me to deal with. I know that at the end of my move comes the beginning of a new move, but at the end of their move, they have to turn around and come back after me once I make my cut. So I've put myself in a position where I'm going against the grain, against their flow. The defenders' perspective, thus, changes dramatically. They're no longer pursuing me. They know they have to stop me and they only have a split second to do it. If they waste that second, I'm gone. Going against the grain changes it from being pursued to being confrontational, because now they have to deal with me coming at them. I'm the one calling the shots.

I'm not sure Shula understood this at first. I'm not sure he'd ever had a runner like me. But excellent coach that he was, he caught on quickly, and pretty soon he was inventing plays for me. If the hole wasn't there on an off-tackle play, I was to bounce to the outside and blow past the corner. We had one play called "37 trap outside." If the trap wasn't there, then the guard (Larry Little) was supposed to bounce outside and block for me.

I rarely concerned myself with an opposing defense. I didn't see the people out there. I only saw green turf and was thinking, wherever I can go, wherever I can maneuver, that's where I'm going. Most often, that was against the grain.

My running style was one of the few flamboyant aspects of the

1972 Dolphins. Execution, not flash, was our password. The key was to control the game and make the fewest mistakes possible.

In many ways the season was surreal. A game would start. We'd march down the field and score. We'd sit on the bench. The defense would be in for three downs and hold the opposing offense. We'd go back in and score again. And before you knew it it was halftime and we were leading by something like 17–0. It's a helluva feeling to know that when you step on the field that you have to do something to mess up to lose, that you have a team that is that good. That's how we felt in 1972 and 1973.

While we realized we were special, we didn't think we got that recognition from others. Maybe people were still skeptical of the old AFL, maybe people still viewed us as an expansion club. There was talk that our schedule was easy. But the fact remains we went 17–0 in 1972 en route to winning the Super Bowl. No team had ever done that and no team has done it since then. And we did it without our starting quarterback who had been All-Pro the year before.

People forget that although we entered Super Bowl VII undefeated, the Redskins were the favorites. We dominated the game and won 14–7. Kiick started, but I saw plenty of playing time, mostly as a decoy. My 100-yard performance during the exhibition season against the Redskins had made Coach George Allen wary of me and our ability to score from the outside. He later explained his game plan was geared to contain my outside runs. It did. But this left the door open up the middle for Csonka and he ran for 112 yards. We controlled the game on the ground so much that Griese threw just eleven passes all day. He was his usual self, completing eight, including a touchdown to Twilley. Kiick contributed a 1-yard touchdown run.

Our defense was even more impressive. Fernandez and Buoniconti had excellent days, while Jake intercepted two passes, running one back 55 yards from our end zone. He was voted the game's MVP. The Redskins scored their only touchdown on one of the more memorable plays in Super Bowl history when our kicker Garo Yepremian picked up the ball after a botched field goal attempt and tried to throw a pass to who knows who. He threw as only a former soccer player could throw. The ball slipped from his hands to Washington's Mike Bass, who ran 49 yards for the score. Garo was lucky to escape with his life when he returned to our bench.

While this was not one of my great games from a statistical stand-point (I had 10 carries for 34 yards), I felt that I had contributed and was proud to accept my ring. The victory was a total team effort. (Juice Simpson's glory years began in 1972. He received more recognition than I did, and he deserved it. But when people ask if I would rather have had his career or mine, I answer truthfully, "Mine." You can only break so many individual records, but when you have the opportunity to play with a team like the one I was fortunate enough to be with, a team with that much talent and the ability to control both sides of the line of scrimmage, it is a privilege and a thrill.)

Looking back, I'm somewhat amazed that I was able to achieve what I did in 1972. I played every game that year, including the Super Bowl, after taking Dexemil. To understand my use of Dexemil, which is commonly called "speed," you have to put it into the context of the times. Sports merely mirrors society. In the late 1960s and early 1970s, the use of speed was quite common in society. Business people and truck drivers used it as they crisscrossed the country; students used it to pull "all nighters"; dieters used it to take off weight; and football players used it to get up for games. Doctors liberally prescribed it. (The mind-set then simply said that speed and Valium and such were okay. They weren't *really* drugs. Neither, for that matter, was alcohol. This was the period when Dean Martin and Foster Brooks were getting huge laughs with their drunk routines, and drunk drivers were considered more amusing than lethal.)

Actually my first experience with pills in the locker room came in 1969, my rookie season. One night before a game I told our trainer that I was having difficulty falling asleep. "Take this," he said. It was Seconal, or, in street terms, a "red." Now, when a trainer who has reached one of the elite positions in his profession—working with an NFL team—tells a 22-year-old rookie to take a pill, who's to argue?

Astonishingly, he gave this to me *the night before a game.* Seconal (we now know) is something they sold on the corners for junkies to go into a nod. Take one tonight, there's a good chance you won't wake up tomorrow until noon. And when you do wake up, you're gonna have a hangover. To make matters worse, the Dolphins provided us free beer on the night before a game. Barbiturates and alcohol. That can be automatic death.

I woke up the next morning in a fog. I told the team doctor how groggy I was. He pulled out two pill vials and gave me two green pills and one brown pill. "Take these," he said.

"What are they?"

"Mood pills," the doctor said.

"What do they do?"

"They get you in the mood."

Now, not only a respected trainer, but a team doctor is telling you that pills are okay. As the doctor is nothing more than a yes-man for ownership, you don't have to be a genius to conclude that such behavior must be condoned at the highest level.

This was the only time I took any pills my first two seasons, but late in 1971, I started using them before games on a regular basis. We were on the road, and on game day the weather was quite cold. In the locker room, a veteran said to me, "Take this yellow pill right here. You won't feel that cold out there."

I said, "Okay. I'm running kickoffs back. I'm not really out there that much anyway." Then I asked what it was.

"An old yellowbird." Translation: Dexedrine.

For the remainder of 1971, I found myself taking Dexedrine. In 1972, I switched over to Dexemil. One pill every game day. That was it. But that was enough. I'd take the pill at 10 a.m. or 10:30. By game time I was banging. And then I wondered why I would stay awake until 3 a.m. and chew my gum for fifteen hours without giving it a second thought.

How widespread was the use of such pills? It wasn't pervasive, but a lot of backs and defensive people and some offensive linemen used them. Linemen in the trenches, whose sole task it is to hit, feel the pills take away that trace of hesitancy and build that edge of confidence. Backs think, "Hey, I'm running faster, running stronger."

But you're not. After a while I realized I was *at* the game, but I wasn't really *in* it. I'd sit in front of my locker and say to myself, "Should I go with this or not?" My conclusion was always the same: "We haven't lost a game all year. I don't want to take the chance without it." Those are the very words I said to myself at Super Bowl VII. It had become a game-day psychological crutch.

I wasn't the only one "under the influence" on the field. There were jars of these pills over some players' lockers. Did the coaching staff know? In my opinion, they must have. Taking these pills, which we now call amphetamines, was accepted in the locker room as it was accepted in the world outside the locker room.

I finally quit after the first game of 1973. We were playing the San Francisco 49ers in the Orange Bowl. It was so hot that the 49ers had wilted by the end of the first quarter, and their quarterback, John Brodie, was kneeling in ice on the sidelines. However hot it was, add 25 degrees; it's always 25 degrees warmer on the field. Maybe the Dexemil had given me a boost when it was cold out, but I didn't need to be jump-started this day. The pill threw everything off. Here I was jumping for balls instead of timing them right, fumbling—doing all kinds of erratic things because I didn't have control of my mind. I think it was after my third fumble that I threw my helmet from midfield and it hit the wall in the Orange Bowl on one bounce; a gargantuan heave.

Shula said, "Hey. I think you better sit down."

I never took another pill again. (Did I ever use cocaine on game day? Absolutely not. Nor did I ever use it during the season. There were quite a few players in the NFL, myself among them, who smoked pot periodically during the season—never before games—and of course there were even more who drank alcohol, which, let us not forget, is also a drug. I did not begin using cocaine heavily until well after I retired, and I was not even introduced to the stuff until 1973 or 1974. At that time, I was like almost everyone else in society and viewed it as a purely recreational drug. I snorted occasionally during the off-season. It might sound funny, but I was a professional and I took my work on the football field very seriously. It never even occurred to me to take cocaine during the season, and to this day I'm amazed when I read that professional athletes have actually used the drug during the season, on a game day, or in the clubhouse. I was floored when baseball player Tim Raines admitted that in 1982 he would slide into the bases head first so as not to damage the vial of cocaine which he kept in his back pocket.)

Stopping the pills dramatically increased my productivity. On paper the 954 yards I gained in 1973 may not look that different than the 1000 I gained in 1972, but I carried the ball 41 times less in '73. (My average of 6.4 yards per carry was best in the league.) More important, I was breaking off longer runs. In 1972, my longest run from scrimmage had been only 33 yards. Now I was ripping off runs of 50, 60, 70 yards. I'm certain this was because, off the pills, I was returning to my natural form and I was once again in touch with the God-given talent and ability that I had. I didn't need any chemicals. I was producing enough myself to give me the lift I needed to excel.

The message was clear: The pills didn't add to my performance; they took away from it. The nervousness, the edge that people try to lose by taking the pills, is something they actually need to keep in touch with the reality of where they are. (I have heard of linemen taking speed who jumped offsides when they saw movements in the stands. Who needs that?) You need to be *at* the game, *in* the game, *with* the game.

Despite the fact that I had gained 1000 yards in 1972, despite the fact that I was playing even better in 1973, I still hadn't locked up a starting role in the backfield. Shula was still alternating me with Kiick. I started the opener against the 49ers, but Kiick started the next week against Oakland. We lost for the first time in twenty games, 12–7. Our third game was at home against New England. I thought for sure I would start, but Shula gave Kiick the nod. All I could figure was that this was some sort of way to appease Jim for the fact that he wasn't seeing as much playing time. And all I could think of were Shula's words from the Super Bowl VI loss that he liked to stay with the combination that was bringing success. I thought that was me and Csonka.

When I finally did get into the game, I was more than pissed off. I was obsessed. The first time I touched the ball—Boom!—I went 37 yards for a touchdown. The next series—Boom!—I went 71 yards for the score. I came off the field wanting to shove the ball in Shula's face. By halftime, I had gained 138 yards on ten carries. By game's end I had 197 yards on just fifteen carries. This was and still is an Orange Bowl and Dolphins' record. It could just as well have been 297 yards. Everything was clicking that day—one of those rare occasions where you know they can't stop you, regardless of what they try to do. You know they may hem you up a little while, but you're going to get away. Although pleased with my performance, I would have liked the opportunity to gain 200 yards. Shula pulled me early in the fourth quarter. I don't know why he did, because the year before that, despite an ankle injury, I was pushed out onto the field so that Csonka and I could be the first backs on the same team to rush for 1000 yards in the same season.

I thought this performance would certainly earn me a start against the Jets in the Meadowlands the next week, but Shula started Kiick again, explaining that Jim's family would be at the game. There were other slights, too. In 1972, I had scored twelve touchdowns rushing, tops in the league. Almost all of my scoring was done from close in to the goal line. In 1973, that was impossible because Shula started bringing Kiick in when we got down to the goal line. Wait a minute, I'll stop this, I thought. So I started scoring from 40 or 50 yards out.

An obvious question arises: Did Shula set up these obstacles for me so I would work harder and perform better? I don't know. But he was a master at playing those games to motivate a guy. While I was always able to motivate myself to play to my peak in a game, I have to admit that I did do my best in the games where I wanted to kill him for something he had done to me. Some people sit down when a coach gets on them. I always stood up.

Up to this point I had remained virtually injury free for the better part of two seasons. When I finally did get hurt, I did it in a big way. I broke my neck in the twelfth game of the '73 season against the Steelers. I still remember the play—119 arrow—a delay to the tight end. (A pass! I was hardly ever in on passing downs; that was Kiick's specialty.) Unfortunately, our tight end was covered. Griese, who had originally looked me off, now came back to me in the flat. By this time the Steelers' All-Pro Mel Blount was standing behind me like we were in the pay line. The moment I caught the pass, Blount hit me. Normally, you break your fall to the polyturf—which was nothing more than a hard, streetlike surface covered by a rug— with one hand. In this situation, however, I had to cover the ball with both my hands. I didn't break my fall at all. I hit the ground with my neck bent underneath my body. The combination of my weight and Blount's weight on the bent neck literally snapped two vertebrae (although it was some time before we found that out).

If you're a real hero, you try to come off the field after an injury as cool as possible. You trot over to the coach, and say something like, "Hey, coach, I think I've got a broken arm." With this injury, there was no mistaking me for Mr. Macho. I came off the field screaming. "Aaahhh." It felt as if someone had taken a blow torch to my shoulder and opened it wide. I ran past the coaches and crawled underneath one of our benches. I was making sounds like a dog who's just been hit by a car, a dog you can't do anything for.

The team doctor found me. He bent down and said, "Eugene, if you don't come out from under that bench, I can't help you." Eventually I crawled out. I was certain I had a broken collarbone or a cracked collarbone and broken clavicle. The doctor took x-rays at the stadium and again at the hospital. Nothing was broken, he told me. I had a bad neck sprain.

I had been averaging about 7 yards per carry before I was hurt, had more yards rushing than Csonka, and was well on my way to another 1000-yard season. I played the next week, but was held out of the final game of the regular season so, it was explained, I could be healthy for the playoffs. As a result, I fell 46 yards short of 1000 yards rushing, and Csonka and I were denied the chance to become the first tandem ever to gain 1000 yards each in a season twice. Apparently the team doctors thought me quite well recovered the next week. I carried the ball twenty times for 105 yards and two touchdowns in our playoff win against Cincinnati. We beat Oakland for our third straight AFC championship, and it was on to Super Bowl VIII and the Minnesota Vikings.

I finally got my Super Bowl start. Again I was primarily a decoy. I had played an excellent preseason game against the Vikings and the team's coach Bud Grant had proclaimed me the most dangerous back they faced all year. The Vikings' efforts to keep me from breaking off long runs outside again opened the field up for Csonka, who never needed much of an opening anyway. He was awesome, rushing for a then Super Bowl record of 145 yards on 33 tough carries and two touchdowns. He was the game's MVP as we won easily, 24–7.

For the third year in a row, it was on to the Pro Bowl. Juice was there for the second time after a spectacular season in which he broke several records, including most yards in a season, 2003. He had more than doubled my output, but since he was a one man team in Buffalo, he had also carried the ball more than twice as many times as I had. In my mind, the rivalry was still in full force. Almost all of the players who had finished between his first place and my ninth place in the Heisman Trophy balloting in 1969 had fallen by the wayside. It was now me (with excellent individual stats and two Super Bowl rings) and him (with incredible personal achievements but no playoff experience much less two Super Bowl rings). I loved playing Buffalo. During my years under Shula, we never lost when I went head to head with Juice. I was so psyched up for the games that I generally outperformed him.

We would have played in the same backfield at the Pro Bowl, but before I could play I had to have my neck x-rayed again, as well as my wrist (which had been injured in the AFC championship game). John Madden was coaching our squad and I remember he looked troubled as he gave me the results. The good news was that the wrist was okay. The bad news was that the neck was broken, the fifth and sixth cervical vertebrae were fractured.

The difference between a sprain and a fracture, which can easily lead to paralysis, is dramatic, as are the respective treatments. When the doctors at the Pro Bowl read my x-rays (I later learned), they sent word that I should be driven back to the stadium very gently. A bad bump could cause the broken bone to damage or even sever my spinal cord. After I talked with Madden, the doctors told me they wanted me to stay for a few days until a metal neck brace with heavy posts could be made for me. The doctors advised me that I should have been placed in the hospital immediately after the injury, but as the fracture was now over a month and a half old there was no sense in doing that. "But if you don't wear this brace for the next four to six months," they said, "you'll have trouble for the rest of your life."

I wasn't terribly worried or scared. This just seemed like one more injury that needed to be taken care of. You put yourself in the hands of the doctors and do what they tell you to do. If they want me to wear a heavy brace, I'll wear a heavy brace.

After getting the brace, I made arrangements to fly to Miami. When bad weather forced us to divert the flight and land in Los Angeles, I ended up with an evening to kill in the City of Angels. Another passenger on the flight invited me to dinner and then took me to a hip after-hours club called Pip's.

As I was sitting at the bar in Pip's, the owner came up to me and told me one of the patrons would like to meet me. I was led down a corridor into a private room at the back of the club. The room was dark. I could see several people seated on couches, but I couldn't make out their faces. One of these people stood up. He was a man who appeared to be in his fifties. I moved closer. He stuck out his hand, "I wanted to shake your hand," he said. "I made a lot of money off you guys last week." He was referring to our Super Bowl victory. As he spoke I could make out his features. They were familiar. Damn, it was Frank Sinatra!

The next day I flew back to Miami. I immediately went to see the Dolphins' team doctor. "What's that brace for?" he asked. I gave him my x-rays and told him what the Pro Bowl doctors had said. He looked over the x-rays. "Yeah. It is a fracture," he said. "But you don't have to wear the brace." He explained that he thought the other doctors had overreacted because they had been happy to find the fracture. He told me that all I had to do was wear a soft collar. You do what your doctor wants you to do. If he says soft collar, soft collar it is.

Three weeks later I was in such pain that I had to go to the hospital, where I was put in traction. Now I was worried. I didn't like the idea of being bothered by something that had happened so many weeks earlier. You're not supposed to store pain.

So, our team doctor—the same doctor who had left me on my own after I hurt my thigh, the same doctor who gave me mood pills— was wrong. (The Pro Bowl doctors were right. I eventually required complicated surgery on the neck, and I will have trouble for the rest of my life.)

How could the team doctor of a Super Bowl champion football team, a man charged with the responsibility for overseeing the health and safety of such valuable commodities, have been so wrong? I realize doctors often have honest differences of opinion with each other, but this seems to have been a case in which the team doctor blew the diagnosis. An alternate explanation is that the doctor correctly diagnosed the fracture from the beginning and then withheld that diagnosis from me, calling what he knew was a fracture a sprain. I don't like saying this, but my experience, and I think it is the experience of many who have played in the NFL, is that too often teams and their doctors are concerned not with getting a player well, but rather getting him "well enough" to play. It is possible that in the team's desire to see me play, a "misdiagnosis" would have been most advantageous.

And so, my greatest two years in football ended up with me in a hospital, flat on my back in traction.

CHAPTER 6

THE END OF THE LINE, 1974–1976

I was back on my feet by the time the 1974 exhibition season was to begin. That was a busy year. On the domestic front, it was the year I broke up for good with Dorothy and began a lengthy battle for custody of Maceo; it was also the year I met Bobbie (although we would not marry until December of 1979). As for football, 1974 was the year in which several key members announced they would be leaving the Dolphins for the greener pastures of the World Football League, a circumstance which led to the renegotiation of my contract; a year in which the NFL Players Association went out on strike; a year in which a knee injury kept me out of action most of the season; and a year in which I consulted the "root man" to get Don Shula off my back.

Turning first to football: In between our victory in Super Bowl VIII and the beginning of the 1974 season, Csonka, Kiick, and Warfield announced they had accepted a $3.3 million package to leave Miami and join the Toronto Northmen franchise in the fledgling WFL beginning in 1975. Before the 1973 season, I had signed a three-year contract for $190,000. Now, the Dolphins, fearful that I, too, might jump ship, were willing to tear that contract up and offer a five-year deal worth $675,000. That was more money than I had ever seen, an average of $135,000 a year. I signed.

The first thing I did was buy a Ferrari. It wasn't the first exotic car I'd purchased and it wouldn't be the last. Ferraris, Corvettes, Porsches, "Beemers," Benzes—over twenty during the course of my career. Were they wise investments? Probably not. But what was there in my own experience that told me that? I did have a management group handling some of my financial affairs, but they proved so incompetent that I, along with several other players the group represented, had to sue. (This isn't unusual. You would think that athletes should be able to get top financial advice, just as they should be able to get top medical care. This is rarely the case.) I know myself well enough to admit that even if I had been counseled to be a fiscal conservative after signing the new contract, I still would have bought the Ferrari. Until long after I retired, I had a preoccupation with speed, with fast cars. I had no fear of driving over 150 miles per hour for 6 or 7 miles at a stretch. Every time I'd drive down to the Florida Keys, I'd try to set a new personal record for speed. My best time was 95 miles in 55 minutes, and this was on a road where there were some spots where you absolutely had to slow down to 25 or 30 miles per hour for a few miles. The top speed of the Ferrari was 188 miles per hour; the fastest I ever went was 176 miles per hour on the Dade West Tollway. Looking back, that seems a little crazy. But that kind of speed, that kind of testing—the "zoom factor" to me—was important then. It's not now.

There were several interesting stipulations regarding my new contract. First, the Dolphins insisted I come to camp to receive treatment for my neck injury. Because the Players Association was on strike at this time, this put me in the position of having to cross the picket line. I had to explain to my teammates that I wasn't going in to practice, just for treatment. This wasn't as big a problem as it might have been because some veterans—Jim Langer and Bob Kuechenberg among them—had reported to camp despite the strike. The Dolphins also wanted a provision that my new contract would only go into effect if my neck was okay by the beginning of the season. If it wasn't, we'd revert to the old contract. My quick response was, "How about if I sue ya for two million bucks, huh, for letting me play with a broken neck and knowing it?" The Dolphins dropped that demand, and I signed the contract the next day.

After the strike was over, the Dolphins held me out of the early exhibition games while my neck continued to heal. Then, in the fifth exhibition game, I hurt my knee. Now I was really messed up. Physically and mentally. While I managed to play in the first game of the year (scoring the winning touchdown to beat Buffalo and Juice Simpson), I was only able to play in five more games that season.

Some members of the media thought I should have played more. One radio sportscaster said, "If Mercury Morris was half the man Larry Csonka was, he'd be out there playing on his hurt knee." That made no sense to me. My knee was hurt. I couldn't perform unless I was right. You don't put a race car out on the track unless it's right, and that's what I considered myself: a race car, a valuable piece of machinery. To me, being a hero meant helping your team by scoring a lot of touchdowns, not being "a real man" by playing with a broken leg.

When I was healthy, I never dogged it—in a game or practice. In practice, I would run farther than anybody, run 20 or 30 yards past the line of scrimmage. I always tried to make contact with somebody in the secondary, usually Dick Anderson. Dick and I had a deal where he'd hit me with a hard shot and I'd give him a hard shot back. That's why in games I was always in the secondary and always breaking away: because how you practice is how you play.

When I broke into the secondary, I knew exactly where I wanted to go, what I wanted to do. Not enough people practice this. When you run around the left end with the ball in your right hand, you're asking for trouble. Strategically, you need that hand as a weapon. If you have the ball in the wrong hand, not only are you more vulnerable to fumble, you can't fight the defenders off. There is no middle ground. You either have the capability of warding people off with the straight arm or you give that up. It's obvious which is the more desirable option, but you see guys playing it wrong all the time. Maybe it's because they didn't practice it properly. Football is not made of guts. It's made of smarts. That's how I tried to play.

Shula and I had a few confrontations during the '74 season. At one point, he threatened to fine me and suspend me because I hadn't come in for treatment on my knee over a long weekend before a Monday night game. It was my understanding that coming in was optional, so I had chosen to work out at the local Nautilus center on my own, thinking that was better for the knee than the twenty minutes of whirlpool I could get at camp. Shula disagreed, and I heard from Larry Little that Don was looking for me.

When I finally showed up at camp, I saw Shula standing in the locker room. I kind of tapped him as I went by, and said, "I hear you been looking for me."

He said, "Yeah. I been looking for you." He tried to storm past me to his office. Trouble was the corridor was only wide enough for one, and I was in front of him, walking real slow toward his office.

Apparently he wanted to be in his office before me, because he cut through a side office and was in his chair by the time I got there. Our conversation went something like this:

"Where the fuck you been?"

"I was at the Nautilus."

"You were supposed to have been here for treatment. I ought to fine you and suspend you."

"Look," I said, staying amazingly calm and kind of enjoying his anger, "you said it was optional. If I'd have thought putting my knee in the whirlpool for twenty minutes would have got it well, I'd have been here a long time ago." He might have agreed with me on principle, but Shula saw this as insubordination. I, on the other hand, felt fully justified. Shula threatened to fine me several more times. Enough, I thought. I walked out and went home.

I walked out on Wednesday. On Thursday, I stayed home. I didn't really know what was going on, but I felt that this time I was in the right. Before the day was over, I received a telegram from Shula telling me I was suspended from the NFL for good and that the missing of the upcoming game alone was going to cost me nine thousand bucks.

I started to reconsider then. I called Joe Krogan, a popular local sportscaster. My walkout was all over the television. I wanted to give my side of the story. "Well, Joe," I told him. "Shula and I have had our differences, but we both want the same thing. We want to win. I guess that being hurt all year and not able to contribute as I did the last two seasons when we won the Super Bowl, I was disgruntled. That's what I'm really mad about—the injury. But I want to win, and I'm part of that team." I was trying to use television to smooth things over with the public and, more important, Shula. I wanted to get back on the team, and I certainly wasn't interested in taking that $9000 jolt.

On Friday morning, Shula sent Larry Little down to my house to get me. I came back to practice. The press was out in force. Shula told the media something to the effect, "I saw Merc on TV last night, and since he's admitted he was wrong, and since he has said he was sorry, I'm going to reinstate him." Whoa! I didn't say any of that. But Shula was using the media just like I had. He was playing my game. And he was becoming good at it!

I was just happy to be back. So happy that I allowed them to give me an injection in my knee when I didn't even need one.

My walkout had taken place before we played the Saints late in the year. By the time we faced the Patriots on the last weekend of the regular season, I was still out of action. It was a meaningless game. We had clinched the AFC East division for the fourth straight year, and New England was out of the playoff picture. During the warm up, Shula came up to me and told me he wanted me to run back kickoffs. As I recall, he said, "The doctor tells me you're all right."

"Look at this knee. Does this knee look okay to you?" I asked. "It's swollen bigger than Dallas." Again, I was very clear and sure that my "insubordination" was justified.

"Well, fuck," was all Shula said. He was mad. That I could tell. But this time he apparently wasn't up for a confrontation.

"Well, shit," I replied. And I didn't play.

I finished the season with only 214 yards on 56 carries. The team finished the regular season with an 11–3 record and was to travel the next week to Oakland to meet the Raiders in the first round of the playoffs. Shula and I were not getting along. *Reasoning with him has not worked*, I said to myself. So the day before we were supposed to leave, I decided *What the hell? I'll go see the root man.* Seemed like a fun idea.

The root man was a big tall Haitian who operated out of a storefront called King Solomon's Religious Store on 54th and 12th in Miami. The store was littered with such things as animal parts from rituals in which one was supposed to bring a chicken, cut the chicken's head off, and then sprinkle the blood around.

I had consulted the root man earlier in the year for nonprofessional reasons. Dorothy and I had split up for good in January. This was due in part to my lack of commitment to the relationship, which in turn led to her lack of commitment. It was also due to my failure to allow her to fully share the excitement, glory, and spotlight of our remarkable back-to-back Super Bowl seasons. Dorothy, like many of the spouses or girlfriends of my teammates, found herself on the perimeter of all the hoopla rather than in the center. This was inevitable. The world was ours. We were young men who almost overnight had become national heroes. Having to share life with the public created tension in many households, including ours.

Unable to compromise, we parted. It was not an amicable parting. This would have been tolerable if Maceo (who was only 3 years old at the time) had not been involved. But he was. I fought for and received temporary custody of him after the season's end in January. Unfortunately, the court ruled that when I returned to training camp in the summer of 1974, I had to give Maceo up to Dorothy. This didn't make sense to me; I felt I had more free time to give him than most single parents because I was off from work six months a year. The judge disagreed, citing the time and travel demands of football, and set February, 1975, as the date permanent custody would be decided.

It was under these circumstances that I had first consulted the root man. I wanted guidance on how to win custody of my son. The root man told me that he knew a hearing was set for February. I was impressed that he knew. "Don't worry," he said. "*You'll* say when you want to go back to court." I liked that.

So here I was several months later back at King Solomon's. This time it was not Dorothy whom I considered my nemesis. It was Shula.

The root man's clientele was not what you might guess. As I waited my turn, I noticed that many customers were well-dressed men with briefcases. These were professionals—lawyers, bankers, and the like—trying to get an edge, trying to go to the root man to find out what's happening and to have other forces control things.

"Hey, man," I said. "Shula's trying to kill me." I didn't mean "kill" literally.

"Yes. I know."

"Listen, I don't want you to do anything harmful to him."

"I know. If he wins this game, he will go on to mess with you and every other Black ballplayer he does not like, including War-field."

"Damn," I said.

I know this sounds hard to fathom, but I had a certain faith in the man. After all, he was able to tell me about what was troubling me before I opened my mouth. Besides, none of the more conventional approaches that I tried had worked.

"Now here is what you must do," the root man said. "Make a doll. I will give you the pattern, you will get the material, and you will make the doll yourself. You make the doll, place it in a shoebox, you say these psalms, you take this oil, you rub it here, here, here, on the arms and temples." I followed his instructions, putting my little Don Shula doll in a box and then burying it in my backyard.

The root man had also given me a piece of paper with a spider web drawn on it. Across the web was written the word, "Confused." I was to put the paper in my shoe on game day. I did that, too.

I didn't want to hurt Shula; I only wanted him off my back. I really had doubts about this working, but it was fun and took my mind off not playing. So here we are in Oakland. It's a tough-fought game. Al Davis, the Raiders' general manager, has pulled his usual tricks. It's been raining and he has left the field uncovered because he knows we have fast running backs and receivers and playing in the mud will slow them down.

I'm stuck on the sidelines again. My knee is still bad. Shula is mad at me. I can't play. I can't contribute.

It's the fourth quarter and the game is close. I'm sitting on the bench next to Lloyd Mumphord. Lloyd, a cornerback, is my roommate and probably my best friend on the team. He started for us early in the season but then was hurt. Tim Foley took his spot and then, even when Lloyd was healthy again, Shula kept him on the second team.

Now Foley gets hurt. Everyone on the sidelines expects our defensive coach Vince Costello to put Lloyd in, but instead Shula orders Costello to put in Henry Stuckey. We're all surprised. Henry is a swing man—he plays safety and cornerback—who has what we call nose trouble. It has nothing to do with cocaine. His problem is that he's always looking to make that big, crushing hit and is therefore susceptible to getting suckered in on a reverse or, worse, a receiver can fool him by running a short out pattern and then going up the field.

This is exactly what happens. On the first play that Stuckey is in, his man, the Raiders' speedy receiver Cliff Branch, runs a 15-yard out pattern, then comes back 5 yards and catches Snake Stabler's pass. Stuckey makes the tackle just about the time the ball is delivered. On the next play, Branch runs the same pattern. He catches the ball and slips in the mud. Stuckey runs up to make the easy tackle, but he slips, too. Branch gets up, runs by Stuckey, and goes 72 yards for the touchdown.

The guys on our sideline are going crazy. "What's wrong with Lloyd?" everyone is asking. "You hurt, Lloyd?" Lloyd shakes his head. Foley goes over to Costello and asks, "How come Lloyd wasn't in? Is he hurt?"

"I started to put him in, but Shula wanted Stuckey," says Costello.

Shula may have had his reasons, but in my opinion Stuckey was the worst person to put in at that time. He had little experience, except in games in which the outcome had already been decided. Lloyd was not going to make a mistake like the one Stuckey made. Lloyd had big old feet and looked kind of clumsy, but he could cover.

So the sidelines are buzzing about why Shula had insisted on Stuckey. Finally, Shula yells something like, "Because that's the way I want it! Because I made that choice! I make the decisions!"

Right, I'm thinking. Because you're confused!

This was the famous game in which the Raiders rallied to beat us in unbelievable fashion. With very little time left, they started a drive from their own 20-yard line. First, Stabler threw a desperation pass to Fred Biletnikoff, who made a one-handed catch at the sideline (only because, as usual, he had eight tons of stick-em on his hands!). Then, with time running out, Stabler, who was in Vern Den Herder's grasp, threw an even more desperate pass into the end zone. As the ball floated end over end toward the Raiders' halfback Clarence Davis, I was sure we had won the game. Our Nick Buoniconti was on one side of Davis and our Mike Kolen was in front of him. I was sure they'd knock the ball away or knock it out of his hands. Instead, they seemed to slap at the ball, and somehow it eluded them and went into Davis's hands. Touchdown! Final score: Oakland 28, Miami 26.

Do I believe in black magic? Not really. But I'm not so sure that the decision to put Stuckey in the game in place of Foley wasn't a result of some supernatural influence conjured up by me putting those roots on Shula's ass. The coach certainly was confused. Hey, he's still buried in that shoe box in my backyard. Who knows? He may never win another Super Bowl until *I* dig him up!

Shortly before our season ended, I met Bobbie for the first time. She was working as a receptionist at a law firm where I was a client. (Sometimes it seems like half my life has been spent in law firms.) I liked her immediately. I quickly realized that she was something special. She was physically attractive—like all the women I dated. But, more important, Bobbie was different than the other women I'd known. Most of these women were like my mother (Freud would have had a field day with this). They were all free spirits. Maybe by dating them I was trying in some way to "tame" my mother—something my father and everyone else had failed at.

Bobbie was gentle, intelligent, quiet, thoughtful, serious, and hard working. She had come to Miami after going to college in her home state of Tennessee. Like me, she had been raised largely by her grandparents. Like me, she had recently ended a relationship and had a 3-year-old son; his name was Duke. They lived in the projects at Liberty City, Miami's equivalent of Bedford-Stuyvesant or Watts. Finally, like me, Bobbie was a graduate of the high school class of 1965. We were on the same wavelength.

Unfortunately, all of these wonderful traits worked against us the first time around. The timing was terrible. Something inside me told me it was time to settle down and that Bobbie seemed to be the perfect woman to settle down with. But something else inside me told me I wasn't ready to get out of the fast lane just yet. You don't see any passenger cars at the Indy 500.

Realizing that Bobbie was special, I didn't want her to become part of the "field" that I was playing. She didn't deserve to be one of the many. So I decided to stop seeing her altogether. I made the decision as I made many decisions in those days—without consulting her and without thinking about all the repercussions of my actions. I simply cut her out of my life. It would be almost four years before I saw her again.

I was not one for staying alone for very long; it seems I had to be in some kind of relationship, be it foolhardy or wise. But while I needed these relationships to keep me afloat, I wasn't able to provide the commitment necessary to keep them from sinking. Between the time I stopped seeing Bobbie and the time our 1975 training camp began, I married my high school sweetheart, Betty Washington. Betty was a wonderful girl—attractive, understanding, and a talented artist. After having lost touch with her for several years, I made a point of looking her up at our tenth reunion in the spring of 1975. We had a great time.

"Why don't you come down to Miami with me?" I asked before I really knew what I was saying.

Betty smiled. "The only way I'd do that is if you married me." So I did.

The 1974 season was a disappointment because I couldn't contribute as much as I wanted to the Dolphins; 1975 was a disappointment because I wasn't allowed to contribute as much as I wanted to and was able to. With Csonka, Kiick, and Warfield leaving for the WFL, I expected to shoulder much more of the offense, but by the time the exhibition season began, it was apparent that the love lost between Shula and me had not been found. After I hurt an ankle during the exhibition season, the coach announced that he would start Benny Malone at halfback and pair him in the backfield with both Norm Bulaich and Don Nottingham.

Malone had come to the Dolphins from Arizona State in 1974. He was the kind of guy who would run through a brick wall if told to do so and would not even ask why. He was a wild man, and he was always getting hurt running into linebackers. A running back can attack linebackers who are bigger than he is, but he has to use some finesse. Malone tried to beat these giants with brute strength. He frequently lost and ended up injured. He was hurt in the first game of the year.

By this time I had healed. Back in the lineup, I got off to my best start ever, rushing for about 600 yards in our first seven games. Going into week number 8, we were 6–1 and I was coming off three consecutive 100-yard games. I was second in the league in rushing, only about 50 yards behind Juice. Having carried the ball more times per game than any previous year, I thought I might even give Juice a go for the rushing title. Then Malone got healthy again, and Shula, while complimenting me for the job I had done, said he wanted to alternate Benny and me.

As I recall, the coach said he felt Malone could do certain things I couldn't do and vice versa. I was furious. Again all I could think of was Shula's remarks after Super Bowl VI when he had said he liked to go with the guys who got him here. Fair is fair, I thought. I helped get us here so far. I should be in there.

I saw much less action in the second half of the season, gaining less than 300 yards. The team tailed off, too, finishing with a 10–4 record. We missed the playoffs for the first time in five seasons.

After our eighth game, I had stated publicly that I wanted to be traded because I thought Shula was systematically eliminating me from the offense. I felt I had some good years left in me. If the Dolphins weren't going to use me, then it was time to move on.

I probably sealed my fate after our second to last game of the season. We were in Baltimore. We had just lost a tough game to the Colts. The loss virtually eliminated us from the playoff picture. We were sitting on the team bus when Lloyd Mumphord came to the door. He had been traded to the Colts that year. In this game he had intercepted two passes. Each interception had hurt us badly. Lloyd's relationship with Shula had been no better than mine, and after each interception, Lloyd made a point to catch Shula's attention, as if to rub salt in an old wound.

Spotting me on the bus now, Lloyd said, "C'mon, man, let's go." I weighed the options. Standing outside was my good friend and former roommate inviting me to get off the bus and party with him. Sitting in front of me was my coach, who was in a particularly bad mood because of the loss. According to the team rules, you didn't have to come back with the team unless you were injured. I got off the bus. Shula stared at me, and I knew that was it. I got back to Miami in time for our next practice and played in our final game of the season at Denver.

After the season, the Miami papers ran several stories with headlines like, "Good Trade Is All Morris Wants Now." I had previously indicated that I would like to play with a contender—either the Oakland Raiders or the Pittsburgh Steelers—or an east coast team or almost anywhere except San Diego (where the Chargers would post the league's worst record in 1975, 2–12). During the season, Shula had told the press that if I wanted to be traded, "I'll try to accommodate him as I've accommodated others who've asked to be traded." I took that to mean he would trade me to one of the teams I had requested. The only other times I had heard him use "accommodate" he had granted players' trade requests. But by the time camp began for the 1976 season, I was still a Dolphin. I came to camp in relatively good shape despite the fact that in March I had been in a terrible auto accident. My Mercedes was cut off by a sanitation truck. In the collision, I aggravated my neck injury and broke a finger. I ended up requiring two and a half hours of surgery to remove a bone chip and repair torn ligaments in the finger. The doctors also had to put a screw in the finger. (It's still in there.)

If you read Shula's comments from this period, you'll see that he hadn't changed his mind about my role with the team. He still wanted to go with the younger Malone and other backs. The problem, he said, was that he couldn't swing a trade for me. If you read my comments from this period, you'll see that I was being a good boy, working hard in camp, indicating that I'd be happy to stay with the Dolphins, that I appreciated Shula's coaching and the fine offensive line, and that I now realized that even if Shula would never give me the offensive carte blanche that Juice had at Buffalo, at least we were winners. All of this was true... except the business about wanting to stay in Miami. I figured the best way to get out of there was to have a good camp and persuade other teams that I wasn't a troublemaker.

Any second thoughts I might have had about staying were shattered at the club's annual banquet, which took place during the pre-season. At the banquet, awards were given for various achievements. One such award was for "best offensive back." The award almost always went to the back who gained the most yards the previous season. I had never won it, because during my top years Csonka gained even more yards than I did. Having led my closest competitor, Don Nottingham, by almost 150 yards in 1975, I expected to win it. This, I thought, would be a small consolation for not making the playoffs and not getting all the playing time I wanted.

When the time for the presentation came, it was announced that there was a "special situation." The award was going to be given to two men. I thought, Who am I sharing it with? It can't be Nottingham or Bulaich. Alternating at fullback, the pair had combined for only about 150 more yards than I had.

I was right. It wasn't Nottingham *or* Bulaich. It was Nottingham *and* Bulaich. *I* was the odd man out. I'm almost certain this was the first time the Dolphins had ever split the award; they hadn't done so when Csonka and I became the first pair to each rush for over 1000 yards. I was steamed but soon realized I should have expected this. After all, I had barely been featured in the season highlight film. How would it look if you traded the guy you just named your best back?

Attendance at the banquet had been mandatory, but there was one notable absence—Jake Scott. Jake's most recent run-in with Shula had come when Jake cursed a defensive coach in front of Shula for calling the wrong formation in practice. When Shula chided him (much less harshly than he would another player), Jake said, "Well, I wasn't talking to you." I remember looking at Larry Little, thinking that if I had done that, I wouldn't have had to ask to be traded.

Jake had begun to fall out of favor with Shula by 1975 and he, too, was given short shrift in the highlight film. The coach was not happy when Jake announced he was going to the dog track instead of the banquet. "Anyone who's not there will be fined," said Shula.

The next day Jake's wallet was $500 lighter. That's not how Jake looked at it. "I'd have to give half of that to the IRS anyway," he laughed. "And besides I won $700 at the dog track."

Jake was not laughing later in the preseason when Shula suspended him for allegedly refusing to play in a game against the Philadelphia Eagles. Jake had had a painful shoulder problem that our team doctor called a bone spur, but Jake's personal doctor called a bone chip. (Our doctor was the same one who had refused me anesthesia, diagnosed my fractured neck as a sprain, and given me "mood" pills.) Jake claimed that he had not refused to play, but that he had refused to take a shot they wanted to give him before allowing him to play. This was a significant distinction. It was easy to understand why Jake, who was as tough as they come, didn't want to get a shot—which doesn't heal you but only masks pain—in a meaningless exhibition game.

"I've got about ten players as witnesses (that I didn't refuse to play, but refused a shot)," Jake told the *Miami News*. "Shula can intimidate five or six of them, but I know two or three he can't intimidate." I was one of them.

No matter. Jake had gone too far. After a six-day suspension without pay, he was shipped off to the Washington Redskins. I know that must have hurt Shula, who had regarded him like a son.

I'm sure it was less painful for the coach when at about the same time he put me on waivers, announcing he had decided to go with youth and that he had no takers for me. Strangely, however, within 24 hours another team had called about a trade and soon a deal was consummated. Where was the one place I had said I didn't want to go? San Diego. Where was I traded? San Diego. I'm still bitter about this. I know a team has the right to trade a player wherever it chooses, but Shula had in the past accommodated players and had promised to do the same for me. When he put me on waivers, Shula told me in all sincerity, "I tried to make a deal for you, but I just couldn't get any interested people." But how come San Diego took me right away and gave the Dolphins a draft choice? More important, how come Tommy Prothro, the Chargers' coach, later revealed in a deposition taken on another matter that Shula called and told him that he could have me because Shula didn't want me playing on an east coast team? Was it because of spite, or was Shula afraid I'd haunt the Dolphins if I remained in the east? I don't know.

The only thing good about San Diego was the weather. I may have had my differences with Shula, but he was a helluva coach. I may not always have enjoyed his hard practices, but I knew they made for a disciplined, regimented, successful football team. The Chargers were none of the above. I couldn't believe the preseason camp Prothro was running. Players would take off their helmets and sit down on them on the field. "Oh, man, I'm so hot," they'd whine. Miami was much hotter, and Shula would never have tolerated such behavior.

The drills were not as demanding as those in Miami and things were certainly less organized. In San Diego, I could go out and catch a pass or drop it and then take my helmet off, get a drink of Kool-Aid, and relax. In my seven years with the Dolphins, I never had a drink of water on the practice field. A player like me needs that regimentation.

Prothro's preseason remarks that he would be happy if we could improve to 7–7 only reinforced my feeling that this was a bad situation. It was déjà vu—Coach Wilson of the Dolphins all over again.

I fumbled the ball the first time I touched it for San Diego in an exhibition game, but on my next carry I broke off a 60- or 70-yard touchdown run. We had a young team. Most of the guys were in awe of my Super Bowl rings. They knew I came from a championship atmosphere. I tried to instill that, but the situation wasn't right. We had some talented players. However, many of them seemed more interested in their own individuality rather than the concept of the team.

I believe the structure of our practices also hurt. Our morning meetings would end at 11:30. Afternoon practice didn't begin until 1:30. That was much longer than the break we had in Miami and provided too much time to get in trouble. Guys would tape teammates' shoes to the wallpipes, dump ice water into an occupied bathroom stall, or hide each other's street clothes. Sometimes guys would bring a hose inside and turn it on, spraying everybody they could. Staying loose was not our problem!

Another difference between San Diego and Miami was the fines. If you were late for a Chargers' practice or meeting, you were fined 50 cents per man on the team per minute. With 43 guys that added up fast. I was late for one meeting and it cost me $239. The system might have created a needed discipline, but instead of giving the fine money to charity as we had done at Miami, we used it to pay for a weekly party that lasted from 5:30 Friday afternoon until whenever. It would take the guys a couple of days just to recover. By then it was game time. It got so that the players loved it when somebody was late. They'd see him coming and say, "Well, we're having lobster this week because so and so was fifteen minutes late."

The results of all this were evident on the field. We didn't give our all in practice, and as a result, we didn't give our all in games. We started out 3–0, but then the lack of intensity started to hurt. All too often our defenders would try to tackle a guy, miss him, and he'd be gone for a touchdown. You realize on certain plays that if you don't tackle a guy, he's gone. So you have to have the mentality not to let him get by you. That was evident on the Dolphins but not on the Chargers. We had talented players in San Diego; we just didn't have those intense players. In some ways San Diego was like Miami before Shula came.

Another problem was that the coaching just wasn't consistent enough. I don't want to take anything away from Prothro, but he pales when compared to Shula. He was a tall man, but he took such little steps—seven steps to go 5 yards when most people could do it in three—we called him "Half Stride." He spent all his free time playing whist. I actually didn't have too much contact with him because he didn't have much to do with the offense. I'm not sure he even knew the plays. In the middle of the season, I asked him about a play and he said, "I don't know. See Bill Walsh."

Bill Walsh (who has enjoyed such great success as the San Francisco 49ers' head coach and is recognized as an offensive genius) was our offensive coordinator. We had some talent on offense: Don Woods, who gained over 1000 yards as rookie, and Rickey Young, as well as me and Joe Washington (Joe, however, was injured). Dan Fouts was in his early years in the league. Our other quarterback was a refugee from the Cowboys, Clint Longley. He had gained notoriety (and a ticket to San Diego) when he punched Roger Staubach. Nicknamed "The Mad Bomber," Clint was a little off the wall. On Thanksgiving Day he brought a turkey to the stadium—a live turkey—and let it loose. He spent the morning chasing it through the stands.

Walsh deserves his reputation. Unfortunately for me he advocated throwing the ball a great deal; pass receiving was not my strong suit. But I respected and appreciated his demeanor. In some ways he was the opposite of Shula. At Miami if something went wrong, Shula would chew you out. "Make the fucking play," he'd grumble.

Ten minutes after the play was over, he might still be talking about it, "Make the fucking play."

Walsh wasn't that way. He'd just say, "Come on, we just have to come back from that, just take our time." If something didn't work, he'd say, "Okay, we'll try this or this." I liked that.

Ironically, my actions contributed to delaying Walsh's move from assistant coach to head coach. In our second to last game of the season, we played the 49ers. From our fast start, our record had fallen to 5–7. We were losing at the half. Chargers' owner Gene Klein stormed into the locker room. In earshot of the players, he told Prothro that his coaching career was hanging on the outcome of the game. If we lost, Prothro was gone.

I had been seeing limited duty behind Rickey Young. Rickey was a great ballplayer, an asset as both a runner and a pass catcher. He feared for his job with me there and tried to stay in the game as much as possible. He'd get hurt, and I'd go in. Then he'd just say to the trainer, "Tape it up real quick so I can get back in." And he'd be back in, and I'd be out.

Of course this was frustrating for me, just as it had been at Miami. In the San Francisco game, I went in once when Rickey was hurt. The 49ers called a time-out, and before we ran a play, Rickey was back in and I was out of the game. I got so mad that I did the same thing I'd done at Super Bowl VI. I kicked over a table. I kicked a ball, too, and the game had to be stopped to get it off the field.

My tirade and Klein's tirade aside, we tied the 49ers and went into overtime. I was back in the game. We were driving for a touchdown when I noticed that whenever we were inside the 49ers' 20-yard line, the 49ers defensive linemen all seemed to follow the action one particular way. When my number was called in the huddle, I felt it played into their hands. So I decided to call my own play. Instead of running the off-tackle inside trap that had been called, I was going to sprint for the end zone on a naked reverse. I didn't tell my teammates. I knew I'd either make the play or make a fool of myself. I took the gamble, sprinted for the end zone, and scored the touchdown to end the game. Nobody ever touched me because everyone—on both teams—was standing over where they thought the play would be run. It was my last NFL touchdown.

Walsh had been expecting that the head coaching job would be his. But after the game, Klein announced that Prothro would be back in 1977. Walsh was devastated. I'm not even sure if he came to any of our practices that final week. At the end of the season, he left pro football for a while to coach at Stanford.

After the game Prothro told the media that despite my touchdown he didn't think I was worth my six-figure salary. When we were defeated 24–0 by the Raiders the next week, I wondered if he was worth *his* salary. We finished the season 6–8. As for me, I had carried the ball only 50 times all season, but had gained 256 yards, keeping up my high yards-per-carry average. That same year the Dolphins were also 6–8, losing more games than they won for the first time since my rookie season. It was little consolation.

I could have returned to the Chargers for the 1977 season. If I didn't want to go back to San Diego, the team had indicated it would be willing to trade me. John Sanders, the Chargers' general manager, was very kind. He told me, "We can make a deal for you. You can go to Houston. You ought to stay in the league."

While I felt that I could still play, could still contribute to a team, my neck was still giving me problems. My doctors told me a bad hit could result in paralysis. More important, my battle with Dorothy for custody of Maceo was coming to a head. I knew that the only way the court would even consider giving me permanent custody was if I lived full time in Miami and no longer played football, a profession which the court apparently felt kept me away from home too much.

I wanted my 6-year-old son more than I wanted to play football. Maceo came to stay with me and Betty for what was supposed to be a short visit after I returned from San Diego. The days passed. Dorothy seemed to have little interest. I drove Maceo to and from his school, which was almost 30 miles from our home.

Finally, after seven weeks, Dorothy showed up at the school as classes were letting out. Although she lived around the corner from the school, she hadn't even seen Maceo for a month. Now, she declared that he was to come home with her. "No way," I said. She created quite a confrontation in front of the principal. I took Maceo home, called my lawyer, and said it was time to go to court to settle this dispute once and for all. That night, as Maceo and I were watching television, we saw a news bulletin flash across the bottom of the screen. "Mercury Morris kidnaps son. Details at 11 o'clock," the bulletin read. *Bullshit!*

On the day after the schoolyard confrontation, April Fool's Day,

1977, Dorothy, Maceo, and I appeared in court for a hearing to determine permanent custody. Maceo knew the judge was going to ask him some hard questions. "I'm scared, Dad," he told me in the courthouse bathroom before the hearing. "What should I say?"

"Just tell the truth," I answered.

He did, and I was awarded custody.

Now there was no question about my future in the NFL. I quit. For the first time in over twenty years, I would not be playing football in the fall. It took a little getting used to that, but I could accept it. I had Maceo, the memories of two Super Bowl championships, and some personal achievements of which I was quite proud. When I left the game, I had the second-best yard-per-carry average in the modern-day history of the NFL. I was behind only the legendary Jim Brown and one spot ahead of the great Gale Sayers. Not bad company for a guy who many had thought was too small to do anything besides run back kicks.

CHAPTER 7

NO GAME PLAN

I left the National Football League with over $250,000 in the bank, two homes, several cars, some other investments, a lucrative contract to do public relations work for Nautilus, and my good name to trade on. The only thing I didn't have was a game plan. Unfortunately, that would have been more valuable than any real estate or currency could ever be.

A game plan. It happens every Wednesday during the football season. You come to the practice field, you have your aches and pains attended to, and you receive a game plan for the following week's contest. It is a plan of attack, a carefully conceived modus operandi for meeting and overcoming the next challenge, a step-by-step primer for success.

The game plan is handed to you. You don't have to conceive it. You just have to follow it. You're a bit like an actor. Each week you're given your script. You learn your lines (or memorize your plays), and then the director (or coach) tells you how to execute what you have memorized. Yes, there is some room for individual initiative and creativity in the delivery, the performance. But for the most part you accept the fact that somebody else is calling the shots. It's not all that bad having a game plan. You know what's expected of you and how to go about accomplishing it.

When you leave professional football, nobody hands you a game plan for the next week or next year. Certainly not for the rest of your life. This might not be so bad if during the course of your career somebody had been instructing you on how to create your own game plan. That rarely happens today, and it happened even less frequently when I was playing. The Dolphins and other clubs had no in-house program for preparing you for the dramatic and traumatic jump from the sports world to the real world. And just because you've earned a good salary for a few years doesn't mean you will be able to handle things once you make the transition.

When you're a top college and professional athlete, you enter a state of suspended animation in which you really don't have to grow up, take responsibility, or make decisions. Someone is always there telling you where to be at such and such a time, what to wear, and so on. Someone is there to purchase and hand you your airplane tickets and make sure you get that wake-up call. Often someone is even there to write your checks and plan and balance your budget. This setup is not often ideal. In the early seventies, several members of the Dolphins, myself included, ended up suing the management group handling, or rather mishandling, our affairs. But, ideal or not, it exists. (The consequence of this mismanagement was that I became leery of letting other people handle my business affairs.)

The result of all this is that you have little opportunity to practice responsibility. And if you don't have the opportunity to practice—be you the brightest guy or the most illiterate guy—you will not grow. You will be in for a rude awakening when you leave the game and the support system is withdrawn.

I don't have to look any farther than my own doorstep to demonstrate this. I was the classic example of someone who lacked the preparation for being able to do things on his own. At the time I retired, I had done three basic things in life: play football, have fun, and make money. Those are the basics of professional sports. They didn't put me in good stead for life after sports. Of course with my personality and the bravado which being a prominent athlete brings, I didn't realize this.

When I retired I decided to "go into business." First thing I did was get a briefcase. "Hey," I said, "this is all I need. Now I'm ready to do business." What did that mean? I didn't know. During the off-seasons, my activities had been limited to making some public relations appearances for the Dolphins and doing some promotional work for Nautilus. My previous investments—a second home in the Florida Keys and an interest in a Miami Beach fast-food restaurant called Big Daddy's—had only required money, no business expertise. I'd never really done any business before. Still, naive and untutored as I was, I felt ready. Looking back, I see that I had a great deal of enthusiasm and very little direction. I knew where I wanted to go, but didn't have any idea how to get there. I had a feel for the big picture but no grasp for day-to-day detail.

My plan was to build Nautilus facilities in Miami and to build what I envisioned as "Morristown," a huge development in the Keys. I lost money on each of these, a lot of money. The sad thing is that there was nothing wrong with the ideas from a conceptual standpoint. I simply didn't have the background or character to make them happen. Neither did the people with whom I became associated. Having been burned by those handling my affairs while I was a player, I was reluctant to engage too many outside advisers. For a time, a close friend from Pittsburgh who had come to Miami, Rich Didonato, counseled me. But after a while, I wasn't able to compensate him for his services and he had to leave. Rich did a fine job for me. The rest of the lot—partners, lawyers, accountants, consultants, brokers, etc.—did not.

I had been involved with Nautilus from the time of its inception. I had personally benefited from the program and believed in it. I was one of the company's first spokesmen and had a contract running through 1976 to do public relations. The work was simple, required little time, and paid quite well—about $50,000 a year.

Now I wanted to get into the ownership and managerial aspect. I wanted to build a few clubs. An opportunity arose to build a 14,000-square-foot facility in the old Biscayne Hotel which, I was assured, was going to be beautifully renovated. I invested several thousand dollars to have plans drawn up. We were going to have three levels, an elevator, a health food restaurant and bar, the whole nine yards. Unfortunately, before construction began, the hotel's owner, upon whom I'd been relying, lost interest and the hotel went under. So did my plans.

The Biscayne Hotel was a disappointment. "Morristown" was a disaster. Shortly after I retired, I bought 80 acres on Duck Key, a resort island in the Florida Keys, for $1,078,000. Development of the property had begun before I purchased it. The roads were paved. The streets were already in. The land was already plotted. There were to be 284 homesites. My plan was to hold onto the property for a while and then further develop it by building single-family homes and duplexes.

While I put up all the money for the property (much of it was through a loan from the original owner of the land), I only received a 50 percent share. I had an equal partner, the man who had helped me find the property and had arranged the deal. This 50–50 proposition may have seemed slanted against me, but I wasn't troubled. I had ordered an appraisal of the property—at a cost of over $3000—which indicated its worth to be $3,350,000. I was so confident that not too long after entering the deal, I bought my partner out.

Before I could further develop Morristown, I had to get certain zoning changes. I also had to make provisions for bringing in water. This required frequent trips to the state capital in Tallahassee. I felt like quite the businessman flying up there to make my case. In retrospect, I was out of my league. This was OJT (on-the-job training) in a deal where the stakes were too high for OJT.

My expenses during this period between purchase and development were extremely high—$8000 per month in loan principal *plus* taxes and interest *plus* attorneys' fees, travel, etc.

About two years after I had bought the property, I found myself in the position of having to pay the original owner a lump sum of $100,000 by a certain date. The arrangement was frighteningly clear: either I came up with the money by that date or I lost everything— my entire stake in the property and all I had invested to date. As the date approached, I realized I didn't have that kind of money. I was damned if Morristown was gonna go the way of the Biscayne Hotel. With the help of a lawyer, I received $60,000 from the Dolphins in settlement of an old contractual claim (more about this disgusting transaction later). I sent that to my creditor immediately.

Where was I gonna get the other forty grand? I had recently bought a brand new turbo Porsche with candy-apple burgundy metallic exterior and burgundy interior for $43,000. (This was in keeping with my ongoing desire for speed and status symbols, which included the leasing of a big cigarette boat and traveling from Miami to the Keys by private plane or helicopter.) On the day the $100,000 was due, I sold the car, which had only 900 miles on it, for $38,000. I wrote a cashier's check for the remaining $2000 and then hopped a private plane to the Keys so I could deliver the $40,000 balance by a mutually agreed upon 5 p.m. deadline.

We ran into stormy weather on the short trip and radioed that we might be a little late. We were there before 6 p.m. The creditor, a man whom I counted as a friend, refused my payment. There was nothing I could do. Title in the property reverted back to him. Not only did I lose the land and all I had spent to date, the deal was structured so that I didn't even get back the $60,000 (of the 100 grand) that I had paid on time. That wasn't fair, but that's the way the contract read. In all, I lost about $300,000. Way to go, Morris. I felt so small that I could have climbed into my briefcase.

During the period that the Nautilus and Morristown ventures were draining my bank account, I did earn some money doing a car commercial ("Mercury drives a Subaru"). I received $22,000 and a car. But I also lost several thousand dollars on a third project that never got off the ground—Animal Art International. This was to be a home interior business utilizing my wife Betty's artistic skills. Again, it wasn't a bad concept, I simply had no idea how to execute it.

My marriage with Betty didn't fare much better than the business. She is a good person. She was a good wife to me, and she was a good mother to Maceo. Unfortunately, I was not a good husband. I had messed up in marriage with Kay coming into football, and now I was messing up with Betty coming out of football. We really hadn't known each other when we married so spontaneously in 1975 and, as usual, I never made the personal commitment to make the marriage contract work. I was looking for a woman who was absolutely perfect in every aspect. "Compromise" and "understanding" simply were not words in my vocabulary. When we divorced in 1978, Betty could have made things difficult for me financially. She didn't. We remain friends to this day. Again, timing is everything. I couldn't have made a marriage work with anybody in 1978.

I do not want to make excuses, but there were extenuating circumstances which contributed to these professional and domestic failures. One of the factors was cocaine. I blame nobody but myself for that. The other factor was something I had little control over—my health.

My health. Not only did I leave football ill-prepared for business and marriage, I left with a series of physical ailments. This is par for the course. The world is full of hobbling former NFL players. (Indeed, the life expectancy of those who play five years or more in the NFL is only 57. As I played eight seasons, I'm a member of this club.) When I retired, my knees were bad and my wrist was bad. They still go out on me to this day and probably will for the rest of my life. The finger injury I suffered in the auto accident was aggravated on the football field, and on certain days the finger swells up to the size of a small cucumber and hurts like hell. I could (and do) live with these relatively minor annoyances. But I had a major ailment, too: severe complications resulting from my neck injury.

The complications took the form of headaches so painful and debilitating that for several hours at a time, sometimes several days at a time, I could do nothing more than sit in a silent, darkened room and pray for relief. They started in 1977 (before any serious involvement with cocaine), and despite numerous trips to numerous specialists who gave me numerous treatments and medication, they continued until I had major neck surgery in 1980.

I've heard that you cannot remember pain. Thank goodness I can't reexperience the feeling I had during this period, but I vividly remember the effects. It would start on the right side of my body. My right eye would begin to droop and water would come from it. I would have no muscle control over this eye. I couldn't keep the eyelid up or the eye open. My nose would start to run. I would start to drool from the right side of my mouth. I had no way of holding the saliva back. Over a period of time, my entire right side began to deteriorate. Despite the fact that I am right-handed, my right arm was soon much smaller than my left. The right part of my chest also started caving in. There was no relief. I had separate stretches of thirty days, forty days, and fifty days where I had headaches for several hours a day, every day. To put this in perspective, I have heard that something like 20 percent of the people who suffer from this condition commit suicide.

One of the most frightening aspects of the headaches was that I could tell when they were coming—like a train that you see far in the distance, a train that you know will soon be here. I'd "hear" that whistle go off, and I'd know that in about fifteen minutes the agony would begin. It wasn't a question of whether it might come, it was on its way.

The anticipation of this trauma caused me to have a personality change. For the first time in my life, I became frightened. And in this fright, I began to make foolish decisions about my health. I'd want to see a chiropractor three times a day, visit a doctor every night.

The pain itself made the personality change even worse. I either retreated from or exploded at my family. I'd go into my study at home and shut the door. But the slightest bit of noise in the house was enough to bring me out in a rage. I couldn't think clearly and

therefore either avoided making business decisions or made them
rashly. As I said, I don't blame the headaches for my business failures, but they didn't help.

The combination of those failures and the headaches made me a
poor imitation of the confident character I had been. I was no longer
Mercury Morris, the guy who would hit you in the face with the
ball if you hit him late or out of bounds. I went from a situation of
real strength to one of real weakness, and instead of facing that weakness, I hid from it. I found myself hiding from everything and everyone, staying in the bedroom or study.

The doctors and chiropractors were of little help. Several of them
suggested that the condition was merely the result of stress or a bad
case of nerves. They knew of my neck injury but were skeptical that
there was any connection. This may have been because they were
doctors to whom I had been referred by the Dolphins. My regard
for the Dolphins' front office was dwindling rapidly. In some ways,
I saw the headaches as the inevitable result of the team doctor's initial failure to diagnose the fracture and his subsequent dismissal of
the warnings of the Pro Bowl doctors that if I didn't wear the brace
I'd be in trouble for the rest of my life. Every time I had a head-
ache, the picture of the doctor, owner Joe Robbie, and even Shula
came up like the faces on Mount Rushmore. Adding fuel to this fire
was the fact that in order to get the $60,000 for the Morristown pay-
ment, I had settled an old dispute with Robbie over deferred payments by signing a document whereby I agreed not to sue the
Dolphins for *anything* that had taken place during my years with
the team. "Anything" included injuries. The bottom line was that
on my then-lawyer's advice that the contractual settlement Robbie
was offering was the best I could do, I ended up getting less than I
had coming and agreed not to sue for such things as the effects of
a misdiagnosed or concealed neck injury. In my opinion, even if
this wasn't illegal, it was immoral. Robbie had me over a barrel and
knew it.

Looking back over this period, there are few events which would
make my personal highlights film...with one big exception. In
December of 1979, I married Bobbie. We had begun to see each
other shortly after my divorce. I had run into a mutual friend, C. T.
Taylor, and asked about her.

"She's still the same old Bobbie," C. T. said. "She's working in
a bank and living in Liberty City. She won't let Duke go anywhere

and she doesn't go anywhere herself. Her idea of a vacation is checking into that Holiday Inn over on LeJeune Road by herself just to get away from people."

So I called her up. It wouldn't have been in character for me to apologize for dropping out of sight the first time around, so I didn't. I just acted as if nothing had happened over the last three years. That seemed to be fine with her.

There were no more vacations at the Holiday Inn. I'd say, "Bobbie, it's Friday. Let's fly down to the Keys." She'd protest a little. Then I'd say, "Forget about your job." Monday would roll around and we'd still be in the Keys. "Relax, I'll take care of everything for you," I'd promise. We dated for exactly one year and then married. Bobbie and Duke moved into my house in South Miami with me and Maceo.

I wish I could say that my life immediately took a turn for the better thanks to Bobbie's presence. It didn't. The headaches intensified in 1979 and 1980. It was at this time, too, that I began to freebase cocaine. This was the beginning of what I call my automatic downward spiral. Even after the headaches were alleviated by surgery, there was no stopping the spiral.

I don't blame anyone or anything for this entry into the world of freebasing. The decision was wholly mine. It was a poor one. In some ways, it was also an inevitable one—a natural result of being in the wrong place (Miami, where the availability and acceptance of cocaine was in 1979, and probably still is, unlike it is in almost any other American city) at the wrong time (this period of hiding from myself and looking for an escape) in the wrong *times* (remember that in 1979 there was little of the furor over cocaine that now exists; it was viewed as a recreational drug, not a killer).

I had first tried cocaine during the 1973 or 1974 off-season. It didn't seem like that big of a deal. It was considered chic, not dangerous. There weren't any headlines or hot lines, or public service announcements, or First Ladies warning about the hazards. I continued using the drug on a recreational basis over the next five or six years, but I was never addicted to it and absolutely never touched it during the football season. I knew of other players who also used cocaine during the off-season, but not once they reported to camp. Perhaps that's not believable in light of current revelations about players being high for games or receiving cocaine in the locker room, but it's true. When I played, we considered the off-season our own time, but once practice began, because of the obligation we had to the team, there was no place for getting high (with the exception of that deadliest drug, alcohol, and perhaps a few hits of marijuana, which, during that period, was in some circles as accepted and prevalent as alcohol).

Freebasing cocaine is completely different from snorting it. Snorting is a social thing. Freebasing is not. It cannot be. It's an individual thing, a psychological pretender to yourself that everything is fine. When I crossed over the line in December of 1979, there was no going back.

I was introduced to freebasing by Ricky O, a good friend who had access to cocaine. We'd met in 1977 and had bonded immediately. Not because of drugs, but because we were both from that class of '65 era. Also, he had observed my battle for custody of Maceo and had a tremendous amount of respect for me.

I would later become a "master chef" at cooking freebase, but on this first occasion, Ricky O had already cooked the stuff before he came over to my house. I think Bobbie was out. Over the next two and a half years as I sank deeper and deeper, she was aware of my cocaine use, but never participated. She is a deeply spiritual person and didn't need any drugs to find peace. As my behavior began to affect my life with her and the boys, she would periodically suggest I stop. She even stormed out of the house once or twice. But it is not her style to argue or push. She spent more time praying that I'd stop than fighting me over it. I tried my best to make sure she and the boys didn't actually see what was going on.

Freebase is created by cooking and rapidly cooling the cocaine. The result is crack. You put the rock into a freebase pipe. Then you put a torch to the stem of the pipe and inhale the vapor.

My first reaction to the freebase was, "Wow. I like this." It created an instant euphoria, like an orgasm. "Holy, shit," I thought. "I'm almost out of control."

Almost? You can't talk. You can't function. Have you ever been leaning down and all of a sudden stood up so fast that you got real dizzy and almost passed out? That's a little bit what it is like. In fact, one day when I was in prison, I stood up like that and said, "Hey. Wait a minute. This feels just like it did when I hit the pipe. You mean to tell me I spent $100,000 to get high when all I had to do was kneel down and stand up real fast and I could have got it all for free?!"

The euphoric effect of taking your first hit of freebase is so intense that you immediately want to duplicate it. But you can't. You can try all night. I *did* try all night. But it's impossible. It's like in baseball; you can only hit your first home run once. Still, you keep going up to the plate and taking that big swing, trying to recapture that moment which common sense should tell you can never be recaptured. This is why you keep doing it, not because you like the sustained mellow or high feeling that freebasing creates. There is no sustained feeling—no mellow period, no high. You bypass high and go straight to messed up. Ask a guy who's freebasing if it feels good. If he's honest, he'll admit it doesn't.

When you're freebasing, paranoia quickly sets in. It is inevitable. It is oppressive. The walls have ears. The guy with the pipe next to you can't be trusted. The car behind you is tailing you. If you're not careful, your little freebasing group can resemble something like the goings on in *Who's Afraid of Virginia Woolf?*

Example: Once, I was with Ricky O and Eddie Kulins (one of the guys who was later busted with me). We were already high. As we walked out my door, we were discussing going to the home of our supplier Ruth to get a couple more grams of coke. Suddenly, Kulins stopped. "Wait. Is that a microphone in that tree?" he said. "Wait. Do I hear a tape recorder?"

We joined in. "What's that other noise?"

"Did you—"

"No. I didn't."

This paranoia rarely stops you from freebasing. Soon Ricky and Eddie and I were off to Ruth's to pick up the coke where she always left it for us—in the mailbox. On any given evening we might call her and make pickups three or four times. 8:30, 11:30, 2:30 a.m. "This is the last time, Ruth. Promise. We won't call you anymore tonight."

The tab for such an evening might be $1200, $1400. And one thing you always tried to do was pay your tab. You never wanted to alienate a source.

It was a costly habit. You needed at least $200 if you wanted to get started. You needed $100 worth of cocaine; you needed the pipe, which can cost up to $40; you needed a torch; and you needed utensils. The cost of freebasing when I was involved undoubtedly prevented some people from doing it. Unfortunately, the drug peddlers have recently figured out a way to "mass market" the product. Today *they* cook the cocaine before selling it. Their new product is "crack," and it only costs $5 or $10 for a high. Now, unfortunately, almost everybody on the street can afford the stuff.

I still had a fair amount of money when I started freebasing. I hadn't lost my shirt in the Keys yet. I also was laboring under the belief that whatever the status of my business ventures was, I would continue to have money. I had a lawsuit pending against the company whose sanitation truck had hit me in 1976. I figured to collect several hundred thousand dollars when that went to trial. I had my pension coming from the NFL, and if it were determined that the neck injury was disabling, I'd collect a substantial amount. Finally, I had what amounted to carte blanche at a local bank where my ability to secure loans was based less on my balance sheet and more on the fact that I was friends with the owners. Indeed, we sometimes shared cocaine with one another.

The length of our sessions depended on how much cocaine we had and how long we could make it last. Sometimes that would be four or five hours. I once binged for thirteen consecutive days.

When you're on one of these binges, you can't wait for the pipe to come back to you so you can swing for the fences one more time. Waiting for the pipe to get passed around a room can be agonizing. Waiting for a new batch of freebase to be cooked can be unbearable. So you learn tricks to make the time pass. Ricky O was an expert. He'd take a hit; then he'd get up and cook a bit; then he'd clean the pipe; then he'd look at it. I started doing it the same way. Then we came up with an experiment. Let's try and cook it in the microwave. Hey, it only takes thirteen seconds. Hey, I'll cook it in the microwave while you cook it on the stove so we'll have some to smoke right now.

You start to be a real philosopher when you're freebasing, if you can get past the greed factor. Some people can't; they're honed in on the pipe. Don't want to share. There were times when I was like that. Other times I seemed as brilliant as Plato. There was a regular group of us—Ricky, Johnny, Frank, Shakey, Stan, me. We laughingly called ourselves the PBA—Professional Basers of America. We'd talk about the state of the world, our own experiences. How some people were really missing out on life—whatever that meant!

For the first several months after I started freebasing, I did not consider myself heavily involved in it. That heavy involvement began in 1981. Prior to that I would describe myself as one who binged.

I didn't feel the need to freebase whenever I could, but when I did, I really went all out and abused myself.

Those who have never been involved with cocaine stand back and wonder how I could have let all this happen. I don't have any answer. But even now, knowing all I do, I'm not surprised at my behavior. In Miami in 1979 it wasn't that unusual. Add to that the fact that while I had no game plan, I did have a lot of free time on my hands. When you've got free time, especially during the day, you're going to end up in the company of others with free time. These people may not be the best influences.

Why me? Why do some people take a rollercoaster ride and love it and want to stay on the rollercoaster and ride all day, while others take a ride, hate the experience, and vow never to do it again? We're all different. We choose different ways and different levels of abusing ourselves.

While the freebasing initially seemed to help with the headaches, that didn't last for too long. In fact, I soon found it impossible to freebase when I was having the headaches. As 1980 progressed, the headaches intensified. A friend of mine named Larry Napp finally suggested that I see a local doctor named William Scott Russell.

Dr. Russell's immediate impact was more psychological than physical. As luck would have it, he had had the very same problem I was having and had eventually required an operation. He didn't think I was crazy, didn't think that my problems were the result of "nerves." He initially treated me by giving me ergotamine. You spray this into your mouth through an inhaler. It goes into your lungs fast and gets into your bloodstream and is supposed to relieve the headaches. But it didn't work, and apparently it can be dangerous. From ergotamine we advanced to shots of cortisone and xylocaine in the base of my skull. Cortisone! Xylocaine! What an irony. The same drugs used in football were now being used to afford me relief from an injury I got while playing.

Sometimes the injections provided temporary relief; sometimes they didn't. But the headaches were coming every day now and were more intense than ever. When the pain became too intense, I would call Dr. Russell and meet him at his office for another shot.

One night, in October of 1980, I called after midnight. The pain was as bad as it had ever been. Dr. Russell told me to take a cab to his office. I decided to drive. The pain was getting worse and worse. That train inside my head just wouldn't let up. As I approached the intersection of 72nd Avenue and 72nd Street, which even at that hour was busy, something in my mind said, "Here's a way to alleviate your pain. Just drive straight through the intersection without stopping and all your problems will be over."

Obviously, I didn't do that. I found myself saying the Lord's Prayer, and I slowed down. The train in my head was still pounding. Dr. Russell gave me three injections. He said that he couldn't give me any more because it was too dangerous. Despite his warning, I told him, "I've got to have it." He relented, but it didn't do me any good. The train wouldn't go away.

The next day Dr. Russell sent me to a neurosurgeon, Dr. Laurence Guido. Dr. Guido, like Dr. Russell, took the matter very seriously. He wasn't only interested in the symptoms; he wanted to find a cure. After taking various measurements and seeing how small my right arm and chest were, he said, "My God. How come somebody hasn't done anything for you? You need an operation." I started to cry. At last I was in the hands of somebody who might be able to provide relief. After putting me in the hospital for a myelogram, or spinal tap, Dr. Guido reaffirmed that surgery was probably the best and only answer. He cautioned me that one of several things might happen: the surgery might be a complete success; the surgery might have no impact; the surgery might leave me paralyzed; I might die on the operating table.

I had no trouble making the decision. I couldn't live with the headaches anymore. "Let's operate," I said. He did the next day.

Dr. Guido operated on me in November of 1980. He performed a laminectomy, removing a substantial part of my neck—the vertebrae I had fractured in 1973.

The operation lasted about four hours. I remember being very cocky going into surgery. I told Bobbie to have a big breakfast waiting for me when I returned and told the nurses I could remain conscious under the anesthesia longer than anybody they'd ever seen. In reality, I was out like a light. When I came back from surgery, the pain was so great that I wanted morphine rather than bacon and eggs.

My surgery was on a Wednesday. By Friday, thanks to the morphine, I was feeling better. Good enough to go AWOL from the hospital when some friends came up to visit me.

A nurse saw me walking in the hallway. "Where are you going?" she asked.

"I'm just taking a stroll down Memory Lane," I said. Then I snuck out.

I stayed out all night and freebased. I came back the next morning, Saturday, feeling terrible because the morphine and freebase had worn off. By Sunday I had recovered enough to take an authorized trip from the hospital with my doctors to attend the Dolphins' fifteenth anniversary celebration. This featured the halftime introduction of everyone who had ever played for the Dolphins. I entered the Orange Bowl in a wheelchair, but walked onto the field when my name was called. With all the stitches in the back of my neck, I looked like Frankenstein. The crowd knew I had come from the hospital and gave me a tremendous ovation.

The operation stopped the headaches for about a year. The freebasing not only continued, it intensified. It was a logical extension of the hiding syndrome I was going through. I couldn't handle the business failures and the realization that success outside the NFL was hard to come by.

I wasn't actually addicted to the drug—I could and did go for long periods without it—but the number of binges and length of each binge was increasing. It seems that the less I had to do, the more I freebased. And with the businesses failing, I had less to do.

Still, if something arose that was of importance to me as far as commitment and obligation were concerned, I could and did stop. This was the case during the latter half of 1981. First, I was asked to compete in *The Superstars* by ABC Sports. This is a manufactured-for-television event in which former players compete against one another in everything from running to weight lifting to bowling to hitting a golf ball. Despite the headaches, I had been in good shape, weighing in at about 195 pounds, when I began freebasing. Soon I was down to 165 pounds for the simple reason that when you're doing cocaine like that you feel neither like eating, drinking, or working out. (I've never seen an obese freebaser!)

When the offer to be on *Superstars* came, I thought, Here's a way I can pick up a few thousand dollars. I began to train seriously for the first time in over a year. I rode the exercise bike, and soon I was back on Nautilus and off cocaine. I think I ended up in fourth place overall, winning the 100-yard dash and tying former Dallas Cowboy running back Preston Pearson for the weight lifting title with a press of 250 pounds.

After the *Superstars*, I continued cold turkey because the 1981

Pop Warner League football season was starting. Maceo and Duke were 10 now, and I had agreed to coach their South Miami team. I felt an obligation to the kids to stay clean during this period.

It was a rag-tag crew. South Miami, where I had lived since my early days as a Dolphin, is not particularly affluent. I had about 27 kids. Most were from the ghetto. I outfitted them in brand new jerseys. They were blue and white, like the Penn State ones. We had different ones for home and away games. I got them new helmets and bought them emblems for the helmets. I had them looking like a first-class team.

I was a tough coach. My team wasn't allowed to clap. They weren't allowed to cheer until the fourth game of the season. They were regimented. They came on the field like a little pro team. We ran a pro offense and a pro defense. I was toughest on Maceo. My philosophy was to give everyone an opportunity to play except Maceo. I didn't want to put pressure on him where he thought he had to be a superstar, and I had no intention of using the team as a vehicle for my own self-interest, which a lot of parents do. I didn't want Maceo to be out on the field unless he earned it. He played running back, but didn't start (shades of my early days with the Dolphins).

We had one particular play called "19 straight." This is a weak side sweep where the fullback either goes between end and tackle or around end and tackle. The other back has to block the defensive end or linebacker or the play won't work. I worked on this play with Maceo so much in practice that he literally would recite his assignment in his sleep. "19 straight. I'll kick out the end if he comes upfield. Hook block if he doesn't." When I finally put him in a game and called that play, he delivered. He executed the block and our back went over 60 yards for a touchdown. The message I was trying to give him was: You're important here, but first you have to learn how to play the game and not just run with the football. Because that's what had happened to me. I learned to run first and then learned how to play the game. We finished the season with a 6–2–1 record and just missed the city championships.

After the Pop Warner season ended, I again had time on my hands, and I again retreated into the world of freebase. The absence of headaches was not enough to make me a happy person. I still had problems...with my finances and with my character. I just didn't have the same strength or tenacity I'd had on the football field. I felt defeated. I was behind on my payments on the house, utilities, and everything else.

I still was anticipating going to trial and getting a lot of money because of the auto accident. I thought that finally all the suffering from the headaches and everything else would in some way be compensated. But I didn't have the strength to stay away from the cocaine. I had abstained for about six months, but when the opportunity to return presented itself late in 1981, I went back to it. Someone gave me about an ounce and a half of coke, and I was back binging. Again, during this period cocaine was not yet perceived as dangerous. This wasn't too long after Hamilton Jordan, President Carter's aide, was in the news, having allegedly done coke at Studio 54. While the commentators and the public found this titillating, little was said about the horrors of the drug.

There *are* horrors. An extreme example was provided early on to me by my friend Frank Crawford. When Frank and his wife and kids had moved next door in 1978, I had been delighted. For some time I had hoped that for Maceo's sake another Black family would settle in our neighborhood. In reality, I couldn't have asked for a worse situation. It wasn't that Frank was a bad guy; it was just that he was too much like me. We moved in the same orbit, each of our lives revolving around cocaine.

While Frank periodically worked in a body shop, he basically just hung out. I suspect that most of the cash he earned came from less than legitimate ventures. He showed me photographs of himself standing next to stacks of money. Once he borrowed my car for what he said would be a 5-mile errand. Out of curiosity, I checked the speedometer when he returned. Sixty-six miles. I suspect he used my car instead of his to make a drug drop-off.

Frank had the bad habit of using other people's cocaine without paying for it. At one time or another, every freebaser tries to get away with this; freebasing simply brings out the worst in you. But Frank welched all the time. Understandably, this bothered his fellow users who shared smaller amounts with him. More important, it bothered his suppliers, whom he owed a great deal of money. Whenever he was confronted about this, Frank had the same cocky response: "Hey, I'll take a killin' before I take an ass whippin'."

You can only carry on like this for so long. Pretty soon there were people waiting in line to whup Frank's ass, if not kill him. One time a couple of Colombians came to my door looking for him. Eventually somebody found him.

One morning in the fall of 1980, Frank called me on the phone. He sounded desperate. "I need to raise $6000 right now, man," he said.

"It's 7 a.m., man," I said. "Where you gonna get that kind of money?"

"I don't know. That's why I'm calling you. I thought you could take my wife to the bank. Maybe she can get a loan on the house, sell some furniture."

"I can't do anything for you, Frank. And besides, the banks don't even open 'til 9:30."

"I've only got 'til 8 o'clock. Can't you do something?"

I didn't believe that Frank was in trouble. He'd pulled similar scams to borrow money from me before. Hell, I had pulled similar scams to borrow money from friends when I needed it. I went back to sleep.

Frank called again at 8 o'clock. "You get anything done, man?" he asked.

I still didn't believe him. "Frank, nothing can be done. The banks don't even open for another hour and a half."

"I gotta have it. They gave me an extension 'til 9 o'clock." He didn't say who "they" were.

I didn't do anything between 8 and 9. At 9, Frank called again. "Listen," I told him, "even when the banks do open, they're not gonna hand you $6000 right away."

"Well, okay," Frank said. "I want you to look out for my family for me because you won't be seeing me anymore."

Right, I thought. I'll be seeing you tonight like always, and you know it.

As Frank spoke, I thought I heard an echo sound. "Frank, are you on a speaker phone? Is there somebody listening to what I'm saying?" Click!

Although I didn't hear from Frank over the next few days, I didn't think much of it. He often went on binges that lasted that long, checking into a motel on the beach and freebasing until the coke ran out. Once he and I had gone off on one of these for six straight days and nights, getting maybe two hours of sleep the whole time.

On Halloween day, a week after my last conversation with Frank, two plainclothes police officers pulled into my driveway. I immediately got an eerie feeling about Frank. The feeling was accurate. The officers told me they had found Frank in a 55-gallon drum near the garbage cans behind a local hospital. Chains had been wrapped around his neck. His arms and legs had been tied behind his back. He had been shot twice—once in the neck, once in the head. An execution-style murder.

This ending was inevitable. Frank had messed with too many people. In Miami, at least, this is how scores are settled. The frontier mentality lives—no, it thrives. Still, I felt sorry for Frank. It seemed like something out of the movies.

Soon I was in the movie. Frank had owed me money just like he owed scores of people money. His family had told the police about our conversation on the day Frank disappeared. Homicide called me in for questioning. I told them everything I knew. Not just about Frank's last hours, but about how we had freebased together. I had no intention of getting into trouble by withholding information. I honestly didn't know who had killed Frank. Neither did the police.

You might think that Frank's death would have caused me to re-examine my own use of cocaine. It didn't. After all, I reasoned, he didn't die from the coke, he died from a bullet. I kept on freebasing.

Inevitably, my behavior began to affect Bobbie and the boys. Christmas Eve, 1981, was the night I had to steal a tree because I'd been out smoking. Just before this our electricity had been turned off because I was $2000 behind on our bills. I had to borrow the money from a friend. I worked out a deal so that the electric company would take $1700 and I kept the rest to pay for Christmas.

I was still trying to insulate the boys from all this, but it wasn't working. Usually, Ricky O and I would smoke in my office with the door closed. We'd be there for hours and hours. Sometimes Maceo and Duke would poke their heads in, just out of curiosity. They knew what was going on. Dad was wasting himself. I'd just give them some pocket money and tell them to go play video games. I'd find some excuse to get them out of the place.

My freebasing had begun as a nighttime pastime. Often I'd reward myself with a gram or two for accomplishing something during the day. By late 1981, it didn't matter what time it was. If I could get my hands on some coke, I'd smoke it.

It's important to understand the distinction between basing only at night and basing in the daytime, too. Daytime represents responsibility, commitment, obligation. Nighttime is just the opposite; it's

117

do-what-you-want time. When I had played football, I had been able to balance daytime (the season) with nighttime (the off-season). I never reneged on my responsibility to the team; I saved the heavy partying for after the season. Now I couldn't achieve that "balance." I didn't have the regimentation that football had provided.

Time plays tricks on you when you're freebasing. If you're smoking pot, you might look at a clock and see that it's 11 p.m. When you look again, you might think half an hour has passed, only to find a scant five minutes have gone by. When you're smoking cocaine, it's just the opposite. It's 11 o'clock. You call your wife and say you'll be home at midnight. You look at the clock thinking ten minutes have passed, only to find it's 4 or 5 a.m. The sun is beginning to rise. Daylight. Responsibility. How do I escape that damn sun?

In Las Vegas, the casinos throw away the clocks and tint the lobby windows so that the gamblers have no idea what time it is. In Miami, we members of the PBA would put tinfoil on our windows to keep ourselves literally and figuratively in the dark.

Understandably, Bobbie, who had been very patient with me, began to get angry with me as my freebasing increased. She was expecting our child in April. Most of the time when Bobbie got angry, I told her, "Either leave or leave me alone." Freebasing, not family, was my top priority. It was okay with me if she left.

My freebase groove had turned into a rut. Christmas Eve, 1981, I went to a party in a warehouse in a dark and empty part of Miami. There was plenty of cocaine. As the night wore on, I knew there was something else I was supposed to be doing, but I couldn't tear myself away from the pipe to figure out what it was, much less do it. Finally, reality somehow intruded into my haze and I remembered that I had promised to bring home a Christmas tree that we would all decorate. Responsibility. I had been promising all week, but I had been freebasing so much I had never gotten around to it. Now it was almost midnight. Bobbie and the boys would be asleep. They'd come into the living room in the morning eager to open the presents (which Bobbie, not I, had purchased) and, unless I did something about it, there wouldn't even be a tree. You fool, Morris.

I knew I should get my ass home, but the pipe still beckoned. It was like those cartoons in which the angel sits on one shoulder telling the guy what he should do and the devil sits on the other shoulder telling him just the opposite. On this night, the angel finally won. I left the warehouse and headed for a local Christmas tree lot, praying it would still be open. It wasn't. The trees stood on the opposite side of a locked fence. Desperate, I looked around, saw that there wasn't anybody watching, and scaled the fence. I took a tree, tossed it back over the fence, stuffed it in my trunk, and sped off like the thief I was. I don't think I've ever felt as small as I did when I entered the darkened house and put the tree up by myself.

After this fiasco, I decided I wanted to get straight, get my act together. My family deserved it. My trial against the sanitation truck company was coming up in March and I wanted to be straight for it. I told myself I wanted to start a new life.

One consequence of staying up all hours is that you become familiar with everything and anything cable television has to offer any time of the day. My favorite 6 a.m program was the *700 Club* on the Christian Broadcast Network. Every day I would watch, not after I woke up, but before I went to sleep. The show's hosts were Reverend Pat Robertson and Ben Kinchlow, two straight-as-an-arrow men of God. I felt as if they were speaking directly to me. Their message was simple: Hey, man, if you've got a problem, you better seek some help.

Here I was living in a totally disordered world—an unreal or surreal world in which day became night. But occasionally sunlight—reality—crept through the barriers I had built. Robertson and Kinchlow's words somehow snuck in under the tinfoil. Here's what you have to do to straighten up your life.

I think anyone involved in drugs wants to be handed a magic solution, an instant way out of the haze. Here's what you have to do. As comforting as these words were, they were also frightening. These talking heads were forcing reality upon me: Look, we know you're out there, and we know you're screwing up. What should I do? More often than not it was easier just to darken the screen and retreat back into the haze.

During one of the rare moments I was thinking clearly, I decided to take the 700 Club's message personally and do something about it. I went into my backyard, looked up to the heavens, and prayed for two things: that I be released from the bondage of cocaine and that my name be stricken from the drug rolls. Then I called the 700 Club headquarters in Virginia Beach, Virginia. I told the operator who answered that my name was Eugene Morris and that

I had a drug problem that was causing problems in my family. She sent me a $15 pledge book! What, are they crazy? I thought. I don't want this.

What did I want? Help, I thought. I at least wanted to spare my family. I didn't know why I was leading the life that I was leading, but I knew it wasn't the drug. I knew it was my choice to have it and my choice to be involved in the action. I never blamed the cocaine. It was a symptom, not the cause. (I think this is one reason that I now understand what the problem is all about.)

The 700 Club's inane response gave me an excuse to go back to my unreal world. I may even have put the tinfoil on a little tighter. Careful, boy, don't let that happen again.

I did some enormously thoughtless things. Once, my freebasing pals and I took our guns—almost everyone who is into drugs in Miami has a gun—and set out to kidnap some people who had wronged a member of the PBA. Fortunately, we were so messed up that we couldn't come close to pulling it off.

Another time, I actually had the nerve to try and pull a big heist. Of course, I was under the influence when I concocted this scheme. We'd heard there was $300,000 in the trunk of some guy's car. My plan was to have a tow truck pick up the car. Then we'd hot-wire it and drive it up into another big truck and bust the trunk open.

I went so far as to get this big-time gangster from New Jersey. "I want you to help me with a heist," I said.

"Okay," said the gangster. "Let me ask you something. Do you like this guy?"

"What do you mean?"

"Is it okay if I kill him?"

I said, "What? Hold it. I don't mean like that." I started getting scared. This was becoming too real.

Then the guy said, "Do you have an iron?"

"Yeah. My wife has it in the house."

"No. No. No. I mean a gun! I want you riding with me."

Oh, shit, I thought. I'm in a real jackpot now.

Luckily, I found out that the guy who was supposed to have the money didn't really have any. It turned out that the fellow who had given me the information had been freebasing, too. When you're freebasing, even the macabre sounds good.

My "I wanna be a gangster" days ended in the spring of 1982 thanks to Miguel Miranda. Miranda was a Cuban who lived down the street from me. He was mean. So mean he made a guy who dated his niece only one time marry her. So mean that there were machine gun turrets on the fence surrounding his property.

Rumored to be one of Miami's top cocaine cowboys, Miranda was so feared that no law enforcement agency was willing to arrest him for any of the numerous outstanding warrants they had on him, including those for more than half a dozen murders. "I won't be taken alive," Miranda had boasted. The police took him at his word.

Finally, the South Miami police and the Federal Drug Enforcement Administration undertook a joint venture to bring in Miranda. The plan was to arrest him as he came out of Neon Leon's, a local night club. As Miranda reached his car, the cops descended upon him. As he had promised, he opened fire, then sped off in his car. The car chase and gun battle that ensued was so loud I could hear it at my house a mile away; 800 rounds of ammunition later, Miranda was dead.

Not too long after this, the police came to my house and told me that in searching Miranda's place, they had found the gun that had killed Frank Crawford. I wasn't sure if I believed them. I thought they had originally told me that Frank had been killed with a .38. Now they were saying it was Miranda's .22. Maybe they're just trying to tidy things up, I thought. It didn't really matter.

I did learn a lesson from all this: that real life gangsters eventually end up like Miguel Miranda. The thought of driving around with my .459 nine millimeter in my car as I'd been doing for the last few years would never be appealing again.

In March we went to trial on my auto accident. I was represented by Shelby Highsmith, who is a partner of Ron Strauss. (After the bust, Ron would become my lawyer.) The jury awarded me $500,000. I thought my troubles were over. Then Tiffany was born. She was several weeks premature, but she was healthy. Things were looking up.

There were post-trial motions, so I didn't actually receive the money right away. Still, the verdict was good enough to convince my banker friends to loan me $60,000. The first thing I did was buy a brand new Cadillac Seville for Bobbie. Then I bought new appliances—washer, dryer, refrigerator, trash masher—things to make her life easier.

I probably could have made her life even easier if I had stopped freebasing. I didn't. Tiffany had to stay in the hospital for a week. Bobbie stayed with her. While she was away, I'd have the guys over and we'd cook up some cocaine. I didn't stop after Bobbie came home with Tiffany. I just moved the "clubhouse" to another location.

In May, the trial judge, on his own volition, cut the verdict to $300,000. I was shocked (and still am). He simply declared that $500,000 was too much. This judge was previously indicted on bribery charges and was acquitted. I couldn't help but wonder if this had anything to do with his decision to cut the jury's verdict by 50 percent.

This decision stung. We appealed the judge's ruling on the damages, while the defendant appealed the jury's verdict altogether. This meant that $500,000 would be kept in escrow until the District Court of Appeals rendered a decision.

So my downward spiral continued. It's hard to imagine sinking any lower than I did at Christmas, but I came close shortly after Tiffany was born. I took the boys with me to Ruth's house. From there I called Bobbie and promised to bring them home and pick up some formula for Tiffany. Instead, I started freebasing. It went on and on. Midnight. One a.m. A neighbor had to get Bobbie the formula. I ended up staying out all night. Maceo and Duke, each only 11 years old, ended up sleeping at Ruth's house.

I wasn't happy with such occurrences, I just seemed powerless to avoid them, to take control of my life. By July, I was at my low point. All my plans had fallen by the wayside, the financial bailout promised by the court case was going to be delayed indefinitely, my bank account was nonexistent, and creditors were breathing down my neck. I was freebasing as often as I could.

Then, to make matters worse, the Dade County State Attorney's office called me in for questioning about Don Reese. Don had been a teammate of mine with the Dolphins. In 1977, he had been convicted on cocaine charges and sentenced to one year in prison and five years probation. Don was broke after he got out of prison. Apparently to pay off some of the debts he had incurred, he went the checkbook journalism route with *Sports Illustrated*. In a highly publicized article, he talked about the widespread use of cocaine in the NFL. The article sold a lot of magazines for *Sports Illustrated*, but ended up sending Don back to jail. Some of the things he admitted having done had taken place during his probation period and were in violation of the probation's terms. (If *Sports Illustrated* had waited a few weeks, the probation period would have been over and those admissions would have been meaningless.)

The article had also stirred up interest in the State Attorney's office. In New Orleans, federal prosecutors had recently convicted Mike Strachan, a former New Orleans Saints player, on cocaine charges. The names of several other players surfaced, generating tremendous publicity. I suspect the Dade County authorities thought the Reese article might be the catalyst to do the same thing in Miami. George Yoss, the Dade County prosecutor who would play such a major role in my story, had visited with the New Orleans prosecutors.

I was called in to discuss what I knew about Don Reese's cocaine use and whether I had ever used cocaine with him, ostensibly to determine if Don had violated the terms of his probation. This brought out the old combative Mercury Morris in me. I answered questions, but I was as evasive as possible. I had gotten high with Don once. I believe I sidestepped admitting this because I was asked if I had gotten high with Don at such and such a place. The place the prosecutor suggested was wrong. The prosecutor doing the questioning was Yoss. This was the first time we met. We did not hit it off.

The trip to the State Attorney's office and the realization that prosecutors had a deep interest in cocaine, didn't prevent me from continuing my fall. As in the past, however, I did periodically reach out for help. In July, there was another rare moment of lucidity. I started asking myself some serious questions. How important is it for you to be the head of this family? Keep in mind, I had no practice. I loved my parents but I had really grown up *with* them and hadn't learned much from them about raising a family. Still, I knew what I was doing was a detriment to my family. I didn't want that. I again called the 700 Club. I was so confused. The spiritual path seemed to be the only way.

This time when I called I was more forthcoming. "My name is Eugene 'Mercury' Morris. I was a professional athlete. I played for the Miami Dolphins. I got out in 1977. Since then my life has really gone downhill. I started smoking cocaine in 1979. My life has the potential to be in shambles, and I don't want that." I asked Bobbie, Duke, and Maceo to get on the line and explain what was happening. They did.

This time the operator responded. She called channel 45, the Christian broadcasting affiliate in Miami. Channel 45 arranged for the pastor of the nearby Sunset Chapel to visit me. His name was Nick Schubert. He came into my house. I told him what was happening and how I felt the need for the spiritual aspect in my life to come alive because I had no direction whatsoever and God would be the only one that could help me. I had been praying. Now it seemed like my prayers were being answered. Pastor Schubert was a tremendous comfort. Bobbie and the boys and little Tiffany and I began to attend his church. We went for three Sundays in a row: July 25, August 1, August 8. I hadn't stopped freebasing, but I was feeling better.

I didn't go to church on August 15. I should have. August 15 was the day that the machinery that would lead to my arrest was set in motion.

This is me in high school, just starting out.

I enjoyed basketball in high school. (*Colao Studio, Pittsburgh*)

Kicking up for the
photographers at West Texas
State. (Van Cook, *Amarillo Daily
News*)

The fruits of victory at State,
with Coach Joe Kerbel and
quarterback Roy Winters.

This picture made *Life* magazine — the big time. (Bob Gomet, *Life*)

On to professional football with the Dolphins. Bob Griese, in the background, has just made the handoff.

Four shots of me running "against the grain" for Miami. (*NFL Properties, Inc.*)

Here I am with four Dolphin teammates in the 1973 Pro Bowl. From left to right, Larry Little, Jake Scott, me, Dick Anderson, and Norm Evans.

Bobbie and me in a happy time.

This is Tiffany bouncing on my knee.

Here is my family, Duke, Bobbie, Maceo, and Tiffany.

Free at last.

CHAPTER 8

THE BUST

I am a great believer that human behavior is best understood in light of the times and circumstances. This is certainly the case with the events that led up to my arrest. Viewed in a vacuum, my behavior and the behavior of those in the Dade County State Attorney's office may make little sense. Put in proper perspective, however, everything that took place is understandable. Not condonable by any means, but understandable.

My actions during these days were neither rational nor intelligent. But I wasn't in a rational or intelligent state at the time. I was still living that unreal or surreal existence. My problem was not so much confronting reality, but getting through the haze and locating reality altogether. You can't deal with the real world if you can't find it. My overtures to the 700 Club and Sunset Chapel were forays out from the haze. Unfortunately, I was still so tied to the freebase lifestyle that I didn't have the power to stay out of the haze for very long. I was a broken man—emotionally, financially, spiritually, and bodily. As my conduct from August 15 to August 18 clearly demonstrates, I was desperate.

In its own way, the State Attorney's office was as desperate as I was. This was a product of the times. In 1979, the popular television show *60 Minutes* had run a feature on drug running gone amok in Florida. It was a big embarrassment to the entire state and resulted in the hurried passage of legislation dramatically stiffening the sentences for drug dealing. Nicknamed the "*60 Minutes* Law," the legislation imposed minimum mandatory sentences for drug trafficking. Trafficking is not quite as sinister as it sounds; it could mean as little as simple possession with no intent to distribute. You don't have to be dealing to fall under the statute. Anyone involved with 28 grams of cocaine, the equivalent of a marijuana smoker owning an ounce of pot, could go to jail for a three-year minimum term. The minimum sentence for over 400 grams—a little less than half a kilo—was fifteen years. By 1982, the new legislation had resulted in harsher sentences for some dealers, but apparently the State wasn't entirely satisfied. According to *Miami/South Florida* magazine, "prosecutors in Florida were privately praising their investigative advantages (but)...They weren't particularly pleased about the law's relative obscurity. The chance to nab Mercury Morris seemed to give them the publicity they needed."

So this is where the State and I were coming from as our pasts and paths merged.

I didn't go to church Sunday, August 15, because I was up all night on August 14 freebasing. The binge continued on the night of the fifteenth at my house. Ricky O was there, as was Eddie Kulins. Eddie's girlfriend, Caroline Taylor, was also there briefly, although she wasn't freebasing. Eddie, who lived in Orlando, was staying with me because he had a legal matter to attend to in Miami. I had met him in the late seventies. We had played a little basketball together and then we had lost contact. He surfaced again in the spring of 1982 at a party at Ruth's house, and we became freebasing buddies. Eddie was about my age, 35 years old. He was a big German guy who worked periodically as a restorer of cars. I'd met Vince Cord at Ruth's, too. Vince and Eddie were friends. Vince was a small Hungarian guy whose legitimate line of work was as a swimming pool contractor.

While we were freebasing in my office, Bobbie and the kids were in the back, entertaining one of our neighbors, Johnnie Belle. By this time Bobbie was so frustrated by my behavior that she just sighed and ignored the coke parties. Johnnie was a woman of about 60 who had been very kind to us. She was Tiffany's godmother. Johnnie left at about 8 p.m. or 8:30. About an hour later, Johnnie's son, Fred Donaldson, came over.

Fred was a tall, thin Black man of about 25 or 26. He had a square crew cut. I had met him for the first time in March of 1982 . At that time I had been planning to hire his brother to do some yard work, but Johnnie asked if I would hire Fred instead. Fred had then worked in the yard on and off for a few months landscaping and trimming.

During that time he had become a friend of the family. He was particularly kind to Bobbie and the boys. He often ran errands for Bobbie—it was he who had gone out to get Tiffany's formula on the night I was AWOL—and he frequently took the boys fishing. At the time, he struck me as a little odd—he didn't relate well to adults—but I counted him as a friend, almost like a younger brother. He broke bread at our table and on a few occasions joined me and my freebasing pals at the pipe.

I knew Fred had had some run-ins with the law and apparently needed money to make restitution for something he had done, but I didn't know the specifics. I knew, too, that he periodically tried to peddle drugs. Shortly after I met him he had tried to borrow $330 to buy some marijuana which he thought he could resell for $900. I'd like to say I made the moral judgment that this would have been wrong, but the reason I turned him down was because I didn't have the money.

Earlier in the spring, when I had some money, I had paid Fred several hundred dollars for the yard work he had done. He insisted I owed him more. I thought we were squared away. We had had several discussions about this over the course of the summer, the most recent and severe being on August 1, when he had threatened to take me to court and get even with me.

I considered Fred harmless and dismissed the threat. "Where are you gonna get the money for a lawyer to take me to court, Fred?" I laughed.

"Okay, buddy. I'll get even with you," he said.

After my arrest, I learned what he meant. In late July or early August, Fred called the Dade County State Attorney, Janet Reno, and made certain allegations regarding my involvement with cocaine. There are hundreds of lawyers employed by the State Attorney's office, but Fred's call was referred to Chief Assistant State Attorney, George Yoss, presumably because Yoss had already dealt with me in July on the Don Reese matter. Yoss then told Fred to call George Ray Havens, the State Attorney's chief investigator. There are some twenty investigators in the State Attorney's office. Why was the chief investigator immediately put on the case on the basis of Fred's phone call to Yoss? Because, as Havens later explained, the call regarded someone of the stature of Mercury Morris.

Fred called Havens and, according to Havens, said, "I want to talk to you about Gene Morris selling cocaine and he owes me some money, but he hasn't paid me the money and every time I go to ask him for the money he's always got some excuse. But he's always got a lot of cocaine."

Havens wanted more information. He arranged to meet Fred at Matheson Hammock, a park in southwest Dade County. Fred said what kind of car he had, Havens described his own car, and the two agreed to rendezvous. While it was beginning to look like *Miami Vice,* it didn't have to. Fred could have walked into the Criminal Justice Building and seen Havens in his office.

Fred got into Havens's car and they talked. They talked about many things. About how Fred had done work for me and how he thought I owed him money. About how I was freebasing cocaine. About how in July Fred had seen mounds, "kilos," he said, of cocaine in my house. About how I had asked Fred if he wanted to partake, but he refused because he didn't like cocaine. About how I had told Fred that I had $60,000 but couldn't pay him because I had to invest it in a cocaine deal. About how I had offered Fred the cocaine for $58,000 a kilo and suggested he could sell it for $60,000 and make a $2000 profit. About how Fred had turned down this opportunity saying he only wanted the money I owed him and that I had promised him that money after the deal went down. (None of this was true.)

"Why are you coming forward with this?" Havens asked Fred.

Fred gave two answers. First, he wanted the money he said I owed him. Second, he said that although I was a hero to the kids in the neighborhood, in reality, "He's only a coke dealer." Fred told Havens that he didn't like that.

The pair also talked about Fred's arrest record. Fred explained that he had been arrested for larceny and for assault. Fred didn't give the specifics of the assault charge, which later surfaced; believe it or not, Fred had literally bitten off the ear of a man who Fred claimed was trying to steal Fred's cockatiel. The bird, Fred explained, had been a personal gift from God. It was for this act that Fred had been put on probation with the order to make restitution. The court had ordered him to pay his victim $2500, the cost of a plastic ear. Payments were to begin in August. If Fred didn't make good, he could be jailed for violating the terms of his probation. He needed money or some kind of waiver from the State. Havens doesn't recall whether Fred told him about his recent arrest on marijuana charges at this meeting, but Fred didn't mention he had also been arrested on several other charges, including stabbing a man with a screwdriver.

I bring up this record only because it is important with respect to Fred's own credibility or lack of it. Here was a man the State Attorney's office didn't know from Adam making some serious charges. As Havens later said, at the time he received the call from Fred and in the days that followed, he (Havens) had no information that I had ever used, much less dealt, cocaine. And he had no information that I was the subject of any local, state, or federal investigations (I wasn't). So who was this man Donaldson making the charges? What was his background?

Havens claims he reached no conclusion as to whether Fred was telling the truth or not, although he admits to having been suspicious regarding Fred's professed lack of experience with cocaine. Still, he was interested enough to pursue the matter so that he could "determine who the man (Fred) was and his validity and background and whether there was any substance to what he was telling me."

The meeting concluded with Havens asking Fred when he would next see me. Fred said he hoped to visit and collect the money over the weekend (August 7 or 8). Havens remembers, "I told Mr. Donaldson...to ask Mr. Morris if he still had this cocaine, and if he did, to tell Mr. Morris that Mr. Donaldson had somebody that he knew might be interested in buying some of these kilos of cocaine." Fred was supposed to call back with the results.

Fred called Havens back on August 10. In the meantime, Frank Gilbert, an investigator in Havens's office, had been running a background check on Fred. The check appears to have been incomplete, not revealing the probationary requirements of the restitution. Moreover, at this time there was an outstanding fugitive arrest warrant out on Fred for the alleged sale of marijuana to undercover agents. You might think that if Havens and Gilbert had run a check on Fred and uncovered this, they would have arrested him then and there. But that never happened; he was never arrested on it. These are important in establishing Fred's motive. For example, did he make up the story with the hope he might benefit from the State in some way? While Gilbert ran this check on Fred, he ran no check on me to see if any governmental enforcement agency—presumably more reliable than an informant with a long arrest record—might be able to verify what Fred was alleging. So Havens still had no other information about any cocaine involvement on my part.

My only contact with Fred between August 6 and August 10 was when he came over briefly on August 7 to drop off a camera he had borrowed some time earlier. Nevertheless, Fred called Havens back on August 10 and, according to the investigator, related that we had met and I had said I didn't have any cocaine at that time but was expecting a shipment and that when the shipment came in, I'd contact Fred.

I did not see or talk to Fred between August 10 and August 13. Still, on August 13, Fred phoned Havens and told him that I had contacted him and said that if he (Fred) and his associates were interested in buying the cocaine it would be in kilo quantities and that Fred should call me back if he was interested. Shortly after this, Havens requested a Black undercover agent from the Florida Department of Law Enforcement to work on the investigation. This man, Joe Brinson, would play the role of the buyer Fred had mentioned.

Of course, at this point Fred hadn't mentioned any buyer or deal to me. This brings us back to August 15. Fred, having started in motion the machinery for setting me up, now appeared at my door. We sat down at the kitchen table, away from where the freebasing was going on in my office. Fred wasn't threatening or angry. He simply told me that there was a way for me to pay him back some of the money he thought I owed him. I didn't feel I owed him anything, but I was beginning to think that this might be an honest misunderstanding.

Fred said he had these friends coming in from New York and that if I could help him by introducing them to the people I knew that had cocaine—one or two kilos—it would be a chance for us to get square and for me to score some coke and some cash. The buyers, Fred said, were willing to pay $60,000 a kilo. If we could get the stuff for less, we could make a nice profit.

My first response was negative. I didn't know if anyone I knew had access to that much cocaine, and I didn't think that the people who supplied me with user's amounts of cocaine would want to be involved with someone like Fred for one or two grams, let alone one or two kilos. I told him we'd look like clowns. I didn't have any coke left at all. He asked me if I would, in effect, serve as a middleman. Could I meet with Fred's people and then meet with my supplier?

I was still reluctant. "How do you know you're not dealing with the police?" I asked. "Why don't you just use the stuff like I do? Don't deal it."

Fred said he needed the money and again reminded me that he thought I owed him several hundred dollars. He said he might end up in jail if I didn't help him. About this time, Caroline Taylor slipped into the kitchen for a glass of water. Unaware of her presence, Fred gave me a user's quantity of coke. "What's this for?" I asked.

"Show it as a sample to the buyer," Fred told me.

Then he left. I still hadn't agreed to introduce him to my supplier.

I'll say one thing about Fred. He was persistent. He came back about half an hour later. He reminded me how he had run to the grocery store for Bobbie when she had only a few dollars to put food on our table. He told me that if I helped him I'd be able to get some money so I could feed my kids. I told him I was expecting my disability pension from the NFL in September—$125,000. (This was iffy. If the players went out on strike as they had threatened, payment might be delayed for several weeks.) "Besides," I said, "I don't know any of these people you're talking about."

Some months earlier, Fred had told me that a friend of his from Miami Beach wanted to buy two kilos of cocaine. "I don't know anyone who has that much coke," I had said. And the matter had been dropped.

Now the man came up again. Fred said the guy was a big dealer on the Beach, who sometimes supplied him. But, Fred continued, he had been busted a year or so ago and couldn't be involved in the deal. His brother-in-law was coming from New York to be the money man, the buyer.

Fred assured me they could be trusted. All I had to do was introduce the brother-in-law to my source. "Okay," I said.

Did I know this was wrong? Yes. Why did I do it? Because I was operating in that surreal society where right and wrong weren't always the litmus test for behavior. Because I was in the midst of a freebasing haze. Because I thought if it worked I'd be able to get Fred off my back, get a few bucks to tide me over, and feed my habit. I was messed up and so were my values. And who knows? Maybe deep down inside, I realized the only way I could stop the downward spiral was to get caught doing something wrong. In crossing over the line between mere use of cocaine to play the new role of middleman, I was inviting disaster. Maybe I realized that Mercury Morris couldn't jitterbug his way out of the corner he had got himself in; that Gene Morris needed some disaster to start him on the road to reason.

I wasn't so sure I could even do what I promised Fred. The electric company and the phone company weren't the only ones I owed money. My two so-called sources, Vince Cord and Ruth, weren't having anything to do with me at the time because I owed them, too. Remember, the first rule in dealing with a supplier is: keep your tab up to date.

Ricky O was in the other room freebasing. I asked him if he knew of any way to get a kilo or two. "Let me check tomorrow," he said.

I told Fred we would talk on the sixteenth. Before he left he reminded me that the user's quantity of cocaine he had given me was to be used for show if we met the next day and I hadn't located the two kilos. This would stall the buyer until we could find the coke, he suggested. His actual motive was quite different. Once I gave the undercover agent any coke, I'd be subject to criminal charges.

After Fred left, I talked with Kulins about the deal. We both had a funny feeling that something was fishy. Still, we decided to go ahead with it. (Throughout this entire period, something kept moving me forward—often against my better judgment. I still don't know what it was.)

According to the State, Fred called Havens early the next morning, Monday, August 16. Fred again (falsely) confirmed that I had received my shipment of cocaine. He said that I was willing to sell it in kilo quantities and that I wanted $60,000 a kilo (when in fact Fred had told me this was what the buyers were willing to pay). Fred also told Havens that he had told me that he (Fred) would contact his associates and would be willing to meet with me and my associates to discuss the sale. Understandably, Fred did not mention that he had been to my house the night before and that I didn't have any cocaine beyond what we had been freebasing and the samples he had given me.

At this point, Havens called in the undercover agent Joe Brinson to meet Fred. Fred told him that he, Joe, was supposed to be Gene Gotbaum's brother-in-law from New York, and a plot was hatched. Fred was instructed to call me at home and tell me that his people were ready to meet me and my people. At this point, Havens later acknowledged, Fred was considered "an unreliable source of information." Why was the State moving forward? It was hoped, Havens said, that the phone call would either verify or contradict Fred's statements. Would the State have moved forward if Havens had known that the information Fred had provided to date—namely, that I was in possession of two kilos of cocaine and wanted to sell them—was false (which it was)? No, Havens said. He would probably have closed the file.

Where was I while all this was going on? At City Hall in South Miami arguing over the upcoming Pop Warner football season. Practice was to start in two days. I was trying to make sure that I could coach the same team that I'd coached the year before.

I was back home by the time Havens instructed Fred to call me. Not only was the call made, it was taped. This was done without seeking a court order. In fact, Havens later admitted that there wasn't even probable cause to obtain an order from the court authorizing such wiretapping.

The call was made at about 2:45 p.m. I was sitting around the house with Eddie Kulins. Ricky O had been trying to come up with a kilo. He'd had no luck. Vince Cord and Ruth were still possibilities, but I wasn't confident I could persuade either to deal with me.

Here is a partial transcript of the tape:

DONALDSON: What's up?

ME: Nothing. What's the scoop?

DONALDSON: All right. He's going to do it like this here. He said he'll show you the money.

Fred went on to explain that at 4 p.m. his buyer wanted to meet me in the parking lot of Dadeland, a huge and crowded shopping center near my home. I could either look over the money and satisfy myself that the buyer was legitimate and then go back and get the cocaine, or we could consummate the deal right then and there. I asked if Fred was sure this wasn't a setup. He assured me he trusted Joe. Fred described the car he'd be in, said it would be parked near the J.C. Penney's at the shopping center, and said he'd have on the same outfit he'd worn the night before. (He slipped up here. He hadn't told the authorities he'd seen me the night before and given me the so-called sample.)

I pulled up in my Seville a little before 5:30 accompanied by Kulins. We were observed, it turns out, by several agents stationed in surveillance vans and in various stores around Dadeland. I can't prove it, but I suspect the press was there, too. I say this because within a minute of my arrest on the eighteenth, the camera crews, including news helicopters, were in my yard, obviously tipped off by the State Attorney's office. It's reasonable to assume the crews were on call during this entire period.

By the time I drove to Dadeland, I had talked to Ruth, who thought she might be able to come up with a sizable amount of cocaine. She had advised me not to transact any business at Dadeland. It was too public, she said, too many cops around. Little did she know!

Meeting #1, August 16

Brinson, we later learned, was wearing a body bug.

BRINSON: Joe.

ME: Hey, man.

BRINSON: Hey man, you, ah, got the stuff?

ME: You got the package? Ah, here is the deal.

"Package" was slang for "money." Even though I wasn't a dealer, I thought I knew how to talk like one. I could provide rhetoric if not cocaine.

Although I still didn't have any cocaine and still wasn't sure I could get any, I told Joe that I could come up with two kilos. He said he had $120,000 with him. I asked him if he was a cop. Of course he said "No." He didn't look like a cop. His hair was too curly. He seemed too short; he was wearing heels, yet he still was quite small. If I had been thinking clearly it might have struck me that it was odd that Gene Gotbaum of Miami Beach—someone whom you would assume was Jewish—had this Black dude for a brother-in-law!

I said that I could meet Joe and Fred in twenty minutes with the cocaine. This was a stall. I was far from certain that I could deliver.

I proposed meeting in a different place. Joe said that with all that money in his car he wanted to stay at Dadeland. So I agreed to come back.

"Throw that sample over here, Gene," Fred said as I was leaving.

How did he know I had a sample? He had given it to me the night before. I tossed the sample. I could have been arrested then and there. But the State had bigger plans for me.

Meeting #2, August 16

Eddie and I returned at about 6:15. Again, we didn't have any cocaine. Brinson's body bug caught the conversation.

> ME: Nine o'clock tonight. He wants to wait, hurry up and wait to see everything is okay.

"He" was actually Ruth, who still thought she *might* be able to come up with some cocaine. Again, I was stalling.

Meeting #3, August 16

At 9:15 we met at Dadeland again. I still didn't have any cocaine.

> BRINSON: You got it, man?
>
> ME: Right.
>
> BRINSON: Huh?
>
> ME: It's down the street.

At this point I was still stalling. I thought Ruth would be able to come up with some cocaine and that in my capacity as middleman, for making the introduction, I'd make a little money. Ruth wanted the deal to be made on her turf. Joe was wary. I tried to assure him that this would be okay. My words would later be used against me.

> ME: Hey, man. You ever heard of a motherfucker who use to play for the Dolphins?
>
> BRINSON: Yeah.
>
> ME: Named Mercury Morris.
>
> BRINSON: Oh, yeah.
>
> ME: Well this is me...so what I'm telling you is I got kids, I got just as much to lose as you, and I won't fuck with nobody who doesn't have as much to lose as me.

Still playing for time, I told Joe the cocaine was just down the street. Joe said he had to make a phone call. If I'd have been thinking clearly, I might have been scared off by this. I might have realized that the call was to his backup team to see what he should do. But I wasn't thinking clearly...or else, I really did have some hidden wish to get caught. We agreed to meet in half an hour.

After I left, Brinson's body bug was still on. The tape recorder caught him saying something very telling to Donaldson.

> BRINSON: I don't believe the motherfucker's got the shit, man. I think he's bullshitting.

Brinson would later admit that not only did he think I didn't have any cocaine, he didn't think I had access to any significant amount. Remember, Fred had told them I had two kilos in my possession.

Nevertheless, Brinson's superiors told him to continue to pursue me. If, as seemed evident, I didn't have two kilos of cocaine, they wanted Brinson to encourage me to go out and find that much. This is why I remain so disturbed by the State's behavior. Perhaps they had a right to initiate an investigation of me based on Donaldson's wildass story. But at this point they knew the story wasn't true. Instead of stopping, however, they not only manufactured a crime for me to commit, they created the level of punishment that I would be subject to. If I could deliver two kilos, I'd be in for a lot more time than I would for delivering a user's sample or even an ounce. They didn't want me on simple possession; they wanted me for trafficking, which carried a hefty mandatory minimum.

Meeting #4, August 16

We met again at about 9:40. Again, I didn't have any cocaine. I told Joe he should go over to Ruth's house. One might think that the State Attorney's office would have done so. After all, if their primary purpose was to get to the supplier of cocaine, then Ruth's house was, apparently, the place. Instead

> BRINSON: I ain't dealing with no broad...ain't too many whores I trust because I work with them sometimes...I only want to deal with you.

Distasteful as this and other remarks both Brinson and I made over the course of the evening were, I understand them. We were both role-playing that night. He was playing a gangster-buyer and I was playing a gangster-middleman. The difference was he had a license (badge) to play; I didn't.

I also understand why Brinson didn't want to deal with Ruth. This would have taken me out of the picture. And it was definitely me they wanted in the picture. After I was arrested, someone in the Criminal Justice Building told me that when the investigation began, someone in the office had ordered a special cake baked on Monday, the sixteenth. "I wish I'd have known how to get in touch with you to warn you," he said. (I had an unlisted number.) On the cake was the number 22—my jersey number from my days with the Dolphins.

Meeting #5, August 16

Our fifth and final meeting that night took place at about 10:15 in a parking lot near where Ruth lived. Brinson again refused to come to Ruth's house. I told him he should trust me and, in words that would also come back to haunt me, I said that I was the kind of connection he was looking for and that we could do business again and again. This was the empty boast, not of a cocaine dealer, but of a man who had been caught up in the excitement of the evening. I wanted the deal to materialize. I needed the money. I stood to get $1000 per kilo. We left it that maybe some time in the future we'd get together and try to swing a deal.

Between these various meetings, I had been going home and making calls to Vince Cord (who hung up on me because I owed him several hundred dollars) and Ruth, who kept trying to get the cocaine required to swing a deal. I didn't know then but later found out that Ruth was calling Cord in an attempt to locate the coke. It was my understanding and hope that if we stalled long enough, Ruth might be able to come through. But when I told Joe that the cocaine was already at her house, I was lying. I was just hoping that he'd come over and that something would eventually happen.

As I drove home, I honestly thought the deal had fallen through, that Joe was no longer interested. I admit that I was disappointed. Yet, at the same time, I was relieved. Our first Pop Warner practice would take place in less than forty-eight hours. In the past, the responsibility of coaching had forced me to abandon the surreal world for the real one, if only temporarily. To be involved with the kids translated into not being involved with cocaine. For the next two days, as the deal was on-again one moment, then off-again the next, these opposite emotions of disappointment and relief would share quarters in the pit of my stomach. I was almost schizophrenic—one minute longing for the daylight and the responsibility that coaching demanded; the next minute longing for darkness and the escape from responsibility that cocaine provided.

So where did things stand when I went to bed on Monday night? The State had set a plan in motion on the basis of information from an informant with an arrest record a mile long, an informant in whose interest it was to help the State because of a pending marijuana charge and the possibility of violating the terms of his probation on another charge because he couldn't make restitution. The target was me, and me alone—someone about whom, they acknowledged, they had no reason to believe was engaged in anything illegal. The information upon which the State was relying—that I had received two kilos of cocaine—was false. The State Attorney's investigators didn't know this at first, but after they put their elaborate sting into action, their own undercover agent reached that conclusion. Five meetings were held in which Brinson kept dangling $120,000 in front of me. Yet, me, big dealer supposedly in possession of all this cocaine, could never deliver anything... except for a user's sample given to me by Fred and requested by Fred at our first meeting. Later, chief investigator Havens would say that if he had known the sample had been provided to me by Fred he would have questioned Fred's reliability and would have considered me not a suspect as a dealer but as merely Fred's errand boy.

I admit that I don't come off any better than the State. I was talking tough and profane and sounded like a guy who could deliver. But the proof is in the pudding. I couldn't deliver because I didn't have any cocaine. At best I could introduce Brinson to someone who might be able to get some. But the State wasn't interested in going over to Ruth's house. The State wanted the man for whom it had baked a cake—number 22. Only trouble was, I hadn't worn

22 for seven years, and I wasn't the man they thought I was. I wasn't a dealer. I was a down and out cocaine user, totally broke, who couldn't stand to look at himself in the mirror.

When I woke up late in the morning on the seventeenth, I had no idea that the potential for a deal still existed. My houseguest Eddie Kulins and I were sitting around the house when Fred called. He told me he was at Gene Gotbaum's house and then put on Joe. Actually, Fred was at the State Attorney's office and the call was again being taped.

> BRINSON: You know, I thought about it and everything, I talked it over with Gene (Gotbaum). I'm willing to meet you halfway.

Joe went on to explain that, without passing any money, he wanted to take a sample from each of the two kilos I supposedly had. Then he would go back and test them. If the cocaine proved pure enough, he'd come back and make the purchase.

> BRINSON: Now we're still going to be dealing with the girl now?
>
> ME: Yes. Everything is fine.

The problem was that we weren't still dealing with "the girl"—Ruth didn't have anywhere near that much cocaine, and everything wasn't "fine"—I still didn't know where I could get any coke. Cord was a possibility, but he still wasn't returning my phone calls. Kulins called him. Cord said he'd see what he could do.

I didn't show up at Dadeland, but I talked on the phone with Joe and Fred a few times during the afternoon. Joe asked if I could deliver "one Z." Translated, this slang meant that Brinson wanted to buy an ounce of coke, a substantially reduced amount from the two kilos I was supposed to have at my house. Why? It's my opinion that having baked the cake, tipped the press, gone to all this trouble, the State wanted to make sure it could get me in some fashion or else there would be a lot of frosting to wipe off of a lot of faces. If they never got the two kilos they were angling for, they at least wanted something. Moreover, it's clear to me that my behavior over the years had really pissed off the powers that be in Dade County to the point where they relished nailing me. It was more than the Don Reese confrontation with Yoss. I suspect it went back to the mid-seventies when, amidst unsubstantiated rumors that I was using cocaine, I had defiantly parked the turbo that was unmistakably mine in front of known dealers' homes. For years, I had flaunted my flirtation with the underworld, never going far enough to warrant the intervention of law authorities. Until now. They were going to make damn sure they didn't let me slip away.

I answered Joe back in the same lingo. "One picture will be delivered from the art gallery." Then I gave him directions to my house.

The picture from the gallery was coming from that distinguished "collector," Vince Cord. Eddie took my car and brought back Cord and the ounce. Ricky O was at my house, too. Cord handed me the ounce outside my house. I brought it in and immediately scooped some out and hid it in the cupboard for me and Ricky so that we'd have something to smoke after Cord was gone. By taking it out of this sample, I wouldn't have to pay for it. This is standard operating procedure by a user. You're always scamming to get coke without having to pay for it.

Fred and Joe pulled into my driveway shortly after Cord arrived. Joe wasn't too talkative. I showed him the sample and told him to take a hit. He said something like: "That's all right, man, I don't want to mess with it. I just want to take a sample back to my people." This made sense to me. I thought *he* might be scamming, saying he wanted a sample when he had no intention of buying. Well, I thought, that's okay. It's Cord's sample. Joe put the powder in some tinfoil. He asked me how much the ounce would cost. "$1800," I said. Cord had told me to charge $1800 and that $200 of that would be my cut. Brinson could have arrested me then and there on a simple possession charge, but, again, that wasn't the crime for which the State wanted to arrest me. So Brinson and Fred left.

Fred called me back in less than half an hour and put Joe on the phone. Again, the conversation was taped without my knowledge or a court order.

BRINSON: It was good, man. It wasn't the best, but it was good. I see you're a man of your word. (I later learned that after Brinson left he gave the State Attorney's investigators the sample. It was tested immediately and deemed high quality cocaine.)

ME: Well, I try to be.

BRINSON: Right. So I want to take the whole thing? How much you got?

ME: Well, everything is cool.

BRINSON: How much you got? I want some more besides the Z.

ME: Oh, yes. I know that. You have to come talk to me, man, all right?

BRINSON: Okay. Okay. Good-bye.

I don't exactly sound like I've got anything. Do I?

Joe and Fred were back within a few minutes. In the meantime, Cord had left, taking the ounce with him. He knew I couldn't be trusted with it!

Joe told me he had the money to buy the sample ounce and asked how much he could buy. Could he get a kilo, a pound? Once more he was encouraging me to get enough to ensure big headlines and a big sentence. I told him I'd check with my people. We agreed to meet at a nearby park later that evening.

Before we were scheduled to meet, Ricky O came over. Of course, we started freebasing the portion of Cord's coke that I had scooped out. In our coke-induced infinite wisdom, we hatched our own plan to make sure the meeting went all right.

"Rick, what should I do?" I asked.

He said that he'd drive down to the 7–Eleven store near the park to scout things out. "I'll make sure it's not a ripoff or they're not the cops," he said.

Ricky had previously given me another method for determining if Brinson was a cop. "Ask if you can pat him down," he said. "If he doesn't have a wire on, he won't mind." At some point on the seventeenth, I passed this information along to Fred, suggesting he do the pat down. Shit. That was like asking the wolf to watch the sheep.

At about 9:30 I drove to the park. I didn't have any cocaine with me, but Cord was on his way to my house with half a kilo. He wasn't going to let me out of his sight with it. The plan was for me to get Joe to come back to the house. Our conversation at the park went something like this.

"Do you have it?" Fred or Joe asked.

"No. You gotta come around my house," I said.

"No. We can't right now. We'll call our people and then we'll give you a holler."

"Why can't you just follow me?" I asked. "I'm right here."

"We can't. We gotta do something."

Again, I should have seen the red flag. I was suspicious. But what the hell. We'd come this far.

I later learned that there was a van full of officers nearby. They were prepared to bust me then and there when I delivered the cocaine. But I didn't deliver. The reason they didn't want to come to my house was because they didn't have a search warrant.

I went home. Eddie and Cord and I waited, but nothing happened for about forty-five minutes. "What is this bullshit, Kulins?" I asked. "They can come. They can't come. I don't understand."

"Yeah," he said. "Something is wrong here."

"Tomorrow's the last day," I said. At some point in the evening, I had told Joe and Fred that Wednesday, the eighteenth, was absolutely the last day I was going to be involved with them. After that Pop Warner practice began and I didn't want to be mixed up in anything else.

More time passed that night.

"Man, these guys aren't coming. I don't even want to deal with it," I finally said. And I took my phone off the hook. Cord took his coke and left. And for the second night in a row, the deal didn't go down.

On Wednesday, the eighteenth, my three-day quest for my old Pop Warner football team ended. I won. That same day the State Attorney's quest for me ended. Unfortunately, they won. But they weren't playing by the rules.

Fred called me a little before noon. He put Joe on the line. The conversation was taped. Both Joe and I professed fear of being set up.

BRINSON: When the change of plan came up, I didn't know, you know, how to take it.

ME: Yeah.

BRINSON: You see, I was very surprised because I thought for one time that you might be jerking me off.

ME: Ah, hey, join the club.

Despite these "mutual" fears (mine were real; Joe's were invented so he could keep baiting the hook) we agreed to meet at 3:00 at my house and consummate the deal.

While I waited, the State Attorney's office was busy. Havens and Yoss decided to go to court to seek a warrant to search my home and to seek what is called a "Sarmiento order" to monitor my conversations within the home. Havens had investigator Gilbert swear out a document called an "Affidavit for Search Warrant." Brinson swore out the affidavit for the Sarmiento order, which in effect merely incorporated Gilbert's affidavit.

In the affidavit Gilbert stated that confidential informant Fred Donaldson had advised him on August 6 that he had observed me "sniffing and cutting" cocaine in June and July. Havens later admitted that on August 6 he considered the information both uncorroborated and unreliable, but no mention of this was made in the affidavit. In his deposition, Donaldson later said that he had never said this. Gilbert also swore that Havens advised him that Donaldson had informed Havens on August 10 that I *had received* a large quantity of cocaine. Havens later admitted that this information in the affidavit was false, since Donaldson on that date had merely said I was *expecting* a large shipment, and that it was not until August 16 that Donaldson told Havens I had received the cocaine. No mention was made in Gilbert's or Brinson's affidavits that on August 16 Brinson did not believe I had cocaine or access to it.

Perhaps most telling, the affidavits did not inform the judge that the government had already electronically recorded numerous face-to-face and telephone conversations, including phone conversations inside my home and a face-to-face meeting at my home. (The home is important here. In a sense it is still regarded a man's castle, and there are constitutional safeguards against unwarranted invasions, be they physical or electronic.) At the hearing for the warrants, the State had an opportunity to tell the judge that they had been recording in my home but did not advise the judge of this.

This is very important. Had the judge known that such unauthorized surveillance had already taken place, he probably would not have authorized the warrants. I say this because attorneys have advised me that most judges would have denied the request for the warrants if apprised of previous unauthorized bugging. Also, the particular judge in this case, Criminal Court Judge Gerald Kogan, had previously done just that—denied the requests—in a big case involving police officers suspected of illegal drug activity. Today Judge Kogan is a justice of the Florida Supreme Court.

These are more than legal technicalities. Our justice system is based on certain rules and procedures designed to protect the rights of individuals and the interests of the State. One would think that the State would play by these rules, presenting complete and accurate information in the affidavits. Instead, the State withheld important information from Judge Kogan. Based on the affidavits presented him, Judge Kogan issued an order authorizing agents to search my home and authorizing Brinson to wear an electronic monitoring device and record conversations in my home.

Joe and Fred showed up at my house at about 3 o'clock. Interestingly, although Judge Kogan's order authorized only Brinson to wear the bug, Fred wore it. This was because of my brilliant statement the night before that we should pat Joe down. Fred patted Brinson and found nothing.

Fred and Joe came in. Kulins was with me. He called Cord and told him to bring the cocaine. Cord said he was on his way. We told Joe it would be about fifteen or twenty minutes. In the meantime, we sat down in my living room and watched an old videotape I'd made of the television show *Soul Train*. I remember we laughed because I had taped the show over an old tape of the porno film *Debbie Does Dallas*. *Soul Train* ran out before Debbie was done, and there was about twenty seconds of the film at the end of the tape. Of course, as we were sitting there laughing the government was getting its operation into place. Agents were pouring into the neighborhood, as was the press. (One of my neighbors later told me he had seen the agents getting in place and wished that he had known I was their quarry so he could have alerted me.)

Soon Cord pulled into the driveway. He honked his horn. He parked so that he was blocking all the cars; that way he'd make sure he would get his money before anyone left.

From this point on things happened very quickly. I went out to the driveway. Cord was getting out of his car. We shook hands. He had the cocaine in a brown bag in his glove compartment. "You get the stuff out," he said. "I'm not carrying it into the house."

"Why? It's yours," I said.

"I'm not carrying it into the house."

"Okay, give it to me." I just wanted to get this over. My mind was already on Pop Warner practice that was to begin later in the afternoon. I had my football shoes on.

I carried the bag into the house. "Joe, this is it," I said.

We walked to the back room in my house. Me. Fred. Joe. And then Kulins. Cord didn't come in with us.

I gave Joe the bag. Now all of a sudden, he was in a hurry. "Okay, man, look, I gotta get to the airport."

"Don't you want to test it or check it out?" I asked.

"No, that's okay. I just want to go. Let's get it over with."

The cocaine was sealed in a clear plastic bag inside the brown bag. Cord had brought a scale over the previous evening, a scale which the State initially asserted was mine—thus furthering their portrayal of me as a big dealer. We put the cocaine on the scale. It was about half a kilo, or a little over a pound. I had seen Ricky O with that much cocaine once, but it had been a long time ago.

"Man, I gotta catch a plane. I'm in a hurry," Joe repeated.

This amazed me. Here he was buying this much cocaine and he didn't even want to try it. But it was his choice. We headed out of the house to his car.

I carried the bag under my arm, followed by Joe and Fred. Joe opened his car trunk to get the money. Suddenly we heard sirens. "Oh, shit. This is a bust," Joe said. (He was still playing his role.) He ran off into the yard. Fred ran, too. My house is on a canal. Fred jumped over the fence into the water—a strange move considering he couldn't swim.

So here we are in the yard. I'm panicked, don't know what the hell is going on. All of a sudden there are people all over the place. There's a helicopter overhead taking pictures.

Ricky O had told me earlier, "Put a bucket of water beside you. If it's a bust, you can dump the coke in the bucket and it'll dissolve and there won't be any evidence."

Well, I don't have a bucket. So now I say, "C'mon, God," and I take the coke and throw it toward the canal. My luck, it hits the fence. (One of the few humorous moments during my trial came when my attorney asked me if I had ever completed a halfback option pass. Unfortunately, the answer was "No.") So I run over and pick it up, and this time I get it into the canal. Of course, I hadn't even thought that the coke was still sealed in a plastic bag and wasn't going to dissolve or sink.

Believe it or not, here is what was running through my mind at this time: Hey, if I throw this coke in the canal, hey, I've got my hands up, when the cops see there's no coke on this property, hey, I'll be able to go back in the canal and get the coke and then it'll be all mine. I'm not even comprehending this is a bust, like, "You're going to jail, mister." I'm thinking, "Well," they'll say, "you got any coke around here?" I'll say, "No." And they'll say, "Okay. Sorry." And then they'll leave.

That was actually my first perception as I put my hands up and saw all of these State Attorney's officers—they weren't cops—coming up with shotguns drawn. An officer named Johnson was the first guy to get to me. My hands were already up. Reality set in. "Hey, just treat me like a man," I said.

He took his .38, shoved it in my ear so hard that it drew blood, and said something like, "Get down on the fucking ground or I'll scatter your fucking brains all over Miami."

I was going down real slow, telling him, "Take it easy, man. I got a broken neck, man."

As I recall, he pushed me face first into the dirt, ordered me to put my hands behind my back, and put his foot on my shoulder. Then a woman officer came over with a shotgun and started yelling at me.

I later found out that while this was going on, Cord and Kulins were hiding in the house—Vince in the guest room, and Eddie, as big as a tackle in the NFL, in a closet. As if they wouldn't find them.

Eventually, I was brought inside the open back door of my house. I watched as they kicked my front door out for no reason and started going through the house. Then I was handcuffed and taken back outside. I asked that my hands be cuffed in front rather than in back because of my neck trouble, but the officer refused.

Cord and Kulins were taken downtown and put in a holding cell. I was held outside for about half an hour and then brought inside. At that time, the handcuffs were finally moved from my back to my front. The house was a mess—pots overturned, rooms rifled. I assume that it was at this point, too, that someone fished the cocaine out of the canal.

Bobbie, who, thank God, happened to be at a neighbor's house with Tiffany while all this was going on, now tried to come home. She had heard the sirens, but was too scared to venture out right away. I saw her briefly but never got a chance to talk with her.

I was seated at my dining room table, handcuffed to a chair. As the officers continued to go through the house, I noticed our family Bible nearby. I picked it up and opened it. The first verse I found talked about envying the wicked. I won't pretend that I found God at this time; I was looking for some magical solution to this jackpot, hoping if I, in effect, chanted a passage, walked backward, and stood on my head, everything would all of a sudden be all right. I know now that this approach is not what works. Still, I found the Bible comforting.

The officers were trying to act like *Miami Vice*, but in some aspects they were more like the Keystone Cops. They tasted the cocaine. One of them knowingly proclaimed it "half cut," meaning it was only 50 percent pure (a qualitative analysis would later prove that it was 96 percent cocaine, almost totally pure). One agent found some lactose that Bobbie had been taking for her pregnancy and announced that it was the cutting agent. Someone else found Maceo's chemistry set and said, "This must be the drug testing kit."

On the serious side, while I was at the table, I saw the officers bring out a couple of guns they'd found in the house. One was an antique gun that didn't even work; there was a rusty old goose gun, and Maceo's carbine, given to him by his great grandfather. It wasn't loaded. Indeed, there wasn't even any ammunition in the house. Nevertheless, when I was trotted out in front of the cameras a little later, the officers paraded these guns, too. There's no doubt in my mind that this was to reinforce my image as a big-time gangster. The guns were returned to our family a few days later. Cord's gun, complete with ammunition, was found in his car.

The most disturbing thing that went on dealt with the money. Our half-a-kilo deal was to have been for $29,000. The money had been in a bag in Brinson's trunk. Now, it was brought inside and dumped into a shoebox. But wait, it wasn't $29,000, but over $120,000. The officers had all the money Brinson had been carrying in the hopes of swinging a two-kilo deal. They didn't need it, but it would make a good show for the media.

Now we were ready for the cameras, the same cameras that had arrived on the scene at the moment the sirens went off. The same cameras, I imagine, that had been waiting all week. The coke had been fished out by now. They took it out of the brown bag so it could be seen.

I've watched the footage from that evening's news many, many times. Here come the solemn-faced investigators carrying the coke, the scale, the shoebox full of money, the guns, and finally me—the supposed big-time cocaine cowboy.

What was the cocaine cowboy's cut going to be on this $29,000 deal? $500 and a little coke. That's all. Fred was going to get a little of the remaining $28,000 and the rest was to go to Cord.

As I watch the footage, I see that I am a man who is only partly with it. My eyes are in never-never land. I have that distant look of the frequent drug user. Actually, I look more confused than anything. I *was* confused. Part of me was wondering how the hell I was gonna get out of this. But part of me was just plain relieved that the week—no, not only the week, but that five-year downward spiral that had started after I retired and accelerated after I began freebasing—was finally coming to an end.

CHAPTER 9

DISCOVERY

The Dade County Jail and Metro Dade County Courthouse are connected by a catwalk five stories above the ground. In addition to courtrooms, the courthouse contains the offices of the State Attorney. Lawyers tell me that the normal procedure once someone is arrested is to bring him immediately to the jail, then book him, fingerprint him, take his mug shot, and put his file into a "blind" lottery for assignment to a judge. Then he is put in a cell to await his bond hearing. This is not what happened to Cord and Kulins or me.

Cord and Kulins were put in a holding cell, their booking delayed until mine was completed. And my booking wasn't exactly speedy. I was held in the State Attorney's offices for over five hours before I made the trip over the catwalk. Why? There are a few possible explanations. My lawyer Ron Strauss suggests one possibility: that the State Attorney's office thought it had caught a big dealer and knew that there would be a tremendous amount of press because of my name. The government therefore wanted to get its act together and determine exactly how to deal with the media and what information it was going to release before, in effect, losing control of me when I went to the jailhouse.

A more nefarious possibility exists. It is possible that the State waited those hours to assure that my file would be assigned to a particular judge, a particularly tough judge. I recognize that this explanation raises doubts about the integrity of the blind lottery system, which was designed to assure random assignment of criminal cases to judges. Still, such systems have been corrupted in other jurisdictions, and, as we will see shortly, the result in my case doesn't rule out that possibility.

The 8- by 5-foot room I was held in seemed as busy as Grand Central Station. People from the State Attorney's office were constantly coming in and out. Among the first in was prosecutor Yoss. He said something like, "What happened, Merc?" As if he didn't know! As I later learned, he had been supervising the entire operation.

"Hey, man," I sighed. "I was just trying to make a few bucks." This was my way of saying I fucked up as an introducer, but wasn't a dealer.

I had been allowed a phone call to my attorney. At the time, I considered Shelby Highsmith my lawyer. Shelby, who was and is Ron Strauss's partner, had done a fine job representing me in my civil suit arising from the collision with the sanitation truck. Ron had worked only briefly on that case. As it turned out, neither Shelby nor Ron was in town, so my call was directed to an associate named Peter Gruber. Peter told me that he would try and get me out on bond in the morning. He also advised me not to talk about the case to anyone in the State Attorney's office.

At "Grand Central" there were plenty of people trying to get me to talk. I understand that it is a common practice of the government to try and establish a sense of trust with newly arrested persons in an effort to get them to feel comfortable enough to offer incriminating information. Thus, I was visited by someone who quickly told me that he loved football and had been a great fan of mine. He tried to establish a rapport through sports. I still had my Bible with me and periodically turned to it for comfort. This led to a visit from someone else in the office who told me that he was born again. He tried to establish rapport through religion. But I wasn't offering much information. Quite honestly, I was still in a daze. It would be a day or two before I fully comprehended the jackpot I was in. (Strauss thinks if an investigator had come into my holding area and left a packet of cocaine on the table and then walked out, I would have taken it and used it then and there. He may be right.)

Finally, some time between 10:00 and 10:30 p.m., I was taken across the catwalk to the jail to be booked for the first time. There was a great deal of clamor among the police and corrections officers, many of whom had apparently known about the investigation for three days. Some were happy to see me, others were sad. This is when an officer told me he wished he had known how to get in touch with me to warn me. This is also when another officer told me, "This is a serious, violent crime. Whatever you done, Morris, you deserve."

I was charged with conspiracy to sell a controlled substance (Fred's scheme); sale or delivery of a controlled substance (transfer of Fred's sample and a portion of Cord's ounce to Brinson); possession of a controlled substance (Cord's ounce); and trafficking in cocaine (delivery of Cord's half kilo to Brinson). My bond was set at $600,000. There's no way I'm gonna be able to meet that and get out, I thought. Then I was taken to a cell and put in with two other prisoners, none other than Cord and Kulins.

In the meantime, my file went into the judge assignment lottery. As "chance" would have it, my case was assigned to a former prosecutor, Judge Ellen Morphonios Gable, a.k.a. "Maximum Ellen" because of her penchant, if not delight, in handing out the stiffest possible sentences. Ask anyone who knows anything about the Dade County criminal courts who is the worst judge a defendant can get and I'll lay odds the response will be Judge Gable. The actual odds of me getting her were 1 in 12 (that's how many judges were sitting at the time). As defendants in the same case, Cord and Kulins were also assigned Judge Gable. It just so happens that Fred Donaldson's sale of marijuana charge also ended up before Judge Gable. Justice may be blind, but I have my doubts about the lottery.

I wasn't particularly in good standing with Cord and Kulins. "How come you didn't know, man?" Cord asked me.

"Yeah, man, you should have known," said Kulins.

"Eddie, look," I said, "we were out there freebasing, acting like gangsters, what do we know?"

It was simple. We weren't looking for it. How was I to know that Fred Donaldson, the kid who had cut my lawn, had set me up. (Actually, at this point, I still didn't know Fred or Joe Brinson had been working against me. I assumed that they must have been caught and arrested, too.)

Things settled down in the cell and soon Cord was telling me, "You know, when I came into your house I had a vial on me. When I was hiding, I hid it in that box with your Pop Warner football jerseys."

Bingo! I'm no longer thinking about my charges now. I'm thinking, Hey, well at least when I get out, I'll have something at the house. That is the thought process of a messed-up mind.

My bond hearing was the next morning. My bond was reduced to

151

$150,000, which meant I had to come up with $15,000. Thanks to the efforts of Strauss's office and a local bondsman, I did. Bobbie was at the hearing and so was Pastor Schubert. She was crying and he was crying and I was crying as the cameras followed us down the street.

When we got home, I couldn't wait to get to Cord's vial. I paced about anxiously until Bobbie and Tiffany went over to a neighbor's house. Then I made a beeline for the closet, dug through the jerseys I had bought my 10-year-olds, and found the cocaine. With one eye on the window in case Bobbie returned or anyone else showed up, and one eye on the stove, I cooked up the cocaine and then smoked it.

At some point during the day I read the newspapers. I must admit I was surprised to learn that, according to the press, the bust had taken place at a house I had been renting and that the $120,000 plus confiscated had been mine. These descriptions fit the stereotype cocaine cowboy—a transient who is renting a Miami home and has loads of cash. They didn't fit me. I wasn't renting and, unfortunately, the money wasn't mine. Shortly after I bonded out, my electricity and phone were shut off because I hadn't paid the bills. Later, Strauss would tell Yoss that if the State kept insisting that the money was mine, it should be returned to me.

Later that afternoon, as Bobbie was coming home with Tiffany in her arms, a car hit them. It's a wonder that they weren't killed. Bobbie crashed to the ground and Tiffany flew into the air, only to land on Bobbie instead of the pavement. But they both had to go to the hospital. What more can happen to us, I wondered.

It was at the hospital that I saw Ron Strauss for the first time since the bust. I had decided I wanted Ron to represent me. Shelby Highsmith specialized in civil law, not criminal law. The two practices are very different. Ron was primarily a civil attorney, a highly regarded one at that, but he did have some experience in the criminal field.

Ron was a short but athletic man in his early forties. Like myself, he was a transplanted Pennsylvanian. He had come to Miami to go to law school and had stayed. His practice was a prosperous one. Some in Miami have suggested that he cultivates the media. He is rather flamboyant—his office contains pictures and letters from celebrities he has represented such as Kenny Rogers, Enzo Stuarti, and the comedian Gallagher. But I never found Ron using my case for his personal advancement. If he appeared before the media, it was for my sake, not his. I have been second-guessed for not re-taining an attorney who specialized in criminal law, but I had been very impressed with Ron, in particular his meticulousness, during our limited contact on my civil suit.

My main concern at the hospital was the welfare of my wife and 5-month-old daughter. Fortunately they were not seriously injured, but I was furious when I learned that the driver of the car that had hit them and then left the scene had been drunk. He had injured two people but wasn't in nearly the fix I was; I don't think he was even arrested. I talked to Ron a little about my case, but it was really the next day that we began to run through the events leading up to my arrest.

As I gave a blow-by-blow description of what had happened, Ron kept asking me about Fred Donaldson. At this time, I still had no idea that he had been working with the State. In fact, one of my first questions to Ron was, "How's Fred doing?" I assumed he had been arrested, too.

Ron said that from the way I was describing things there must have been someone working closely with the State, that it was very rare that an informant just called the State out of the blue. He fur-ther explained that the insider was usually someone who had already been arrested for something and was looking for leniency. Ron said he had a gut feeling that this was Donaldson. This was soon con-firmed in a newspaper account of the bust. Under Florida law the State is not required to give the name of the confidential informant, but somehow Fred's name worked its way into the paper.

At one of these early meetings, Ron also spelled out for me the fact that the trafficking charge carried a minimum mandatory sen-tence of fifteen years. Translation: If I was convicted on that count, it would be 1997 before I would be eligible to get out of jail. Ron explained the law did have an exception that allowed a prosecutor to ask a judge to suspend the sentence or waive the mandatory sen-tence of anyone convicted of trafficking who "provides substantial assistance in the identification, arrest, or conviction of any of his accomplices, accessories, co-conspirators or principals" who were in-volved in the same crime. Thus the statute was designed to encour-age those arrested for trafficking to name names so that the State could move up the ladder and nail the user's source, then that source's supplier, all the way, it was hoped, to the top.

Ron also told me that if I was to have any chance at getting out from under this, I was going to have to be intimately involved in the preparation of my defense. This would mean being available for strategy sessions and attending all of the depositions he took. A deposition is the testimony of a witness taken not in court, but under the court's permission. The person deposed is under oath and his words are taken down by a court reporter so that if he says something different at trial, the contradiction can be noted and his testimony impeached. By changing his story, he may even leave himself open to charges of perjury.

It was at this point that I knew that I had to cut myself off from cocaine. As with getting in shape for the Superstars or coaching my Pop Warner team, I now had a task—a task of the highest priority—and I knew I simply had to quit. I did, and while some people imagine that anyone withdrawing from cocaine gets the "DTs" and can't function for several weeks, this wasn't my experience. I stayed clean the entire period with a few exceptions. (Once, after leaving Ron's office with Kulins, we stopped by to visit some of Eddie's friends who had just been released from jail, and got high.)

The Bill of Rights guarantees to criminal defendants the right to a speedy trial. Often, defendants don't want such speed. The State, after all, already has its ducks in place, knows what its case is going to be. A defendant, who is certain to be outmanned and outspent, has to figure out who knows what and who did what, what the evidence is against him, and then build a defense. It takes time to piece together a story, find witnesses, and convince them to testify. The procedure of finding out what the evidence is and what potential witnesses would say in court is called "discovery."

Only 79 days elapsed between my arrest on August 18 and my trial on November 1. To put this in perspective, it was a full year and a half before John DeLorean went to trial on his cocaine charges. We would have liked a longer period to prepare our case, but, despite our repeated requests for continuances, only one was granted, and it was only for a few days. The period was indeed a discovery. I discovered a lot about the facts of my case and a lot about how the criminal justice system works... or doesn't work.

This lesson began quickly. I was released on bond on a Thursday and within a week had been arrested again. This time it was on an old bad check charge. Before the bust, I had bounced a check for something like $46 at the local grocery. The police came on a Friday evening and circled the house with guns drawn. That show of force was hardly necessary. What if Tiffany or one of the boys had strayed into the yard? Of course, I surrendered. I was brought to jail. As it was Friday evening, I was unable to get in touch with Strauss. I ended up spending the night until he bailed me out the next morning.

This happened a couple more times, always on a Friday. Before the bust, I had written several checks which bounced. When we learned that the State had had all the bad check charges at the outset but was arresting me on them one at a time, Strauss went to court and got an order to prevent what was in effect harassment. That each arrest occurred on a Friday was not a coincidence. It's much harder to find your attorney at home or in town or get through to him at his office on a Friday night than a weeknight. Strauss, who by this time had given me telephone numbers where he could be reached on the weekends, was livid. "They want you to see how bad jail is," he told me. "They figure if you do, you'll make a deal."

It was a little early for deal making. We didn't know many of the facts of the case. Still, Yoss was already talking to Strauss. They had squared off in court on preliminary matters and knew of each other from their years of practicing in Miami. At times, the fact that Strauss didn't regard Yoss the personal adversary that I did bothered me. The first time they got together after my arrest, Yoss sat Strauss down in his office, gave a sly little chuckle, and played one of the more damning portions of the parking lot tapes. Then he encouraged Strauss to reason with me and see how much I'd be willing to cooperate. This marked the beginning of informal negotiations between the two of them, each sounding the other out to see if common ground could be reached. Strauss, as was his duty, would periodically approach me with some of his or Yoss's ideas—say, a year in the stockade if I named names—but I was never terribly interested in cutting a deal. I thought I'd be vindicated, and I didn't want to name names as Yoss demanded. I considered the State, as personified by Yoss, my enemy. It had wronged me by charging a user with trafficking, and I wasn't going to let it off the hook by pleading to a lesser charge.

Interestingly, it soon became clear to the State that as far as this case went, it already had the supplier—Cord. But despite the clear language of the law which said the prosecution could only waive the minimum mandatory for cooperation in the investigation of the crime for which the trafficker was arrested, the names Yoss wanted from me—former football players, etc.—had nothing to do with this investigation. It quickly struck me that this guy could in a sense play God with my life, deciding exactly what I had to do in order to get out of my predicament. I never confused his sense of justice with the Almighty's.

Strauss started discovery by taking the depositions of lesser characters in the drama, such as the dozen or so officers involved in the investigation and arrest. The idea was to wait a bit for the major players like Brinson and Donaldson so that we would have as much information as possible when we questioned them.

At the same time, we awaited copies of the tapes of the phone conversations and face-to-face meetings. It was obvious that these would be extremely detrimental to us and that Strauss would try to find some grounds to prevent their use in court. My faith in the system was not bolstered by the way in which Yoss handled the tapes. Strauss and I were in an elevator together after a lunch break during a deposition. Yoss, who had earlier in the day handed the tapes to Strauss, now announced that he was also giving the tapes to the media. Strauss, who hadn't even had time to listen to the tapes because he was busy with the deposition, was furious. The conversation went something like this:

STRAUSS: Why the hell did you do that before I heard them, George? I have a right to try to suppress those tapes. Now you'll try him in the media.

YOSS: The public has the right to know.

So Strauss forgot about lunch, postponed the remainder of the deposition, and drafted a motion requesting that the court prevent the release of the tapes to the media and the printing or broadcasting of the tapes. The State wasn't the only party to oppose the motion. The *Miami Herald* quickly had its high-priced lawyers in court. We lost. The next day, despite the possibility that Judge Gable might at a later date refuse to allow the tapes to be used in evidence, Miami and the world, including potential jurors, saw and heard that "motherfucker" Mercury Morris sounding like the big-time gangster he wasn't.

My family took such setbacks well. While my freebasing had pulled us apart, my arrest brought us together. Bobbie was, as usual, supportive. My parents were also behind me. It took a while to gather the courage to call my mom. When I finally called, I cried and told her that Johnnie Belle's son had set me up. "Just hang in there and pray that you get a fair trial," she said. I broke down. I was more composed when I called my father, who was equally understanding.

One of the tapes raised more questions than it answered. It was tape 4 of a total of nine. It supposedly featured conversation from an August 17 meeting I had with Brinson and Donaldson at my home. It was largely unintelligible, due to an oscillating sound on the first portion of the tape.

Strauss took the tape home one night to see if he could make any sense of it. He thought he heard voices underneath the oscillating sound, but couldn't determine what was being said. He asked his wife Angie, who he said, "could hear a hawk forty miles away," to listen. She picked something up. "Someone was talking about President Reagan and Iowa and somebody named Donovan was mentioned," she told him. "And I heard the name Mitchell or Mitchum, too."

Strauss bought some equipment to amplify the sound and picked up a few more words, but the tape still didn't make any sense. Then he was told of a man in California who might be of assistance. The man, who apparently had some clandestine calling (perhaps the CIA), agreed to help, but cautioned he would not testify in court and said we could not reveal his identity. Strauss rushed the tapes to him. Soon we had a transcript revealing that the tape related information about President Reagan's address to the Iowa Corn Growers Association and the problems of Labor Secretary Raymond Donovan. The name, Andrea Mitchell, was also clearly decipherable. Mitchell was (and still is) an NBC news correspondent. We concluded that the tape had somehow picked up a television newscast. But where? Brinson claimed he had never recorded anything in my house up to August 17.

Strauss called Andrea Mitchell in Washington, D.C., and asked her when she had broadcast the story on the tape. She said she had done several stories on this subject and couldn't recall a specific date. So Strauss sent an investigator to New York to look in the NBC archives. The answer? Not August 17, but August 1. Maestro, a little *Twilight Zone* music, please.

What did this mean? It was the responsibility of the *State*, not us, to explain this. But there seemed to be only two possible conclusions: (1) Someone had been in my house taping on August 1,

157

over two weeks before the State swore in its affidavits that it had begun its investigation. Remember, Donaldson had visited me on August 1 and tried to collect the money. The possibility exists that he was recording then. In one of its first affidavits, the State had claimed the conspiracy to sell cocaine began on August 1, but this was later amended to August 15. (2) The tape had been tampered with in some way. When Strauss took the depositions of the various State Attorney's agents who were involved in the taping, they were unaware that we had deciphered the words under the oscillating sound on tape 4. They all insisted that each tape cassette had never been opened or touched before it was used to record my conversations. There was no chance for a slip-up, they insisted. The investigator in charge of the tapes followed a set procedure, breaking the seal of each tape and then dating it. Their explanation as to what might cause background noise varied. One agent suggested atmospheric interference, another suggested an open mike might have picked up a radio or television set. But our investigation revealed that no radio or television station had played Mitchell's story during the days of the investigation, August 16 through August 18.

Whatever the explanation, it seemed obvious that the tape was not what the State described. This seemed to be wonderful ammunition for our upcoming battle to have *all* the tapes suppressed (kept from being used at the trial). If we could show that even one had been tampered with in some way, we could raise doubts about the manner in which the taping had been done, and thus we might be able to convince Judge Gable to disallow the use of all the tapes at the trial. While Brinson and Donaldson would still be able to testify at the trial about the events leading up to the bust, Strauss was convinced such testimony would not be as dramatic nor as persuasive to a jury as my own damning words as caught on the tape.

During this period of trying to decipher and discredit the tapes, Strauss continued to take depositions. Among the notable admissions he elicited:

- Havens acknowledged that he hadn't considered Donaldson reliable and that he had not exhausted all investigative procedures before instituting the buggings.

- Gilbert acknowledged that he hadn't run a thorough background check on Donaldson.

- Brinson acknowledged that when the tape caught him saying to Fred, "I don't believe the motherfucker has the shit. I think he's bullshitting," he believed that I neither possessed nor had access to the cocaine as Donaldson had suggested. Nevertheless, Brinson stated, at the instigation of Chief Investigator Havens, he had continued to encourage me to go out and find some cocaine so that we could consummate a deal. This, Strauss told me, may have been more than entrapment. It may have been prosecutorial misconduct. The State was creating a crime for me to commit.

In my opinion Brinson did not come off as wholly truthful. The most glaring example of this was how he initially stated that he had not been wearing a body bug to tape conversations when he visited my home on August 17. Only later did he concede this.

I attended each and every one of these depositions and became immersed in the case. When something didn't sound right to me, I'd pass Strauss a note or whisper to him. At the same time, I was actively involved in helping to piece together background material on Donaldson. I found family members and neighbors who were willing to testify against him. Most important were the statements of several kids in the area that Donaldson had sold or given them marijuana and other drugs. Meanwhile, Strauss's investigators found what Gilbert had apparently never looked for—a Donaldson arrest record a mile long. There were several dozen arrests, ranging from larceny to several cases of assault, to the pending marijuana charge, which had nothing to do with the kids. This last charge was important, for if proven it would mean Donaldson had violated the terms of his probation and would have to go to jail, unless he did something like help net a big-time drug dealer to warrant the court's leniency.

By the time Strauss took Donaldson's deposition in October, we had put together a picture of what we considered to be a mentally unstable, drug-using, violent criminal with a motive for setting me up. The set-up aspect was important if I was to undertake the defense that I had been entrapped. At this time, we had yet to make a final determination if that was the route we would take; that would depend on how Judge Gable ruled on our motion to suppress the tapes and other evidence.

Donaldson's deposition took place over three days and runs 497 pages. I was present the entire time. Also present were Strauss, a lawyer from the State Attorney's office (Yoss and Gregory Victor took turns), Cord's attorney Jeffrey Weiner; Kulins's attorney Arthur Huttoe; and, at various times, Lawrence Stein, the public defender representing Fred on his marijuana charge and the charge that he had violated his probation by failing to make restitution to the man whose ear he had bitten off. We were all crammed into a small room at the State Attorney's office. I believe the space was generally used to interrogate suspects, because once the doors were locked they could only be opened from the outside.

It was the first time I had seen Fred since my arrest. He had moved out of our neighborhood to what we eventually found out was a room paid for by the State Attorney, which, interestingly, had refused to acknowledge that Fred was an informant and insisted on calling him a "concerned citizen." The State Attorney was also providing him with food, transportation, and money. (This showed. I had never seen him dressed so well.) As this unfolded, I started referring to him privately as "Mark." He reminded me of the Black character by that name in the old Raymond Burr television series *Ironsides*. Mark worked for "the Man" and so now did Fred.

Knowing that he had set me up, I probably would have done serious damage to Fred if we had been left alone together. Of course, we weren't. I was cautioned before the deposition began that any effort on my part to intimidate Fred would result in my being asked to leave.

The deposition only reinforced our portrait of Fred. His behavior was so unusual that only a few minutes into the proceedings Arthur Huttoe asked him to step outside, and then stated: "For the record, it is my opinion that this man is under the influence of drugs at this present time. His whole demeanor, his reactions, and the pupils of his eyes indicate that he is under the influence of some sort of drug. In my opinion, it is probably Quaaludes, from my experience having observed a lot of people under the influence of Quaaludes."

Yoss disagreed. But Weiner added: "I would like to join in that. This man is definitely not normal, he is not responsive or alert, he does not appear coherent, he cannot answer the questions in a normal fashion without undue delay without his eyes rolling up and down." Strauss joined Huttoe and Weiner and proposed a recess so that Judge Gable might be requested to order an immediate examination and urinalysis. A compromise was agreed upon: the deposition would continue, and at a suitable break the request would be made. Unfortunately, when it came time to bring this matter to the attention of Judge Gable, Weiner and Huttoe did not join Strauss in court. So Ron went by himself and asked the judge to order a test. The State opposed the testing, which was interesting since Donaldson was supposedly a "concerned citizen" and not the State's agent. "What do you want me to do, Ronnie?" she shrugged. "I can't make the man pee into a bottle." So there was no test.

In addition to acting strange, Fred seemed to have left his memory at home, at least parts of it. He was able to recall many of the events leading to my arrest, but had a hard time remembering facts about his own arrests. "As my re-memory serve me, I don't recall," seemed to be his standard refrain.

When he did recall facts, he didn't always remember them accurately. For example, he remembered a fight with an individual which led to his arrest on an assault charge, but denied that he had stabbed the individual, even though that is what the State Attorney's report said. Another example: he denied having bitten off the ear of the man whom he claimed had stolen the cockatiel which God had given to him (Fred). Strauss showed Fred the State Attorney's report describing how Fred had indeed bitten off the ear. Fred disputed the report. This was his amazing version: "I flipped him on the ground. I tried to restrain him to the ground by having both of my hands on his right hand. He took his left hand, put it up to my ear, put his fingernail in it and I took my right hand and pushed his left hand down. At this point I am pinned down over the man. I am biting him. . . . All of a sudden he reaches up at my ear with his mouth, and by having fast reflexes I grab his ear first and by pressing down to the ground obviously I'm going to pull up, and his ear ripped from his body. Now you have the right facts."

His description of how he collected exotic birds was equally fantastic:

DONALDSON: I have talked to several dudes who are trappers of birds. . . . In fact one of them is the president of the Wildlife Association of Canada.

STRAUSS: How did you meet him?

DONALDSON: I was walking down the street and I had in my possession or rather was trying to catch a parrot which had a yellow head and I couldn't catch it and the gentleman came up to me and told me how I would go about doing it.

STRAUSS: And he walked up and announced who he was and how you could catch it.

DONALDSON: No. He told me how to catch it and then told me who he was.

This would be funny... if the stakes hadn't been so high. Remember, this was the man whose accusations—which were every bit as fantastic as the stories above—set the State Attorney's office on its merry way.

Fred's ability to distinguish right from wrong was also suspect. Strauss, while looking at Fred's rap sheet, asked him if he had ever been caught removing gasoline from a vehicle.

DONALDSON: Yes.

STRAUSS: Were you stealing the gasoline?

DONALDSON: I was borrowing it.

STRAUSS: Did you know the person who owned the vehicle from whom you were borrowing the gasoline?

DONALDSON: No.

STRAUSS: Your last statement [is] that you were borrowing the gasoline from somebody you didn't know?

DONALDSON: Excuse me. I meant to say that I was getting it.

STRAUSS: Is that stealing in your mind?

DONALDSON: It depends on how you look at it.

STRAUSS: Well, how did you look at it?

DONALDSON: There was a need.

Strauss caught my attention and then rolled his eyes.

Strauss repeatedly asked Fred about his use of marijuana and cocaine. Fred admitted to only being a casual reefer smoker and repeatedly denied ever having used cocaine or peddled marijuana or other drugs to kids in the neighborhood. These appeared to be lies, for we had members of Fred's family and the kids themselves willing to testify otherwise. This would be very important at the trial in establishing Fred's truthfulness and whether or not he had violated the conditions of his probation.

If it sounds like Strauss was putting Fred on trial at the deposition and that I'm putting him on trial here, that's not so far from the truth. The background, credibility, and motive of an informant are most important, particularly if a defendant is going to argue that he was entrapped. As for motive, Fred admitted that he was mad at me because he felt that I had intentionally withheld money from him knowing that if he couldn't pay restitution he would go to jail. But he insisted his main motive for contacting the authorities was to save the kids in our neighborhood, that he was a concerned citizen. No mention was made of the fact that by helping the authorities, this "concerned citizen" might save himself from the pending marijuana charges or a return to jail for failure to pay restitution. Those payments were to have begun September 1, and the trial on the marijuana charges was scheduled for later in the fall. When Strauss brought this up, Fred admitted that he had in the past cooperated with the government and received leniency on other pending charges. Fred also admitted that Chief Havens had talked to the police about his (Fred's) marijuana charges shortly after he (Fred) had come to him with the story of my cocaine dealing.

Having discussed motive, Strauss now moved to the specifics of my case. Fred stated that he had never told Havens that he had seen me sniffing and cutting cocaine. This directly contradicted the affidavits the State had presented to Judge Kogan in its successful effort to get a search warrant.

Who had brought up the amount of cocaine to be purchased? Strauss asked. Fred was a bit confused. First he said he had told me that he had a friend who wanted to buy a "key," or kilo. Then, he changed his mind and said I had told him that I had two kilos.

There was more confusion about whether he had actually been at my house and if so had seen cocaine on the dates he told Havens. He finally concluded that he couldn't recall.

Fred was certain that he hadn't given me the cocaine sample that I had tossed to Brinson at Dadeland on August 16 and equally certain that he hadn't encouraged and instructed me to throw the sample to Brinson; he did not know I even had a sample. This was interesting, since on the tape of that conversation Fred was heard to say, "Throw that sample over here, Gene."

We also had a witness who was prepared to testify she had seen Fred give me the sample. This was Kulins's girlfriend, Caroline Taylor, who had been at my house when Fred visited on August 15. As we had listed Caroline as one of our witnesses, the State knew she might testify on our behalf. My respect for the State was further diminished when I learned that Caroline was dragged down to the State Attorney's offices on a Sunday morning, given a polygraph test, and interrogated for eight hours about everything from the events of August 15 to her own drug use. During this grilling, she denied, then admitted, having used marijuana. This prompted the State Attorney to threaten her with perjury. Frightened of the consequences, she finally signed a prepared statement recanting her statement that she had seen Fred give me the sample. At the trial, however, Caroline's desire to see the truth come out overrode her fear of the State and she testified that she had indeed seen Donaldson give me the sample.

In addition to the tossing of the sample of coke, Strauss was interested in something else from the taped conversations of August 16. During the first tapped phone conversation, I had asked Fred if he was sure that this wasn't a setup. Fred had assured me that it was not.

STRAUSS: You lied to him, didn't you?

DONALDSON: I guess so.

STRAUSS: You would have continued lying to him until such time as he brought cocaine for them. Isn't that true?

Fred danced around that question and continued dancing despite Strauss's repeated attempts to get him to answer it. This was an important exchange, for it demonstrated the intent to lead me on until I finally committed a crime.

Strauss touched on numerous other points, including Donaldson's statement to me that Joe (Brinson) was the brother-in-law of a Miami Beach cocaine dealer named Gene.

STRAUSS: Do you know a cocaine distributor on Miami Beach by the name of Gene?

DONALDSON: No, sir.... There is no such person as Gene...

STRAUSS: You created the name Gene?

DONALDSON: Of course.

This exchange took place on October 6. At the end of the day, the deposition was continued until October 14. On October 7, Strauss took Joe Brinson's deposition. Brinson provided a fictional last name for this fictional "Gene" from Miami Beach. "Gottbaum" was how the court reporter spelled it, since, Brinson said, "I don't know the correct spelling."
Strauss's curiosity was raised.

STRAUSS: Did Fred tell you there was a real Gene Gottbaum? I can't imagine anybody making up that last name.

BRINSON: No.

STRAUSS: Fred has never been a standup comedian of sorts, has he, to your knowledge?

BRINSON: Not to my knowledge.

STRAUSS: Therefore [did you ask], "How'd you come up with that name?"

BRINSON: Yes.

STRAUSS: What did Fred say when you asked him that question?

BRINSON: "He is Jewish and he lives on the beach side."

As he read the transcript of this deposition later that week, Strauss couldn't help but be struck by the oddity of Donaldson's selection of the name Gene Gotbaum. He mentioned this to his wife over dinner. "Let's look it up in the phone book," she said.
There was nothing under Gottbaum, but there was a listing for a Dr. Irving Gotbaum. Strauss did not know the relevance of Gotbaum to my case, but he felt every angle should be pursued. He called the doctor's office the next day and asked the doctor's secretary if the doctor had treated Fred Donaldson. The secretary said she couldn't give out such information.
Strauss tried another tack. "I think the doctor went to school with Fred. How old is he?"

"Sixty."

"Does he have a son?"

"No, a nephew," said the secretary. "He's an x-ray technician at Jackson Memorial."

Armed with this information, Strauss brought Gotbaum up again when Donaldson's deposition resumed. Donaldson at first maintained that "Gene" was fictional, but finally admitted that he had gone to school with a Gene Gotbaum.

Strauss still had no idea of the importance of this, but filed it in his mind to be pursued if time permitted.

Our motion to suppress was filed in court and argued in front of Judge Gable a few days after Donaldson's deposition was completed. The major points of the motion were: (1) that the initial wiretap on my phone without a warrant on August 16 constituted an unconstitutional invasion of the privacy of my home and that it and all subsequent tapes of phone conversations and face-to-face conversations must be suppressed, and (2) that the State's failure to apprise Judge Kogan of all pertinent facts at the August 18 hearing for a search warrant and Sarmiento order to wiretap required that the tapes from that day and any evidence obtained as a result of the search that day be suppressed. Upon first learning of the State's deception of Judge Kogan, Strauss was so outraged that he had Yoss arrange a face-to-face meeting with State Attorney Janet Reno, Yoss's superior. Yoss was present at the meeting. Strauss thought Reno might be equally outraged and take internal action after hearing the disturbing facts. Apparently she did nothing. After this, Strauss filed a motion alleging improprieties by the State Attorney's office but nothing came of it.

How could we argue that all this evidence be suppressed? Our motion was based on the well-established "fruits of the poisonous tree" doctrine. Translation: in order to protect individuals from unwarranted invasions of privacy and in order to prevent the State from abusing its power, the courts have consistently ruled that any evidence obtained as a result of illegal searches and seizures or wiretaps must be suppressed. This is because such evidence is considered tainted. In effect, the evidence is the fruit of a poisonous tree and must be thrown out.

We knew the ruling on this motion would be the most important decision made involving the case. If we won, the State would have to rely solely on the in-court testimony of Donaldson and Brinson (whose credibility had also been shaken during his deposition). And just as important, it was possible that the State might not be permitted to introduce all the evidence obtained at my house at the time of the arrest, including the cocaine. We were confident of our chances, but realized that Judge Gable would not be the most sympathetic decision maker.

In the motion and at the hearing we recounted to Judge Gable how the State had failed to get a court order for the August 16 taping of my phone conversation, how the State had failed to exhaust all investigative procedures (as required by law) before instituting the wiretapping and taping, how this was initiated on the basis of the uncorroborated allegations of an informant whom the State conceded was unreliable. Then, we recounted how the State had misled, misinformed, and withheld information from Judge Kogan when seeking the search warrant and Sarmiento order to bug my phone on August 18. Specifically, the State had failed to tell Judge Kogan that it had considered Donaldson an unreliable informant and that it had not revealed that it had already been taping conversations without court orders for two days.

We lost. Judge Gable ruled the search warrant and the taping of my phone conversations legal. She did rule that the tape made of a face-to-face conversation at my house on August 17 was not legal and suppressed it as well as the infamous Iowa Corn Growers tape 4. But the State would be able to use everything else at the trial. Strauss later told me that as long as the judge was going to rule in the State's favor, it would have been more to our advantage if she would have allowed tape 4, too; that way we could have given the jury the opportunity to decide if there had been any tampering with the tapes. In a sense, by disallowing the two tapes, Judge Gable trimmed the fat off the State's case and left Yoss with a juicy filet mignon.

I was devastated by Judge Gable's ruling. Man, you're being peeled like a banana, I said to myself. Will justice ever be served? Still, we had to press forward. The trial was only a few days away. The ruling really narrowed our options down to two: I could plead guilty and try to make a deal with the state by naming names, or I could go to trial and try to prove that I'd been entrapped.

As for playing "Let's Make a Deal," Strauss and Yoss were still batting proposals back and forth. Strauss, for example, tried to establish ground rules that would enable me to name only names of individuals (primarily football players) who had already acknowledged cocaine involvement or who had already been mentioned in the press as involved with cocaine and could not be prosecuted because of the statute of limitations. Yoss refused, saying, in effect, he would only make a deal after he heard the information I had to offer. No way! I didn't have the kind of names and information he wanted (but even if I had, I wouldn't have given it to him).

It seemed to me that the facts of the case were clearly in my favor and that we'd win easily if we showed the jury how I'd been entrapped. Briefly, entrapment is what is called an affirmative defense. Although it seems that I've spent a major portion of my life around lawyers and in court, I don't presume to be a legal scholar. So here is how Supreme Court Justice Hughes described entrapment: "[It occurs] when the criminal design originates with the officials of the Government and they implant in the mind of an innocent person the disposition to commit the alleged offense and induce its commission in order that they may prosecute." This seemed to describe my case to a tee. The criminal design had originated with Fred Donaldson, who as the State ultimately admitted by the time of the trial had become the State's agent, and then was working for Chief Investigator Havens. They came to me, an innocent person, implanted the idea that I should sell cocaine, and then continued to induce me to do so until I finally arranged the transaction for which I was arrested. I made the distinction in my mind that I was a user, not a dealer. Although personal use was wrong, the State had no right to persuade me to become a dealer and no right to choose the crime for which I was to be charged by setting the amount of cocaine desired. Surely, any jury will see this, I thought.

I was even more confident when, just a few days before the trial, Strauss followed up on the Gene Gotbaum lead. He did this by sending his investigator, Doug Gazboda, over to Jackson Memorial Hospital to find Gotbaum and see what he knew about Donaldson and cocaine. Gotbaum wasn't at the hospital, so Gazboda left a card asking him to call Strauss. Gotbaum called, but when Strauss explained that he was representing me, Gotbaum hung up. Gazboda then went back to the hospital, but Gotbaum was not interested in talking. Strauss thought he had hit a dead end, but then Gotbaum called again and said something like, "I don't want you to bother me. I'll tell my lawyer to stop you. This is harassment. I don't know anything about Morris and don't want my name brought up."

Strauss answered, "You don't understand. Your name has already been brought up."

"I don't care," said Gotbaum. "You'll hear from my lawyer."

Strauss still had no idea where, if anywhere, Gotbaum might fit into the equation, but he threatened to subpoena Gotbaum. Gotbaum hung up but called Strauss at home later that night. As Mr. Gotbaum spoke to Strauss, Mrs. Gotbaum got on the other line and started yelling at her husband not to talk. Strauss tried to calm her down. Gotbaum continued. The conversation went something like this:

STRAUSS: Your name was mentioned by Fred Donaldson as a coke dealer in Miami Beach.

GOTBAUM: That lying s.o.b. I've never done that. He should know.

STRAUSS: How?

GOTBAUM: I went to high school with him.

At this point, Strauss saw Gotbaum as joining the parade of those who could impeach Donaldson's testimony at the trial.

STRAUSS: What do you know about him?

GOTBAUM: He's a drug user; he's hallucinated with LSD; he's a habitual liar.

Strauss sensed Gotbaum knew something else but was afraid to offer it because by coming forward he might ruin his reputation at the hospital.

STRAUSS: I can't stop Donaldson from talking. I feel your name will surface. Do you know more about this? I feel you're holding something back.

Strauss later told me there was a pregnant pause, that the silence was deafening.

GOTBAUM: I'll tell you this. I bumped into Freddy months ago and he told me he was gonna set Gene Morris up.

STRAUSS: Months ago?

GOTBAUM: A few months before Gene was arrested.

They weren't even investigating Morris at that time, Strauss thought.

STRAUSS: Will you give me a sworn statement even if they may not allow you to testify?

GOTBAUM: I'm already too involved. No.

STRAUSS: Will you at least meet with my investigator?

Gotbaum reluctantly agreed. After talking with Gazboda, he said he'd help us. Just a few days before the trial, he gave a sworn statement that he knew Fred Donaldson and that Donaldson had told him several months earlier that he was going to set me up in a drug deal.

So from Donaldson's statement that he had made up a fictional "Gene," to Brinson's statement that this fictional Gene's last name was something like "Gottbaum," to Strauss's trip through the phone book and call to Dr. Irving Gotbaum, we had located a witness who swore that Donaldson had planned on setting me up months before he went to the State Attorney's office and told investigators that *I* had approached him about selling cocaine. Things were looking up.

CHAPTER 10

THE TRIAL

I went into the trial confident. I felt that I had the truth on my side and that a jury of my peers couldn't help but see that. Unfortunately, I didn't exactly get a jury of my peers. Of the seventy prospective jurors, only a handful were Black. As was the rule rather than the exception at this time in Miami, none made it to the jury box for the trial. The State either found cause to dismiss these Blacks or exercised its peremptory challenges. These permit the dismissal of a prospective juror by either side without having to state a cause. Each party is permitted six such challenges. But because there were three defendants—me, Kulins, and Cord—the State had eighteen challenges. (Not too long after my trial, the Florida Supreme Court ruled that certain jury selection procedures were biased against Blacks and reforms were instituted. This in the 1980s.)

Call me naive, but despite the makeup of the jury, I still thought I'd win. Maybe it was my faith in God; maybe it was my attitude that you never think you're gonna go 7–7, you think you're going 14–0; maybe I'd seen too many *Perry Mason* reruns.

The trial began on November 1 with Hamilton Burger, er George Yoss, presenting the opening statement for the prosecution. This portion of the trial gives lawyers for all parties the opportunity to lay out for the jury what they believe the evidence will show. Yoss, a little round man in his middle thirties who was losing his hair ahead of schedule reminded me of the actor Danny DeVito. He summarized the charges against me, Cord, and Kulins, and then gave a straightforward presentation of what the State felt the facts would be. As might be expected, the State's version of the facts didn't entirely jibe with our version. Of course, Yoss didn't present the facts that were detrimental to the State's case.

As I had pleaded not guilty by reason of entrapment, Yoss anticipated my argument. "The evidence is going to show in this case that the defendant was not entrapped; that he wasn't forced into committing a crime that he wouldn't ordinarily have done," he told the jury. Then he detailed the fine distinction the State was going to make: "But the evidence is going to show that he was given an opportunity, an opportunity, under the law, to commit a crime if he wanted to."

A trial is a battle. It reminds me of a football game, what with all the strategizing. You come into the arena with a game plan that you've tried to keep as secret as possible. Maybe you've even got a few new wrinkles which might throw the other side off. Until Strauss went to the podium to present his opening statement, none of the other parties knew for sure what our game plan was going to be. They knew I was pleading entrapment, but they didn't know if I would be taking the stand in my own defense. That may sound strange, but oftentimes defendants exercise that Fifth Amendment right and sit silent through an entire trial while their lawyers poke holes in the State's case and challenge the credibility of the State's witnesses in an effort to create a reasonable doubt in the minds of the jurors. That's all that is required for the defendant to prevail—a reasonable doubt. Donaldson, and to a lesser extent Brinson, Havens, and Gilbert, had proved themselves less than credible at their depositions. So Strauss did have some ammunition if he determined it wasn't advisable for me to take the stand. Whatever tack we took, it would determine to a large extent how the State and the other defendants presented their cases.

After Yoss concluded, Strauss began his opening statement by telling the jury that this was not an open-and-shut case. "We're here to tell you there is a need for a trial," he said. "We're here to tell you it is entrapment, misconduct by police officers. We're here to tell you there were lies, deceit, misrepresentations; here to tell you they took advantage of a broke, former celebrity football star."

He explained that in pleading entrapment, "That means, basically, he (Morris) admits he was there. He does not admit that he had criminal intent. . . . He was lured, entrapped, ensnared."

Strauss then moved to the "man that's the heart of their case, named Fred Donaldson. And if you believe Fred Donaldson, then you can't believe Mercury Morris. If you don't believe Fred Donaldson, Mr. Morris was indeed entrapped."

So here was our strategy. The jury could listen to Fred on the stand and the jury could listen to me and they could determine which of us was more believable. To help them make that decision, Strauss gave a laundry list of Donaldson's prior offenses and provided a motive for entrapping me: to get out from under the pending marijuana charges and potential charges of failure to pay restitution for the ear he'd bitten off. Strauss told the jury he had witnesses who would come to court and testify that Donaldson was a liar, a liar when under oath.

Strauss then provided our version of the facts, stressing that I didn't have any cocaine, was broke, didn't even have access to cocaine. "It's not complicated," he said. "He's a user. But if they want to arrest a thousand users tomorrow morning, they can go out in the street and do it."

He concluded by once again putting Donaldson on trial. "Donaldson is the reason Gene Morris is here. Take Donaldson away and they don't have a case."

The battle lines had been drawn. It was getting late, so Judge Gable adjourned the trial before the lawyers for Cord and Kulins gave their opening statements. We would pick up there tomorrow. . . . So we thought.

As is often the case, what took place outside the courtroom that day was probably more important than what took place in front of the jury. At about 11 p.m. that first night, Strauss received a call at home from Yoss informing him that Cord had pleaded guilty to a lesser charge and was going to testify against me. Strauss realized this could be the kiss of death. If Cord testified against me, the State might decide it didn't need to put Donaldson on the stand at all. We had the right to call Donaldson as a witness, but rarely, if ever, will a defendant call the informant as a witness if the State hasn't called him. This is because if *we* called Donaldson to the stand, he would be considered "our" witness, and the general rules of the court say that you can't cross-examine or impeach the credibility of your own witness unless you can persuade the judge that the witness is hostile. The way Judge Gable had ruled up to this point suggested that we would have little chance of getting a favorable ruling on this point from her.

Cord's decision to plead guilty was a direct, although not foreseeable, result of our strategy to plead entrapment and let me take the stand in my own defense. Strauss's opening statement had suggested that I would be taking the stand. He had confirmed this to the attorneys for Cord and Kulins in a private meeting outside the courtroom.

Aware that I would basically have to admit that what the State said happened did indeed happen, Cord's lawyer had warned Strauss that this would hurt his client. He implied I was betraying the cause. Strauss countered by reminding the lawyers for Cord and Kulins that he (Strauss) had sought to separate my trial from their trials on the grounds that Cord and Kulins could testify about the entrapment if they weren't facing justice at the same time I was; conversely, they would have been protected from my testimony admitting entrapment if they had been tried separately. But Cord's lawyer and Kulins's lawyer had refused to join in the motion, and Gable had denied it. "I asked for separate trials," Strauss said. "Now we gotta do what we gotta do."

The next morning in court, day 2 of the trial, Cord informed Judge Gable of his decision to plead guilty. "Your counsel has probably done the greatest service that could be done," the judge told Cord forcefully. She was an imposing figure of about 45 years old with long blonde hair and steel blue eyes. That look led some in Miami to call her Medusa behind her back. Others called her Lady Law because she was on record as believing justice should be rendered swiftly and without mercy. In her early years on the bench, she had expedited trials by ordering witnesses to stand as they testified. The reasoning was that they wouldn't take up as much time if they couldn't sit down. The appeals court had finally put an end to this practice. Judge Gable was also rumored to keep a gun under her robes. "You would be doing the 40 years with a mandatory 15 years and not one day less [if you had been convicted]."

Strauss expressed shock at Cord's decision. He moved for a mistrial on the basis that Cord, according to Yoss, had cut a deal whereby he agreed to testify against me in exchange for a waiver of the mandatory minimum sentence. In addition, as Cord's attorney had helped pick the jury for the defense, we were now saddled with a compromise jury that wasn't entirely of our own choosing. Not surprisingly, Judge Gable denied the motion. "A defendant is on notice that people he is charged with can flip (plead guilty and turn state's evidence)," she said. "Co-defendants flip all the time."

Strauss then asked for a delay so that he could take Cord's deposition. It was essential we gather evidence as to Cord's background and attack his motive for testifying against me. Again, Judge Gable said "No." If Strauss wanted to take the deposition, he could do it after the day's proceedings. At this point Yoss must have begun to feel like we Dolphins did during that 1972 season when we won each and every game and knew we couldn't lose! The State was prevailing on every motion.

We had expected that Yoss might call Donaldson as his first witness, but he did not call him at all on day 2. Joe Brinson was on the stand most of the day. He played the tapes that we had tried to suppress. There is no escaping it. The tapes were damning and damaging.

On cross-examination, Strauss tried to lessen the impact of the tapes, discredit Brinson, and demonstrate the lengths to which the State had gone to catch me. Strauss first suggested that Brinson may have been so moved by the desire for the notoriety that my arrest would bring that he was willing to go to any length to arrest me, even entrapment. He asked Brinson if he had ever investigated Gene Gotbaum, whom Donaldson had identified as a cocaine dealer in Miami Beach. When Brinson said he hadn't, Strauss sarcastically asked, "Did Gene Gotbaum ever play football?" The implication was that the State was only interested in netting me. Strauss also created the implication that despite Donaldson's portrayal of me as a big-time cocaine cowboy—and in Miami everyone knows that means machine-gun-packing dealers—the State must have had its doubts. Otherwise, it had acted totally irresponsibly by picking such a busy place as the enormous Dadeland shopping center parking lot for a transaction that had the possibility of turning violent. Brinson admitted that he was armed during the time with a .357 Magnum and that other agents hidden in the area were also armed. If I had been an armed cocaine cowboy and a shootout had occurred, many innocent bystanders might have been hurt.

Throughout the cross-examination, Brinson's memory was at odds with things he had said less than a month earlier at his deposition and with the events as they had been recorded on the tapes. For example, Strauss asked him how Donaldson knew I had a sample of cocaine on me at the first meeting at Dadeland. Brinson indicated that I had mentioned this at the meeting. But it was nowhere on the tapes, which Brinson acknowledged had seemed to pick up all the rest of the conversation. This explanation just didn't seem believable. It was an important point, because one of the counts against me dealt with the delivery of that sample (which I maintained was Donaldson's). Also, Havens had said the delivery of that sample was an important element in convincing the State I had access to cocaine. Delivery in Florida is the equivalent of sale.

While my words on the tapes were coming back to haunt me, now Brinson's were haunting him.

STRAUSS: Tell the jury in your own words what you said to Fred Donaldson outside the hearing of Gene Morris while you were in the undercover vehicle.

BRINSON (AFTER YOSS'S OBJECTION WAS OVERRULED): To the best of my recollection, I believe I said, "I don't believe the motherfucker's got the dope."

STRAUSS: Got the "shit"?

BRINSON: Something to that, yes, sir.

Strauss asked him what his next line was. Brinson couldn't remember.

STRAUSS: "I believe he's bullshitting." Isn't that your language?

BRINSON: That's street language, yes, sir.

Brinson's memory about just what he meant had to be refreshed by Strauss's referral to Brinson's deposition.

STRAUSS: So, you believed that he didn't even have access to it, he might not be able to get it, and you scheduled another meeting, didn't you?

BRINSON: Sir, that conversation was made off the record.

A weak reply.
Strauss now went on to establish whether Brinson encouraged me to commit the crime.

STRAUSS: Was your motive in continuing the discussion and the role-playing of Gene Gotbaum's brother-in-law to encourage Gene Morris to bring you cocaine?

BRINSON: I at no time encouraged Gene Morris to make that sale. I gave him an opportunity to make the cocaine sale.

Strauss asked the court's indulgence while he quickly reviewed a portion of Brinson's deposition, found what he was looking for, and read a question from that deposition.

STRAUSS: Question: 'Were you instructed by Chief Ray Havens at any time during the breaks in the meetings (with Morris on August 16), the five of them that you had, to continue to solicit and encourage Gene Morris to get the cocaine and bring it back to you?' And your answer is: 'Yes.' (At the instruction of Chief Haven.)

Strauss found several other sections in the deposition where Brinson had admitted "encouraging" me. Now, at trial, try as he would to deny that he had encouraged me, Brinson had to concede that he had admitted the same on several occasions at his deposition.

I thought Strauss did a fine job of handling Brinson. For that matter, Strauss had been by far the best prepared of all the defense lawyers. The lawyers representing Cord and Kulins didn't even come to most of the depositions. I heard that Cord paid his lawyers something like $20,000 and all they really did was plead him guilty on day 1.

Cord's deposition on the evening after day 2 of the trial lasted until midnight. It was a revelation. I thought he was a swimming pool contractor and also a relatively small drug dealer. But upon questioning, we learned that he was actually in the big time. There were federal fugitive warrants out against him for smuggling and importation of Quaaludes. In that matter, Cord's co-defendant had been murdered (word on the street had it) just before he was to turn State's evidence and testify against Cord.

We knew that when Cord testified against me the next day he would indicate that he had given me the cocaine to sell to Brinson and that I was going to profit off the venture. We suspected, too, that the State would question him about past dealings with me. If the State could prove we had done deals like this before, it would be easier to convince the jury that I had the required criminal intent.

It was obviously in Cord's interest to cooperate with the State, to give it information it didn't already have that would be helpful in convicting me. Otherwise, there was no reason for Yoss to agree to waive the minimum mandatory. Still, it was highly unusual that a *supplier* was being granted the waiver for testifying against the *middleman;* the purpose of the waiver was to get higher-ups, not lower-downs. You might think Yoss would have withheld the waiver unless Cord named his own supplier—the person the next rung up. But apparently Yoss made no such demand. So why the deal? It appears that the State was more interested in convicting me than it was in finding the supplier of Cord's cocaine. Strauss told me that Yoss didn't think that Donaldson would be believable under oath and felt he needed to substitute Cord's testimony for Donaldson's if he was to have a chance of convicting me.

Our approach would be that self-interest rather than interest in seeing the truth come out was Cord's motive. Strauss would try to raise questions in the jury's mind about whether Cord was being honest or had manufactured a story so the State would cut a deal with him. Information about his criminal activities and anything on which we could impeach him would be important. That Cord might play loose with the truth wouldn't have shocked us. Before Cord had "flipped," someone in his camp suggested that I conceal the truth about Cord's whereabouts at the time of the bust.

Before the jury came into the courtroom on day 3, Strauss tried to subpoena Federal Drug Enforcement Administration (DEA) records concerning Cord with the hope that those documents would reveal information about Cord that he had concealed at the previous night's deposition and that such information could be used to destroy his credibility. At about the same time, a lawyer friend of Strauss's presented Strauss with much of the information that was in those DEA records. It did indeed show Cord was lying. Strauss asked for a recess to gather more information on Cord. Gable refused (this was getting all too predictable). Then we got a double whammy. The U.S. Attorney's office in Miami refused to turn over the "official" DEA records concerning Cord and argued that we not be allowed to introduce anything in those records into evidence, saying that to do so would expose other ongoing investigations. Over Strauss's objection, Judge Gable sided with the U.S. Attorney.

So Cord took the stand, and all Strauss could do was shoot holes in his testimony with blanks instead of real bullets. Strauss succeeded at raising questions about Cord's motive for pleading guilty—a reduced sentence and immunity for the things he testified to in court—and did bring out some information about his criminal past. But Cord refused to admit many things about his past we knew to be true from our copy of the DEA records. Prevented from introducing the DEA material into evidence and showing these authenticated documents to the jury, Strauss wasn't able to raise doubts about the truthfulness of Cord's testimony to the extent we would have liked.

Cord's testimony did not help my cause. Cord said I owed him money from buying cocaine from him and that he hadn't liked dealing with me and that he had only gotten into this deal at the urging of Ruth. Cord indicated that I had approached him with other deals and that we had transacted one prior deal for $3500. That was not true. I would have to refute it when I testified.

By day 3 I was totally frustrated. To hear witnesses like Havens and Gilbert and Brinson give a different version of the facts every time they were questioned—from the time they swore out affidavits in front of Judge Kogan, until their depositions, until their actual testimony in court—was disgusting. These men were law enforcement officers and it seemed to me they weren't being honest, hadn't been honest from the beginning. To hear Cord and know we couldn't bring up information to impeach him was also discouraging. And not seeing Donaldson...boy, did I want to see him take the stand. I knew Strauss had meticulously outlined the three volumes of Donaldson's incredible deposition and was prepared to walk him through the coals.

During this time, I tried my best to stay on top of things, passing Strauss notes during testimony and taking part in strategy sessions. All the while I was preparing myself for my testimony. Here's where I'll finally be able to tell my side of the story, I thought.

After Cord testified on day 3, the State rested its case. Yoss had not had to put Donaldson on. We sent home the twenty or so witnesses, among them fifteen police officers, who had come to court prepared to testify that Donaldson was a liar and perjurer. One potential witness was Detective Vincent Gable, the judge's then husband. He had signed the arrest report regarding Donaldson's pending charge for sale of marijuana.

Now it was our turn to present our defense. Strauss called sev-

eral witnesses, including Dr. William Scott Russell, who told how
he had treated me for my headaches, and Caroline Taylor, who, despite the State's gestapo-like tactics in threatening her with perjury,
testified that she had seen Donaldson give me the sample of cocaine
on August 15. That was important testimony. But it was clear that if
there was any hope of getting out of the jackpot, it would rest with
me.

I took the stand on day 4. I was ready and willing. My adrena-
line was pumping just like it did before I took the field for the Dolphins. Strauss wanted the jury to know who I was and where I had
come from. He began by having me review my career and the awards
I had won. We then moved on to my neck injury and the headaches
which had begun after I retired. Strauss hadn't wanted the jury to
think I was exaggerating about how devastating the headaches had
been, so he had already called Dr. Russell to testify about them. As
I told the jury about the night I had almost tried to kill myself by
driving through the intersection and then had said the Lord's Prayer,
I broke down and cried. A short break was called so I could regain
my composure.

From the headaches we went to my business failures. And from
the business failures, we went to my relationship with Fred Donaldson. I explained about our dispute over the money and how we had
had a falling out on August 1, how I had visited him on August 2 to
see if we could work something out, and how on August 7 he had
dropped by to return a camera.

As I recounted these events, I acknowledged to the jury my own
cocaine problem.

ME: I had a drug problem at that time, a frequent drug problem, not a habitual problem, but a frequent one.

STRAUSS: Were you a user of cocaine?

ME: Yes.

Strauss asked me if Fred used cocaine and if we had ever used
cocaine together. I answered each question "Yes." Then we moved
on to Fred's visit on Sunday, August 15. This was important. Strauss
was hoping that if we raised sufficient doubts about Fred's, the State's
agent's, motive for setting me up, Yoss might be forced to call Fred

as a rebuttal witness and we would finally have our opportunity to cross-examine him.

> ME: Fred started in about the fact that I owed him money, but he wasn't mad about it and he said that he had a deal with some friends of his from New York and that if I would help him by introducing him to the people I knew that I could get cocaine from, it would be a chance, or excuse me, an opportunity, for us to be square.

Further questioning by Strauss established that I had been told by Fred he had money problems arising from his need to make restitution, that I initially balked at the proposition, and that Fred gave me a user's sample of coke before he left the house. Strauss then asked me who supplied me with my cocaine. I explained how I purchased user's amounts from Ruth and Cord. I also indicated that at the time Fred approached me with the proposition, neither one of those suppliers was answering my calls because I owed them money.

Now Strauss attempted to rebut Cord's testimony about my involvement with more than user's amounts of cocaine.

> STRAUSS: Did Vince Cord ever talk to you about a couple of ounces of cocaine?

> ME: Yes, he did.

I explained that Cord had talked about buying a 1976 Chrysler from me, offering to pay me 2 ounces of cocaine instead of cash.

Now we moved back to the chain of events leading to my arrest.

> STRAUSS: Now, we all heard the taped conversation on August 16, 1982. Did you have available to you any source of two kilos of cocaine?

> ME: No.

I acknowledged how I tried to get the cocaine from Ruth and how she had told me to call Cord and how he had hung up on me because I owed him money, and how Kulins was the one who got a reluctant Cord to participate.

STRAUSS: What was your function in the entire two or three days?

ME: Well, what I thought then was that I—I would introduce Fred, or Fred's person, but they didn't want to meet them. They didn't want to meet them and—

STRAUSS: Did Agent Brinson talk to you about going to Ruth's house?

ME: He didn't want to go see Ruth.

STRAUSS: Who did he want to deal with?

ME: He wanted to deal with me.

I further explained how Brinson and Donaldson turned down my offer to see Ruth, how Fred suggested the price of $60,000 a kilo, how the ounce Brinson took from my house on August 17 was Cord's, how I kept telling Brinson that I thought my contacts could come up with the cocaine, but in reality never was sure they could.

Strauss finished his examination of me by questioning me about the events of August 18, the day of the bust. Then Kulins's attorney conducted a brief cross-examination in which he tried to establish Kulins never knew what was going on. Yoss's cross-examination, which we all knew would be the roughest, was scheduled next.

Judge Gable ordered a recess for lunch. As the jury left, I moved to Bobbie and Tiffany, who were sitting in the courtroom. I took hold of Tiffany.

The court reporter recorded the following dialogue:

YOSS (TO JUDGE GABLE): I'm just as compassionate as anyone in the courtroom. I think that was totally improper in front of the jury. It's not needed. You can do that as soon as they leave. I would object to what happened between him and his wife and holding the child in front of the jury. That's improper.

JUDGE GABLE: Noted.

STRAUSS: I will instruct my client not to hold his baby in front of the jury again, knowing no one is uncompassionate in this case.

Strauss's sarcasm was apparent.

After lunch, I took the stand again. Yoss played hardball for the next couple of hours. It was about as grueling as anything I'd ever faced.

On the subject of my contemplated suicide, for example.

YOSS: Did you say the Lord's Prayer in contemplation of what would happen to those persons that you might hit going through the intersection?

ME: No.

YOSS: You didn't care about them, did you, or you weren't thinking about it?

On why I didn't tell Donaldson it was wrong to distribute marijuana, despite my assertions that I considered him a kid brother.

YOSS: Did you give him any advice that you would give a kid brother?

ME: No.

YOSS: You didn't care who he was going to sell it to?

ME: No. I didn't care. . . . At that point I didn't care if he was concerned about making money with drugs because I had a drug problem myself.

YOSS: What would you do if one of your children . . . wanted to borrow money . . . so they could [sell] pot?

ME: I wouldn't let them do it.

YOSS: But you didn't care if Fred did it?

And on the subject of cocaine.

YOSS: Just so there's no misunderstanding, you know that cocaine was illegal to possess?

ME: Yes, I did.

YOSS: It's illegal to distribute it?

ME: I never distributed it.

YOSS: I didn't ask you that, Mr. Morris. I asked if you knew it was illegal to distribute it.

ME: Yes.

YOSS: So long as you mention it, are you contending that you did not distribute a sample of cocaine to deliver or hand a sample of cocaine to Joe Brinson on August 16, 1982?

ME: Yes, I gave it to him.

On my testimony in my civil suit against the sanitation truck company. Here Yoss quoted from my deposition in 1981 in that suit in which I had said, "I don't use drugs."

YOSS: Did you lie under oath?

ME: Yes, I did.

YOSS: You lied under oath because you were suing for a million dollars in cash; isn't that true?

ME: No, I lied under oath because I couldn't admit to myself at that time that I had a drug problem. I don't know anybody that would have used drugs, especially with the way I used them...and admit it to the public.

Yoss took this little sidetrip to demonstrate to the jury that if I lied in a civil suit, I would lie in a criminal case in which I was facing jail. But as I saw it, there was no reason to lie in this criminal case, in fact if anyone was lying it was Donaldson and Brinson and Cord.

Yoss next tried to establish my motive.

YOSS: You weren't a hero like in the days of '72 and '73 at the Orange Bowl?

ME: Well, no...

YOSS: People weren't paying a lot of money to watch you play football?

ME: No. I wasn't playing.

YOSS: You weren't making any money either?

ME: No, I wasn't.

YOSS: Couldn't even afford to pay Freddie Donaldson the $400 you owed him?

ME: Yes, that's true.

YOSS: You wanted to make money?

ME: Yes, I wanted to feed my kids.

YOSS: That was the reason you did this then, you wanted to feed your kids?

After questioning me about my participation with Don Reese in cocaine dealings (I admitted I had used cocaine with him in 1977), Yoss asked how Strauss had prepared me for this testimony. I told him that Strauss expected me to tell the truth.

YOSS: Is that the same truth you told back in that deposition in November?

ME: No, it's not. Mr. Yoss, you're asking about a lie that's based upon a lie to myself. That's the same syndrome as a person who is an alcoholic and refuses to admit it to himself, even though the family and everything else may be destroyed, that person will not admit that.

YOSS: You're saying you kicked the habit, you're a different Gene Morris?

ME: I'm saying I kicked the habit and I'm a different Gene Morris.

Yoss seemed skeptical and, in what I would describe as a somewhat sarcastic tone, questioned me about my calls to the 700 Club and the visit from Pastor Schubert. He asked me when I found God. I told him that I hadn't found God. God had found me. Yoss wanted me to pinpoint the precise moment of my turnaround.

ME: I think when I went to jail and what seemed to me to be the most devastating situation I had ever been in. I saw other miracles happen in my life that could come from no other place.

YOSS: So, the approximate cause of your becoming the new Gene Morris was across the street when you hit the Dade County Jail that night.

ME: No, sir. It was that man sitting over there.

I pointed to Pastor Schubert.

If all of this seems tough, the next hour was even more demanding. Yoss cross-examined me on the events of August 16 through August 18, step by painful step. I stuck to my story, even when it didn't jibe with the State's account. For example, I maintained that *I* was the one carrying the cocaine to Brinson's car, not (as Brinson had asserted) Brinson. I also said that, contrary to Brinson's testimony, I did not transfer the cocaine to him when we went to his car. The cocaine, I said, did not leave my hands until I tossed it toward the canal. I never touched the buy money, either, I asserted.

YOSS: Are you saying Joe Brinson's lying about when you gave it to him, he carried it out, put it in the trunk of his car?

ME: Yes, sir. I am. Not only am I saying that, I'm saying I'm telling you the truth and if you let me finish, I'll continue to tell the truth.

I did continue to tell the truth. When I left the stand I really thought I had swayed the jury in my favor. I wished that they could go into the jury room and begin their deliberations right away. Unfortunately, Kulins still had to testify.

If my testimony was dramatic, Eddie Kulins's testimony was comedic. His strategy was to try and convince the jury that he had been drunk or high during the days leading up to the bust and had been, in effect, an innocent and uninformed bystander. Some of the tapes and testimony, however, said something else, and Eddie may have come pretty close to perjuring himself. In what may have been the trial's funniest moment, Eddie, who kept insisting he always had a six-pack with him, was asked if he had had a six-pack at a particular time before the bust. "No, sir," he said, "but I sure wish I had one now."

Day 4, one of the most demanding in my entire life, closed with each side resting its case. Donaldson never took the stand, and neither did a witness we tried to put on ourselves—the mysterious Gene Gotbaum. Judge Gable refused to allow him to testify, reasoning that, since Donaldson had not testified, Gotbaum had nothing relevant to say. Strauss did persuade the judge to allow Gotbaum to come in during a break and, out of the presence of the jury, read for the record his statement about Donaldson. The whole thing couldn't have taken more than a couple of minutes. But as the events of the next few years would prove, they were a very important couple of minutes.

Gotbaum was a tall, thin fellow with dark, curly hair. Here is what his statement said:

> I have known Fred Donaldson since 1974 during my high school years. We did not however attend the same school. During our high school years, I have seen Fred Donaldson on several occasions use L.S.D. (Acid), Quaaludes, and marijuana. During the times of influence and non-influence of drugs, Fred Donaldson displayed acts of irrational behavior.
>
> Several months ago, Fred Donaldson called without having called in several years to ask my advice concerning Mercury Morris and the money that Morris owed Donaldson. Donaldson stated that he wanted to get back at Morris by setting him up in some sort of drug deal. I then advised Donaldson to stay out of trouble and forget such a ridiculous idea.
>
> Since I have known Donaldson, he has been very inconsistent in telling the truth.
>
> (signed) Eugene M. Gotbaum

Day 5, November 5, was set aside for closing arguments. But before the State could begin its argument, there was another development. Kulins, following Cord's lead, pleaded guilty. Apparently his testimony had been such a fiasco that Yoss had threatened him with perjury. From three defendants, we were now one—me. Against the grain—as always.

Gregory Victor, an Assistant State Attorney who had worked on the case, gave the State's closing argument. Strauss followed with ours, and Yoss concluded with the State's rebuttal.

Victor gave a straightforward presentation of the facts brought out during the trial and how those facts required a verdict of guilty. He wasn't particularly dramatic. Strauss, on the other hand, gave Sir Laurence Olivier a run for the money. This was our last shot at the jury.

Strauss began by telling the jury it was on a search for the truth. Then he tried to disassociate me from Cord and Kulins. "Both pled not guilty (but) when they realized Gene Morris was going to tell the truth on the stand, they pled guilty....Mr. Cord and Kulins worked a deal where there would not be a minimum mandatory sentence without parole of fifteen years. It takes a man who believes in himself, who believes in what happened, who told the truth to sit here and ask you to find him not guilty by reason of entrapment."

Strauss impressed upon the jury the importance of its role. "There are two paths that go from this courthouse for Eugene Morris. One path goes directly across the street to the jail and from there to the state penitentiary. The other path goes to his house. Standing in the middle of that path is this jury."

Then Strauss moved to the theme he would come back to again and again during his two hours at the podium: the absence of Fred Donaldson. "I will ask this question throughout my closing argument: Where is Fred Donaldson?... Fred Donaldson is the only other living being that can corroborate, disprove what was said outside the presence of those tapes. Fred Donaldson has a face. He's a live human being and he is upstairs on the ninth floor in the State Attorney's investigator's office."

Strauss explained to the jury that if he had called Donaldson as a witness, he could not have called him a liar. He recounted that the State had begun the entire investigation of me based on Donaldson's uncorroborated allegations. "They (the State) believed Fred Donaldson," he told the jury. "But they wouldn't present Fred Donaldson to see if you would believe him."

The tapes had been damaging in suggesting I was a big-time dealer. Now Strauss attempted to dismiss the rhetoric and focus on reality. "Did Gene Morris ever deal in cocaine in kilo quantities? That's the issue... Gene took the stand, said he had no predisposition, never had any money, never could...."

Having framed the issue, Strauss now moved on to explain the entrapment defense. Judge Gable would explain this when she gave the jury its instructions, but she had a reputation for giving instructions so rapidly that juries couldn't even understand them. That usually benefits the State, not the defendant. Strauss wanted to make sure the jury realized that I should be found not guilty if it found that I had no prior intention to sell or deliver, possess, traffic in cocaine or conspire to traffic in cocaine. "Possession, we admit—his [Morris's] own," Strauss said. "In this case to deal with Agent Brinson, we deny. He was pursued, induced, lured into committing the offense."

Strauss took those three magic words one at a time. *Pursued.* Morris was pursued by Fred Donaldson, he said. Who could controvert that? "Where is Fred Donaldson? Ninth floor, upstairs, secreted." Each time Strauss would mention the ninth floor, he would point a finger up to the ceiling. It was very effective. Pretty soon observers in the courtroom were doing it. *Induced.* Could Morris have walked away? Remember, Donaldson was saying it was Gene's fault that he might not be able to make restitution. And it was Donaldson who gave him the sample. *Lured.* The State kept dangling money in front of Morris, who was broke, Strauss said. He compared it to having a police officer don skid-row garb and lie down in an alleyway with a $100 bill sticking out of his pocket. What happens when the bum who is hungry and doesn't have any money comes by? "That's what luring means," Strauss explained. "They not only extended a hundred dollar bill, they extended a hundred and twenty thousand dollars to a man who could not feed his family and they knew it. Fred Donaldson knew it. Where is Fred Donaldson? Ninth floor."

Strauss then moved on to the specifics of the State's case, recounting the discrepancies, if not outright lies, in Brinson's testimony about the sample and his "off-the-record" statement that he didn't believe I had access to cocaine. Strauss really let Cord have it, too, reminding the jury of Cord's role in the proceedings, the deal he was given to testify, and his background as a drug dealer. "In my opinion the fires of hell were built not warm enough for that individual," Strauss said. "He's a scavenger in the soul of man and he gets immunity and he gets a deal. If this investigation was about the source of cocaine, if this investigation was to take a user...and get to their source...they have him. And what do they do once they get him, they invite him to testify, to bring his dirty hands into this courtroom for their case. Why? Because they replaced Fred Donaldson with Cord."

Strauss went through the events of August 16 through August

18, noting how the State had encouraged me to locate the cocaine, how Brinson had refused the opportunity to go to Ruth's house and nab an apparent supplier, how the State had made phone call after phone call, visit after visit. Then he began a series of questions to the jury.

"Who are these people who create crime, entice people to cooperate? ...Who are these people who set up people with slime like Fred Donaldson? ...Who are these people who immunize the likes of Cord to get Mercury Morris? ...Who are these people who intimidate witnesses (Caroline Taylor) so they will not be willing to appear and testify? ...Who are these people who secrete testimony of Fred Donaldson from the jury? ...Who are these people who for the sake of national media coverage encourage a user of drugs to go out and locate drugs for them on a trafficking felony charge?" Strauss answered each of these questions, after he asked it, the same way: "They are the investigators of your State Attorney's office."

Strauss concluded: "The purity of (Gene's) being was exposed to you. His past glory lives only in our memories. He was lifted to paradise and fell into purgatory, but as few of us can really say, his soul has received the Lord. Mercury Morris is no more, but Gene Morris has begun to live. Send him from the courtroom in God's care. Thank you."

I think everyone in the courtroom was deeply moved. I know I was.

Yoss spent much of his rebuttal shifting the spotlight back on me from Donaldson and trying to distinguish the difference between giving someone an opportunity to commit a crime and encouraging him to do so. Then, Strauss's attempts to bury the old Mercury Morris notwithstanding, Yoss dug me up and put number 22 back on me: "For a lot of years in Dade County there were a lot of cheers for Gene Morris. We all went out there and cheered...when he ran over the goal line.... We booed him, we yelled, we complained, we cried when he dropped a pass or fumbled the ball or he didn't go over the goal line. But let me tell you what he did fumble. He fumbled a lot more than a football game. He fumbled his life away...."

And so my trial ended. As predicted, Judge Gable rushed through the jury instructions. Then six of my so-called peers went to determine which pathway I would indeed take.

I waited and prayed with Bobbie and Strauss in the hallway while the jury deliberated. After about an hour, the jury sent word out that it wanted more information about the elements of pleading entrapment. I thought this was a good sign. "They agree that I was entrapped," I said. Strauss was pessimistic. "They're coming down with trafficking," he said. A little later, the jury sent word out that it needed to know where it should put the checkmark in the box for trafficking. My heart sank. I knew I was cooked.

After only three hours, the jury returned. I was pronounced guilty on four of the six counts, including trafficking, the offense which carried a minimum mandatory sentence of fifteen years. I was found not guilty of two of the lesser counts dealing with the sample Donaldson had instructed me to toss to Brinson. Judge Gable set sentencing for January.

I was allowed a quick good-bye hug with Bobbie and then taken to jail, directly to jail. Do not pass go. Judge Gable denied Strauss' request that I be allowed a few days to get my things in order before reporting to jail. The trafficking offense was such that anyone convicted of it could not stay out of jail while appealing or until sentencing or even to get their things in order.

As I was led to jail, Strauss and Yoss met a horde of reporters in the hallway. Yoss drew all of the attention, telling everyone that justice had been served. Strauss told the only reporter who came up to him that the piece of paper he held in his hands—it was Gene Gotbaum's statement—would play a crucial role in the months to come.

Cord and Kulins would not be joining me. By virtue of pleading guilty, they were given the gift of freedom until sentencing. Fred Donaldson, it turned out, would not be joining me either. When his case concerning the sale of marijuana came up before—guess who? Judge Gable—the next week, the State had to drop the charges. It seems the evidence—the marijuana itself—had been lost.

CHAPTER 11

DADE COUNTY JAIL

It seemed fitting that a cold rain was coming down as, handcuffed, I crossed the catwalk from the courthouse to the jail. It was about 9 p.m. on Friday, November 5. In the old days, I would have been out with Ricky O and the guys freebasing. In recent days, I would have been at home where I belonged with Bobbie and Tiffany and the boys. Now I was on my way to a cold slab, or the floor in cell 5A3.

After crossing the catwalk, I was put on an elevator which led to the fifth-floor cell block. I hadn't been off the elevator for two seconds when a corrections officer approached me. "You're Morris, huh?"

I didn't respond.

"Well, let me tell you something," the officer continued. "In about two months, they'll forget all about you. You'll just be another inmate around here."

I had been in a daze since the jury had announced its verdict, but this woke up the bull in the ring. "Well, in about two seconds, I'm gonna forget about you," I frowned. "Why don't you try doing the same for me now."

This exchange set the tone for how I was to do my four and a half months at Dade County Jail until I was shipped "up the road" to prison. I simply wasn't going to bend, wasn't going to Toby and say, "Well, you've got me by the gonads now, so I'm just gonna be real submissive." Oh, no. My attitude was: "If you're gonna kill me, but you want me to beg first, you better bring your lunch and dinner. Because I'm not begging." It pissed the guards off that I wasn't humble.

The guard who had fired the opening shot was a tall Black dude named Mason. We fought the entire time I was at the jail. He'd make a smart remark and I'd be in his face.

"Well, I know karate," he'd boast.

"Well, they'll use those two black belts you've got to lower you into the ground if you come in here messing with me," I'd counter.

My entry into cell 5A3 was something of a reunion, not on the order of the 1972 Dolphins homecoming that would take place in two days, but a reunion nonetheless. This was the cell I had been brought to when I was arrested on the bad check charges in the days following the bust. Many of the guys sitting on the bunks had been sitting on those same bunks since August. Equal protection under the law? Many of them had been awaiting trial for over a year, while I had been rushed through the system in seventy-nine days.

Everybody was glad to see me... for different reasons. Some were glad because I was Mercury Morris and others were glad because I was Mercury Morris! More guys were sympathetic than not. After all, they were criminals. They knew a setup when they saw one.

I took a seat on a metal slab that masqueraded as a bed. Bobbie had gone home to get me a change of clothes. For now I was sitting on the dank, dirty rectangle in the light suit I had worn to the courthouse. I couldn't imagine sinking any lower.

Eventually my change of clothes did come, but not without the inevitable hassle. A search of the blue jeans Bobbie brought revealed a pill in the pocket. It was Inderal, which had been prescribed for my high blood pressure. Until Bobbie produced the prescription, the jeans were considered too dangerous to pass on to me.

The cell had a television set. As I had all week, I watched clips of the trial on the 11 o'clock news. It's an eerie, unreal feeling seeing yourself on a tiny screen, watching as you're convicted of crimes which carry such a stiff sentence.

If I slept that first night, it was only for a few hours. My mind was racing too fast. Besides, the guards wake everybody up at about 4:30 for breakfast. You learn quickly: if you don't get up, you don't get breakfast.

I spent most of Saturday doing interviews. Strauss came to the jailhouse and together in a private room we faced a number of reporters from the print and electronic press. Strauss was portraying me as this poor, broken guy hanging on the gates of Rome like Spartacus. I heard him use that imagery so many times that pretty soon I began to believe it. We had been through so much together over the last few months that we were like brothers. I knew he was having conniptions about having lost such a high-profile case. At the same time, although in my heart of hearts I knew he had done the best job he could have done under the circumstances, I couldn't believe how he had allowed this course of events to transpire. At times, he hadn't seemed aggressive enough. At times he seemed to be accepting the fact that the prosecutors could lie and get away with it. He seemed too friendly with Yoss. I mean, I had been set up, entrapped, and everybody knew it. The press was generally sympathetic, but not one reporter seemed interested in getting to the bottom of the story itself; they just wanted to portray me as the fallen hero.

I was in a fog until Paul Warfield visited on Sunday. Despite the television news, the questions of the reporters, my conversations with prisoners and guards, it really hadn't struck me that I could be in prison for *fifteen years*. When it finally did sink in, I was totally bewildered by the injustice of the whole thing.

The only way I could make any sense of what was going on was to turn to God. I had my Bible. There were skeptics, Judge Gable among them, who thought I only turned to God after I was arrested. I had, however, begun the journey before that—on those occasions in January and July when I had prayed for release from the bondage of cocaine. At my trial, Yoss had asked me whether or not I thought it had taken getting arrested to be released from the bondage and I had said, "Yes." But *convicted?* I couldn't understand that. I was certain that I would prevail in some way, be vindicated, be freed.

The avenues to freedom were, admittedly, somewhat limited. Strauss had filed a motion for a new trial, arguing everything from error by Judge Gable in refusing to allow Gotbaum's testimony to inconsistent verdicts by the jury. The reasoning here was that if my only defense was entrapment, and I was found not guilty by reason of entrapment on two counts, then I must have been entrapped the whole time, for all the charges. As these motions would be argued in front of Judge Gable, the odds of success, based on our prior experience with the judge, were not high.

A second possibility for leniency centered around a grand jury appearance scheduled for December. This had to do with a bank with which I had been involved and the bankers who ran it. The bank had loaned me money during periods of hardship. As it came out at my trial, I had been friends with the bankers to the extent that I had shared cocaine with some of them. Some of the people associated with the bank were alleged to be gangsters. They may have been. I never confused any of them for Mr. Rogers. It was suggested to me that if I provided the federal grand jury investigating these parties with critical information, the State might be willing to waive the minimum mandatory I was facing.

If I lost the motion for a new trial and didn't cooperate with the grand jury, my only hope would be winning on an appeal to the Third District Court of Appeals (DCA) or Florida Supreme Court or by naming names to Yoss in return for the waiver. I couldn't understand why Yoss would be interested in dealing with me *after* my conviction, especially if I were the terrible criminal he had described. Apparently, he still thought I had something to offer. This may have been one reason for the unusually long period between the November verdict and sentencing, which was scheduled for January 20; the State wanted me to get a taste of jail. As in the pre-trial period, Strauss and Yoss frequently engaged in discussions about my cooperation, but nothing was ever firm.

I passed most of my days quietly, writing and reading spiritual material. I tried to distance myself from most of the commotion that is common to a cell housing ten or fifteen murderers. But there were hassles with guards and prisoners.

For anyone accustomed to freedom, especially someone as free-wheeling as I was, being confined requires a terrific adjustment. I felt like a caged animal. This was heightened by virtue of who I happened to be. There were actually people working in the corrections system who made special visits just to look at me. It was as if a rare white tiger or a panda bear was on display. I'd hear the dialogue down the hall:

"Hey, we got Mercury Morris."

"Where is he?"

"Hell, he don't look so tough to me."

"Is that really him?"

I did look different than I had during the trial. Within a week after the conviction, I had shaved my head. I'm not one for seeking hidden psychological meaning in everything one does. One friend suggested to me that I went the Isaac Hayes route because I wanted to shed my old skin and start anew. I don't know about that. Somebody else hypothesized that I wanted to demonstrate that I still had some control over my environment and myself. All I can say is that you go through changes—physical, emotional, intellectual, and spiritual—during a period like this.

Strauss flipped when he saw my bald head and double flipped when I told him I was growing a beard to go with it. "Don't go the Black Panther route on me," he begged. That was the farthest thing from my mind. As much as I liked Ron, I felt he and I weren't always on the same wavelength. Sometimes I felt that I was the one taking care of him instead of vice versa.

The one person I was on the same wavelength with during this period was Bruce Frumkin, the jail's psychologist. Although I spend little time on self-analysis, I did visit Bruce a couple of days a week. This began not out of desperation, not even because I felt the need to "deal with my emotions," but because it was a way to break up the monotony of life at Dade County. I grabbed at any and every excuse to get out of my cell—meet the press, meet the psychologist, even meet the dentist!

Bruce didn't fit the stereotype I had of a jail psychologist. He was a few years younger than I was and somewhat of a character. He didn't try to play mind games with me, didn't insist on administering a battery of diagnostic tests. Maybe that's why we got along so well from the beginning. Soon I felt comfortable using him as an outlet or sounding board to discuss everything that was running through my mind—my guilt about the past, my outrage at the present, my fears about the future.

One thing we didn't talk very much about was cocaine. Remember, this was 1982, a few years before most of those in the counseling community knew very much about the drug (they knew even less about freebasing). Besides, as far as I was concerned, cocaine had ceased to be an issue the moment the jury foreman had said "Guilty."

My enlightenment came about very simply: the reality of my new environment dramatically reordered my priorities. When you're sitting in a cell staring fifteen years in the face, you learn about priorities real fast. All my energy was devoted to getting out, not getting high. To this day, many people find it hard to believe I didn't go through a wrenching period of withdrawal and depression, that I didn't long for the drug as I sat in my cell, that I didn't need some formalized treatment program to get over cocaine. Such skepticism doesn't disturb me. These people have never been where I was. Without actually being in my shoes, they will never understand how I reacted to the predicament I was in. The literature is replete with examples of individuals who have responded positively to traumatic situations—people who have nobly overcome injuries and illness, people who have overcome the loss of loved ones. In the abstract, such traumas seem impossible to deal with. But when they are real, you have no choice but to deal with them if you want to survive. I wanted to survive.

I kept a diary during the time I was at Dade County. The entries for a particular week give a picture of what life was like.

Monday, November 22, 1982

Yesterday I bet against the Dolphins. I lost four packs of cigarettes, four candy bars, and four Bunkie cream cakes. I liked the Bills in Buffalo. Today I found out that my motion for a new trial was canceled until next Tuesday—very disappointing. . . . I'll have to trust in the Lord to help me live on Thanksgiving. My family is always on my mind. It gets tough when I try to make any common sense of this. . . .

The State has asked me to help with the rehabilitation and counseling of the juveniles here. It's a tough decision, because I have received no fairness from the State, which makes it hard for me to be honest in my feelings with the kids. How can I teach them something as an agent (I like that word) for the State when I have yet to experience any positive steps by them to rectify what they have done to me. I'm still going to try and help. . . .

The Turk (an officer) just came by. He's the man who, when he calls your name on Monday, they ride (from the jail to prison). Fox and Lovejoy were called to go "up the road." Lovejoy insisted he was the wrong man. That makes seven who've gone up the road since I've been here. Tomorrow three more will come in. But only for a while, because in here you either go out the door or up the road. I wonder if it will ever be me. God, I hope not—enter subconscious thoughts of my family and bitterness toward the system. Hide me, hide me, hide me! (Lovejoy's last words). Lord, I know you've got freedom planned for me. The seriousness of the game has now taken effect.

Tuesday, November 23, 1982

A Thanksgiving note to my kids. The Lord is in me now—I feel his presence. It feels good—the faith I've been seeking and the peace of mind that comes with it.

My neck hurts. I'm going to bed.

Wednesday, November 24, 1982

Today I received a semi-jolt when I went to see Russ Buckhalt, the jail's director of social services. He said I'd be working with the kids, but he also said after seeing Judge Gable that she said she always gives more than the minimum mandatory. (Was this to encourage me to cop a plea?) My day was shot, although I tried to hide it. . . .

Ron (Strauss). I haven't seen him in a while. I miss the guy. He and I are very close. It brings tears to my eyes when I think about how hard he worked. Ron has come to know the Lord. Whether he knows it or not, he's been chosen as I have. . . .

Tonight I went to the law library, supposedly to meet the juveniles. None showed. I did meet an interesting man. He's 34. Could be from the class of '65. We talked law and my case. He's the most knowledgeable person I have met in jail. After surveying my case . . . he said, "Run for it and take your best shot, because the justice system has too much pressure (politics) to let you go, even if they are wrong. They (the State) have the winner, and there is little you can do but go crazy thinking about how and why it's supposed to work."

Friday, November 26, 1982

Friday is eggs-grits day. Not bad. Not good, but not bad. This pretty much is my schedule. Sleep at 5:00 a.m. (after breakfast), rise at noon unless I have something to do (class or my trips to see the psychologist). This morning I learned of a medical and dental furlough. Mc-Duffie—Vietnam vet, very wise—says if the judge trusts you, you can get out for a week or two (on such furloughs). God, that sounds great.

Up until the last three or four days, I have been submerged in obtaining knowledge of the word and scriptures. I've been easing up and now, applying my feelings to settle myself. It seems that the "Devil's Police" have been out in full force to try and persuade me to run and/or give up, add the nonrealistic outlook on something so obvious as my innocence. Who else could it be but the Devil?

The attitudes of possession are democratic most of the time. Some go out of their way to share. Some go out of their way to possess. "New York" (an inmate) thinks the world owes him. One morning he argued with "Big Man" (another inmate) over a Danish—not his, Big Man's. Big Man offered him the Danish, but New York said, "No, I want a HBE" (hard boiled egg).

Big Man said, "Hey, man, if you want the Danish, you can have it, but you ain't getting my egg and that's it."

New York—much, much smaller (60 pounds)—mouthed off and, sadly, could not understand Big Man's logic of a gift. Needless to say, there was no fight.

Next day: same circumstance, different people. Trini, a very quiet, giving person. New York wanted his Danish. To make a long story short, he punched Trini over the Danish. If he were starving—maybe. But he had three or four rolls on his plate which he hadn't eaten. I talked to him about this bullshit, lightly, because I couldn't understand his logic. . . .

I just returned from my Friday night "under-the-glass" (separated by partition) visit with Bobbie, Tiffany, and Carol Weber (a close friend from our church). It was as emotional as last time, when my wells were constantly filled. In jail, emotions are circumvented by complacency and something besides saltpeter they put in the Kool-Aid.

When I talked to Ron Strauss today, excited to tell him about some "points of law" I found in the library, he, being the friend he is, told me that I was grasping for any kind of break to free me (other than the truth, which is what it should be). . . . Tuesday, my motion for a new trial comes up. Despite the obvious facts (which will be sidestepped), it will (in general opinions) be turned down, leaving me with the grand jury hearing deal; if I cooperate, they will drop the mandatory minimum (15) which will allow me to get a bond (I pray). I haven't made up my mind yet about cooperating, but my family comes first, next to the Lord.

Saturday, November 27, 1982

It's Saturday night. The radio blasting a song called "High Hopes."

I prayed and wept today. My daughter, close as we've been since her birth, looked at me as if she didn't know me.... I wish some of the people who are responsible for me being here—Yoss, Havens, Donaldson, Gable, Victor—could experience the kind of justice and punishment they hand out. I'm sure some attitudes would change, which would be good for the whole system. It seems at times that Black men from 18 to 40 are being taken out of the reach of understanding and put behind bars. Not to say that there aren't some who obviously belong here. By the same token, there are some who do not....

Someone made some "buck" (wine) which is a three- or four-day process which creates a bread-distilled edition of the Joy Juice of the 4077th. It does not look sanitary enough for me. But in here— what does?

Sunday, November 28, 1982

Tonight, another prison flick, *The Getaway*. Last week, *Escape from Alcatraz*. This type of movie seems to hold a charismatic effect on people who have been up the road before or are here in jail again. Personally, I'd rather see something funny. They all seem to be reminders of where I am.

If I were not here "on the house" (unjustly), I might be thinking about escaping myself, which would make me just what they would like me to be—on the run. I don't run from God, so why would I run from man.

On November 30, Judge Gable denied my motion for a new trial. Although I had anticipated this, it was still a jolt. Short of cooperating with the grand jury or naming names to Yoss, my only hope now was an appeal to the Third DCA. That would take a year or more to be decided.

After the judge ruled, Strauss's partner Phil Glatzer made a special visit. Phil was the firm's highly regarded appellate specialist. He told me that an appeal might very well fail and reminded me that I could be going to jail for fifteen years. "You don't want to put all your eggs in one basket, Gene," he advised. "Maybe you should work out a deal with the State."

"Well, Phil," I said, "I don't have no eggs and I don't have no basket. All I've got is Strauss and you."

I couldn't understand why the State was still interested in making a deal. "If the State suddenly had compassion for me it should admit its wrongdoing and entrapment," I continued. I told Phil I was confident that I'd eventually be exonerated. "I want to appeal the case."

So life went on. Bobbie and the kids would visit. Normally this was "under glass," but occasionally we had contact visits. Tiffany was growing so fast. She seemed to have a new tooth almost every time I saw her, and she was almost ready to walk. It was tough—knowing she was so close, but that she might be fifteen years old by the time I got out.

I organized Bible study classes. I visited the law library. I lifted weights. I gave interviews—ABC's *20/20* shot a feature. And I periodically feuded with the guards.

Another diary entry.

Monday, December 6, 1982

Hassles! It seems that it's becoming difficult to avoid hassles which seem to involve the principles of daily existence. Tonight, while watching the *Monday Night Football* game, I had or shall I say *we* had another incident with the "Hardy Boys" (guards Mason and Canfield). This time it was mainly Canfield.

Terry Towns was real sick. He had been throwing up and when you hold onto these toilets (piss jackets) you have to be sick. Anyway, at about 9:30 p.m., someone started banging the steel door with a wooden scrub brush to get the guards to come down to the cell. He was banging too hard and too much. I told him to cool it, that they wouldn't respond if he kept making so much noise.

First, Mason came down. Then after everyone told him what the problem was (Terry was sick), he left. Twenty-five minutes later, Canfield comes to the bars outside on the catwalk bitching. From a safe distance, he slammed the little pill (medicine for Towns) down on the ledge of the bars, indicating his attitude, which pissed everybody off.

So he began to voice his view on the matter, stating that, "I'm not a doctor and neither is anyone else." The remarks started back and forth between the bars and that's when I got up, walked to the bars, and tried to mediate the situation. One thing led to another—

then it became Canfield and I with the rest of the fellows as my backups and/or witnesses. Canfield insisted on calling me "Dad." I insisted on calling him an "asshole." Meanwhile, poor Towns, looking like the picture of death, still needed to see a nurse or a doctor. I suggested that instead of jacking his jaw, Canfield should take Towns down to the clinic or bring the nurse up.

(Towns was eventually taken to the clinic.) I anguished all night about the incident, saying, "Here I go again, 'Mister Controversy.'"

Mister Controversy and Mason had more than one confrontation. Once Mason told a prisoner to sit down. The prisoner refused. "I don't have to," he said. "I believe in God and only God will tell me when to sit."

"Well, here, I'm your god," Mason replied.

I jumped in. "Hold it. You're telling him you're god? Yeah, with a small "g," spelled backward—that's what you are: a dog." He wrote me up for verbal disrespect, which meant I was reprimanded.

Still the bull in the ring, I was written up several times. Normally, this information is not made public. *Normally.* Someone from the corrections department gave my jailhouse record to the *Miami Herald*—which had never been kind to me anyway—and there it was in the newspapers.

The day after the scene involving Towns, which we referred to as the "Oxbow Incident," I began teaching my classes to juveniles. In this capacity I worked closely with Russ Buckhalt, who had already become a friend, confidant, and somewhat of a protector. I don't mean to suggest that I got special treatment from Russ. I didn't. He did everything by the book, down to opening the door from the cell block to the catwalk. He made me play by the rules, but he also made the guards play by the rules. Unlike many in the county administration, he stood up for me from day 1.

Russ asked me to work with juveniles because he thought it would help both them and me. He felt I could serve as a positive influence with the kids aged 13 to 17 who had "graduated" from the Juvenile Corrections Center to Dade County Jail. At the same time, he realized that such involvement would be far better for me than sitting in my cell and going to waste under the guise of punishment

Physically speaking, Russ was an unassuming man, a pipe smoker given to wearing sleeveless V-neck sweaters. He was in his mid-thirties and rather short. He looked like a young Phil Donahue. Raised in Georgia, where much of the population still yearns for a return to the Confederacy, Russ had married a Hispanic woman and quickly learned the value of adjustment.

Russ was genuinely concerned about the juveniles, who were sequestered on the jail's tenth floor. I termed their quarters a "farm club" for the big leagues of crime. The kids were primarily Black or Cuban, with only a few Anglos. Rodney, Malcolm, and the rest— these young men already had the faces of hardened criminals. Youthful innocence had been replaced by hostility and aggression. They were wild. It wasn't hard to figure out why. If you grow up in the jungle, odds are you're going to behave like Tarzan.

I taught a paralegal class, instructing the kids how to get up on the law so they would know their rights. I didn't want them to fall into the same jackpot I was in. They didn't have the knowledge, experience, education, or big-gun attorneys that I had—and look how I had ended up. They were starting with an even bigger disadvantage.

"Take an active interest in your cases. Work with your attorneys," I told them. They didn't seem particularly receptive. "*Listen!* Do you know why you're here?" I said. "It's because the juvenile court says you've been over there so many times they don't want to fuck with you anymore. You're in Dade County now. And when you're in Dade County that means they want you to do some serious time. This is serious business, motherfuckers."

It took time, but we developed a rapport. Some of them confided in me that they had been beaten by the guards. A little snooping around revealed that the guards had been bringing studded belts from home and banging away. A kid would say, "Hey, I'm glad the Dallas Cowboys lost," and a guard would come in and break his nose.

A guard would say, "Turn that light out."

"Okay."

"I said, 'Now.'" And again the guard would beat the kid.

I suppose the guards figured nobody would ever find out about it.

I told the kids, "Don't ever talk smart to those guards again. Always question them. Ask, 'What did I do to deserve this?' And say, 'I *feel* like you're doing this to me.' Always be plausible and always remember what they said. Write down everything they say and give it to me. I'll give it to Russ Buckhalt and he'll give it to the chief and then we'll get something done. But don't fight 'em with your fists. Fight 'em with the pen and the paper."

The kids got proficient at this quickly. They started bringing me reports. I took the reports to Russ. An investigation was launched. As a result, all the guards were moved from that floor.

This didn't sit too well with most of the guards. A sergeant sent me a note that read, "Morris, we're gonna make it tough on you the rest of the time you're here and when you go up the road."

My response: "Every molecule is quivering over the prospect of what you can do to me."

What they could do to me was write me up for nonexistent transgressions. They claimed I beat up a kid. Not true. They wrote me up for unauthorized physical contact when I tapped Strauss's secretary Debbie on the knee when she visited to bring me legal papers. They even wrote me up for trying to escape. That was the most ridiculous of all.

Russ had started to arrange speaking engagements in the community for me. I would talk to kids about the evils of criminal activity. One day an officer drove me to a youth hall meeting. I was in the backseat of the car, clicking the pen I had for making notes. I was handcuffed. He was armed.

"What are you doing?" he asked.

"Clicking the pen." A pause, then it suddenly dawned on me what his wild imagination had concocted. "I hope you don't think I'm trying to escape. This is just a pen. You're taking me to a youth hall."

"Maybe you just better hand that pen to me."

I passed it through the mesh which separated the front seat from the back.

He wrote me up for attempted escape, claimed I was trying to jimmy the cuffs. Sure. Where was I gonna go with my mug shot? Everybody in the country, much less the county, knew what I looked like.

I had hoped for a furlough for Christmas. This incident didn't help. My appearance before the grand jury didn't either. I really didn't have any information. Besides, giving up people to the law was not my style. I ended up taking the Fifth Amendment. Now it appeared my only hope would be to win on appeal.

I almost didn't make it to the grand jury. Before I left that morning, another guy in the cell, Avery, tried to roust me out of bed and start a fight. "That sonofabitch Mercury Morris. That motherfucker. I don't give a damn who Mercury Morris is. That don't mean shit to me."

This wasn't the first time Avery had been on my case. Several days earlier, I had been interviewed by a columnist for the *Miami Herald* about life in jail. I had mentioned Avery, whose response to the question, "How ya doing?" was always: "The same, man. Three, three, and three." By this he meant, he was in jail on three kidnapping charges, three armed robbery charges, and three attempted murder charges. I had asked the columnist not to use this, but he had anyway, although he hadn't mentioned Avery by name. I had apologized to Avery. He wasn't satisfied. He had already come close to getting my goat several times. His tirade this morning got to me.

"Shit," I said to my friend McDuffie, who was watching this unfold. "To hell with this." I got up, put my tennis shoes on, and prepared to go over and take care of Avery. In fact, I'd made up my mind to kill him, because I had accepted the fact that he was going to try and kill me. This was a logical extension of the sports mentality: kill or be killed. But the stakes here were for real.

McDuffie finally calmed me down.

On my way back from my grand jury appearance, I was still thinking about squaring off with Avery. Fortunately, I never got the chance. While I was away, Avery had tried to mobilize some prisoners to sign a petition against me. Russ had gotten wind of it. Sensing that something was going to happen, he wisely had arranged for my transfer to cell 5B3. This was a much better environment, about 60–40 Black–White as opposed to the all-Black 5A3. About half the guys in 5A3 were in for murder. Not so in my new cell.

By the time my sentencing hearing arrived on January 20, there seemed little doubt that I was going to get the minimum mandatory. The matter really wasn't in Judge Gable's hands. Yoss was the only one with power to waive the mandatory fifteen years. The last effort had apparently been the *Sports Illustrated* fiasco.

Strauss arranged for several character witnesses to appear at the hearing, including Russ and my Dolphins teammate Larry Little, who by this time was the football coach at Bethune-Cookman College. They testified, as did I, that I had learned my lesson and that I could be of much better service to the community if I were not sent off to prison for fifteen years but rather allowed to continue my work with the young inmates and schoolkids whose lives I had already begun to influence. Judge Gable's, "Sorry, Merc," said it all. Her hands were tied (although she had never demonstrated that she was disposed to being particularly lenient when sentencing defendants). I did manage to get one concession. The judge did not levy the quarter of a million dollars in fines against me she could have. (I wouldn't have been able to pay; the court had already declared me indigent. Strauss was now working for me in a capacity as a special public defender.) It was at the conclusion of this hearing that Yoss and I engaged in verbal fisticuffs and I told him it was only halftime.

It would be several weeks before I actually left jail for prison. On the same day I was sentenced, I was back in the law library working on my appeal. Still reeling, I was joined at a table by a new inmate. The inmate looked around the library. The corrections officers rarely entered. None were present now. The inmate took out a pack of cigarettes and said, "Hey, Merc, I know you just got this busload of time, and I feel for you, brother. So here now, why don't you get your bump off of this."

He pulled several Marlboros out of the pack and then emptied out a gram of cocaine.

Hold it. This guy is offering you a drug on the very day you're starting a twenty. Do you want some? "No thanks, man," I said.

"Go ahead, take a bump."

I suddenly got angry. "Hey, man," I said. "Are you high?"

"Yeah."

"Well, I'm here because of that."

"I don't know why I'm here."

"Are you high?" I repeated it three more times.

He answered "Yes" each time.

"Well that's good, because I don't ever want to be high again in my life, particularly on that stuff."

He was bewildered, almost offended.

I was certain that I would never desire, much less use cocaine again.

Shortly after this incident, Russ called me into his office. He told me that my mother was very ill, maybe dying. He had known this for a few days, but had waited to tell me until after the sentencing.

The news shocked me. My mother was only 51. She had visited Bobbie and me in the spring after Tiffany had been born and seemed her usual vibrant self. I had talked to her on the telephone several times since then and she had sounded fine. Cancer now was laying waste to her body.

I was devastated. When I had been arrested, I felt that I had let everyone down, particularly my parents. My mother had known for some time that I had been on a self-destruct course, but she had been patient, never preaching or passing judgment, trusting that I would somehow straighten up. (I later learned that when friends and relatives asked why I hadn't been up to visit in such a long time—it had been over five years—she'd say, "You wouldn't want to see him the way he is now. He's not the Gene you remember.")

I knew I had to see her. There were two major obstacles: George Yoss and money. In order for me to leave the jail, I had to get permission from the authorities, including Yoss. We were not on the best of terms. After Strauss talked to him, Yoss agreed that I could go to Pittsburgh in the custody of the Dade County officers...on one condition. I first had to apologize for the remarks I had made a few hours earlier at the sentencing hearing about catching him in a lie. Damn, I thought. Here we go with this Toby shit again. I knew I was in the right, but what was I supposed to do? Stand up for my principles and not get to see my mother, or, in effect, get down on my knees and humiliate myself.

Strauss and Russ Buckhalt arranged a meeting with Yoss in a small room at the jailhouse. When he entered, I still wasn't sure what I was going to do. He spoke first: "You probably don't even remember what you said."

"I remember exactly what I said."

Yoss sat down. I didn't say anything else for three or four minutes. The room was absolutely quiet. Finally, I stood up, looked straight ahead, and paraphrased the opening lines of the Declaration of Independence. "Sometimes in the course of human events it becomes necessary at one point in time for a man to say he's sorry," I said quickly, trying to control my anger.

Apparently this was good enough for Yoss. He granted permission for the trip.

Unfortunately, the trip was going to cost several thousand dollars. Not only did I have to pay for myself and family, I had to foot the bill for the several officers who would be accompanying me from Miami. This included airfare and a $300 per diem, per officer. Although the State had characterized me as a drug kingpin and had tried to create the impression that the $120,000 they'd brought to my house was mine, it was now understood by everyone that I didn't have a dime. My house was in foreclosure; I had hundreds of thousands of dollars in outstanding loans that I couldn't begin to pay; and now I had legal fees as well.

A reporter wrote an article about my state of affairs. All of a sudden donations for a trip to Pittsburgh started pouring in. People finally seemed to realize that I wasn't a bad guy, just someone who had messed up. Some of the money came from old friends in Pittsburgh. Some came from people in Miami who knew me—even Joe Robbie contributed $1000. But much of the money came from people with whom I had never had any contact. Steelworkers were sending portions of their paychecks. Schoolkids were sending me their allowances. And the Optimist Club of Ben Avon, God bless it, agreed to provide transportation and housing in Pittsburgh for the officers accompanying me. It was extremely moving.

As might be expected, convicted felons don't travel first class. I traveled in handcuffs and leg irons. Wherever I went, the bathroom included, the officers went, too. In Pittsburgh, we were met by more officers and, of course, the press. This entourage went to the hospital.

After I was convicted, my mother had written a letter to me in which she said she wanted the people at the jail to know that she had lived her life and wanted to go to prison for me. I hadn't understood what she had meant by saying she'd lived her life. Now I knew. I didn't even recognize her. Barely conscious, she looked so beaten, so old, shriveled up like a 90-year-old woman. The wig she was wearing could not disguise the fact that her chemotherapy treatments had caused all her hair to fall out.

When my grandmother died in 1970, my mother, who had been such a free spirit, had settled down and assumed much of the responsibility for keeping our family in order. She had worked as a nurse radiology technician. Over the years, she had risen to the top spot in the hospital in which she was now dying. I felt so sad that this fine life was being cut short, felt so helpless that I couldn't do anything for her, felt so guilty that I had let her down, felt so terrible that I would never have the opportunity to vindicate myself for her. I felt that I was growing old, too. But I didn't know if I was growing up. After I left her, I broke down and cried.

If the officers wouldn't let me out of their sight, neither would the press. The cameras were everywhere. I think they even recorded

11-month-old Tiffany's first steps. Their presence made it difficult to concentrate on the reason I had come to Pittsburgh.

While the doctors wouldn't give me a straight answer about how long my mother had to live, the nurses told me she might go at any minute. I called Strauss to see if he could arrange for me to stay a few more days. He couldn't. Unless my mother was absolutely breathing her last breath right now, I had to head back to Miami. Two days after I returned to Dade County Jail, my mother died.

Bobbie and Tiffany and I headed back for the funeral, accompanied again by several Dade County officers. (It cost about $6000 to make these two trips.) Security was even tighter than on the previous visit. We were transported to and from the airport in what the police call a "war wagon."

I delivered the eulogy at the funeral. My mother had many friends. Everyone came to pay their respects. Everyone except my dad. Although they had divorced and my mother had remarried, my dad still loved her. He was so heartbroken that he couldn't bring himself to come.

After the funeral, we went back to my mother's home. I got a chance to visit with my brother and my sisters. We had not seen each other much over the years, but we had always kept in touch. The family bond remained strong.

There were several policemen with me. The house was crowded. Everyone sat around eating chicken and sweet potato pie. My old pal Denny Edmunds was there. After a while, he and I just walked out of the house. Nobody stopped us. I don't think the cops even knew we left.

Denny and I went for a drive through Pittsburgh. I could have gone to Canada. Believe me, I thought about it. I thought it would be kind of fitting for me to find some island in the middle of nowhere and then send back a videotape of me saying, "Hey, hey, hey. Here I am."

Those thoughts lasted only for a minute. I went back to the house. I wasn't a criminal.

I wasn't a football player either. But you could have fooled my fellow prisoners. Ten days after my sentencing hearing the Dolphins played in their first Super Bowl since the glory days of the early seventies. I had never seen such excitement in the cells.

"Hey, Merc? Who do you like?"

"Think we can beat those 'Skins, Merc?"

The questions were neverending. The attempts to draw me into the proceedings never ceased. But I was almost completely detached from the hoopla. It wasn't only that I was thinking about my mother. Football seemed so distant, like a foreign land visited long ago. I watched the game sporadically and dispassionately. The Dolphins lost.

In the days before I left Dade County for prison, I continued to work with Russ's juveniles and continued to speak to community groups. I think both Russ and I somehow hoped that such activity might miraculously stave off the inevitable call that it was my turn to go up the road. One of my speaking engagements may have backfired. I spoke to a convention of sports lawyers at fashionable Inverrary. The press was there. So here I was on the news again. I'm sure more than a few viewers scratched their heads and said, "What's Morris doing at that fancy place in a three-piece suit? Didn't he get sentenced to fifteen years? Get his ass to prison."

Russ was doing his best to keep my ass at Dade County. In mid-March, he went into Judge Gable's courtroom to ask her if she would delay my departure. He hadn't even opened his mouth, when, anticipating his request, the judge spoke: "Forget it, Russ, he's going," she said.

She was right. Two days later, after a jailhouse good-bye to Bobbie and the kids, I was gone.

Prison would be different than jail, I knew. Not too long before I left, I had heard some guards sound an ominous warning. "Two months up the road and Morris will be begging to come back and tell Yoss everything he knows."

I was pretty sure they were wrong.

CHAPTER 12

LAKE BUTLER TO RAIFORD

The transition from jail to prison is a little like the transition from college football to the pros. It's not just that you get a new uniform and number. You're in the big leagues now. Just as all NFL teams have a rookie camp to orient the newcomers, so too does the Florida State Department of Corrections. Everyone entering the prison system is sent to a huge facility at Lake Butler for processing and assignment to one of the five prisons scattered throughout the state.

If you are the average prisoner, you spend six to eight weeks at Lake Butler before they send you to your final home behind bars. If you are Mercury Morris, you are out the door in four days. Four days! If I hadn't earned the nickname "Mercury" at West Texas State, I certainly would have earned it after my arrest. First, a trial in an almost unheard of seventy-nine days. Then, processing at Lake Butler in less than a week. It might not have been so bad if the State had been rushing me off to one of those country club prisons reserved for white-collar criminals. But I was going to the Ellen Morphonios Gable of Florida prisons—tough, dangerous Raiford. I remembered the words of that Dade County guard: "Two months up the road and Morris will be begging to come back...."

Raiford actually consists of two separate facilities: Union Correctional Institute (UCI), where I was going, and, directly across the New River, Florida State Prison. Florida State's East Unit houses a much used death row. Along with Lake Butler, which also serves as the prison system's medical center, UCI and Florida State make up

211

what is called the Devil's Triangle in the northern part of the state. (The northern part of Florida is as deep as the deep south gets.)

I arrived at Lake Butler on a cold March morning after an all-night drive with about twenty other inmates in a twelve-person van. We were met by the prison cops, who seemed to be right out of *Cool Hand Luke*. Big, old, rednecked crackers, they were quick to let us know that they ran the show and would just as soon kick a nigger to sleep. After meeting this "welcome wagon," I was stripped of clothes and valuables, shaved, and given my prison number, 088586.

It's my understanding that the powers that be at Lake Butler decide which prison to send you to based on your attitude, aptitude, and medical condition. One of the first orders of business was getting tested—eye test; ear, nose, and throat test; urine test. The inmates are told to line up in alphabetical order. I got my usual special treatment. "Morris, we want you in the front of each line," a guard told me. Well, Philbrick, I thought, you're in another jackpot. Phase two.

For the first few days, all new prisoners are assigned to a giant cell block. Then it's on to one of several dorms on the grounds. The cell block has about 200 double bunks. Bed time is 8 p.m. You eat, and then it's lights off. There is no television, no reading. You just lie there like a *real* prisoner.

I met some interesting people and heard some interesting stories during my brief stay at Lake Butler. There was a prisoner called "Sailor" who quickly gave me a perspective on things. "Merc, I been in this business for four years," he told me.

"Business? This is prison," I said.

"Yeah, man. But it's a business. You don't see me messing with those guards. See that one over there? He's got brass knuckles in his socks."

Some of the prisoners, Sailor told me, were no better than the guards. I could see this for myself. There were about twenty men who had been shipped to Lake Butler from other prisons for treatment of broken jaws sustained in fights. They sipped whipped Post Toasties or milk shakes through straws into mouths that had been wired shut for six weeks.

On the second night I was there, the guy in the bunk underneath me told me that he had been sentenced to sixty-six years for cocaine trafficking. "One thing about it, Merc," he said. "The cop who busted me in Lauderdale told me that Mercury Morris gave them the info. I told him I didn't know Mercury Morris. Didn't know anybody who knew you."

"Do you know Fred Donaldson?" I asked.

"Yeah."

"Well, there it is. He's the same one who set me up."

The first thing that ran through my mind was that this guy may have been a plant. But plant or not, it looked like the State was trying to scare me into pleading guilty by showing me that there would be people in the prisons who might have a grudge against me. It may sound funny, but there was still pressure to plead guilty. Even after I was sentenced and after I was in prison, Yoss held out the prospect of a bargain in return for cooperation. However, one condition was that I change my plea to guilty. This meant forfeiting my right to appeal, which I would never do. As a man and as a Black man, this was all I had left. I again remembered *To Kill a Mockingbird*, in which Tom Robinson had made a run for it instead of staying to fight.

Another inmate delivered an equally frightening message. "Hey, man. You know you had some paper hanging over your head for a while," he told me.

I knew the lingo. That meant there had been a contract out on my life! "What are you talking about?" I asked.

"That's all I can tell you. But you stood up, and now it's fine."

I had no idea why anybody would have hung paper over my head. Later, when I was at Raiford, a guy involved with an organized crime family in Tampa told me that it was because there were rumors that I knew somebody who knew something and they were afraid I might squeal. It wasn't true; I didn't know anybody.

Just as the Department of Corrections rushed me through Lake Butler, it also rushed me into the prison labor force. It was my understanding that an inmate wasn't eligible to come right off the compound and work in the kitchen. Certain hygiene tests had to be administered; results had to be analyzed. But there I was on KP duty within a day of my arrival. Prison officials don't abide by the letter of the law any more or any less than anyone else in "business"— particularly when the "feds" aren't looking. One night, when the department learned that federal inspectors were coming the next day, it put something like sixty-five inmates on a bus and rode them all over the state until the officials left. The reason? The prison was well over the maximum number of inmates. This scam, called "the rolling prison," enabled the State to avoid detection.

Kitchen duty is no prize for the trophy case. I was awakened at 4 a.m. and marched—you march everywhere—down to the mess hall. "Okay, Morris, you'll be on the serving line," said an officer. He tossed me the kind of paper hat you see in fast-food restaurants.

I started to take my place when another officer came up and whispered something to the first officer. The first officer then said, "Uh, Morris, we want you in the pot room because we need a big guy like you back there."

Believe me, this is the worst job you can have. My orders were to clean the garbage out of the giant cooking vats. This is done by scraping by hand and with a putty knife. Once you get the junk out of the vats, you have to pile it up and then wash it down the drain with a hose that could put out a two-story fire. I repeated the process while something like 1500 people were served. I'll show them, I thought. I worked hard, cleaning everything in sight. Then an inmate came up to me and whispered, "You better watch it, because I heard them talking about you. They said they were going to watch you and see how you react. Be cool, man, because they're gonna try to make you blow your cool."

Learning of this, I began to work even harder. I finished a job that normally takes three or four hours in less than an hour. When I was done, I went over to the officer, smiled, and said, "Is there anything else I can do? Want me to clean this floor? Anybody who needs help?"

He said, "No, that's okay."

If this seems out of character, I had my reasons. When count time came, I went straight to the clinic. The doctors had noted my bad neck and high blood pressure when I checked in. Now a doctor agreed that those ailments were serious enough to keep me from working. When I went back to the kitchen around lunchtime, the officers were expecting me to start busting suds. I was a little late.

"Where you been?" said the officer.

"The clinic."

I showed him the letter saying I couldn't work. He was mad and sent me to a captain.

"Well, it doesn't look like you can do much of anything, does it, Morris?" said the captain.

"No, sir. It doesn't."

"Okay. You can go." He was fuming.

I left the next day, but not before getting into a confrontation with another officer. It was my first clash in prison, but not by any means my last. I was still the bull in the ring and still hadn't found that inner peace or patience that would allow me to walk away from controversy.

The confrontation came during count time. Count time is a prison's way of taking inventory. The inventory, also known as inmates, is supposed to remain quietly in its appointed place. So you sit on your bunk and wait... and wait. When a guard does finally call your number, you are expected to spit it out.

Count time is part of the prison's repertoire for maintaining control over the prisoners, scaring them. I call such tactics the "boo game." Although the count should only last half an hour, it sometimes takes as long as three hours. At Lake Butler, the evening count began at 7 p.m. As we sat on our bunks, I noticed several of the guys were getting up and getting drinks of water, supposedly a no-no. I had been instructed to take my medication for high blood pressure at 8 o'clock. I needed water to wash the pills down. Eight o'clock came and went. Count continued and I stayed on my bunk. By 8:40, I was getting à little nervous. All the Cubans in the dorm were getting up and moving around, so I got down from my bunk to go get some water.

A cop saw me and called my name. Every time your name is called during count, you have to give your number, quickly. I decided to give mine slowly. "Zero... eight..."

"Did you say 'oh'?" the cop asked.

"No. I didn't say 'oh.' I said, 'zero.' Oh is a letter. My number starts with a number."

"You're a wise ass, huh," said the cop.

"Not particularly."

"Why are you off your bunk?"

"I'm getting water for my medication."

"Let me see your slip."

I handed him my prescription. "You can read, can't you?" I asked.

"You got a smart mouth, Morris."

"So do you."

He called a sergeant.

Instead of bawling me out, the sergeant was sympathetic. "I understand you," he said. "I used to have a big car and now I don't. I

215

had this and that, but not any more. I used to like to buy the boys a drink now and then, but I can't even afford to do that anymore. I know you were in a position where you used to have a lot of things, but now that's all gone."

He was dead wrong. Like so many people, he had fallen into the trap of equating where you are with what you have, of equating success with money. These people don't look at the Howard Hugheses, Freddie Prinzes, and John Belushis of the world. Guys who seemed to have everything to live for, but weren't happy.

Still, I appreciated the sergeant's thoughtfulness. I thanked him and went to shake his hand. "No, no," he said and retreated. I understood. Under normal circumstances, he would have been delighted to shake hands with Mercury Morris. Here, however, he was afraid that such a move might be interpreted as favoritism.

Favoritism! I left Lake Butler less than ninety-six hours after arriving there. A group of us were taken from Lake Butler to Raiford in an old bus called the Bluebird. We weren't handcuffed, but the bus door was locked from the outside. The Bluebird's windows were not only firmly secured, but painted so that you could not see out. Previous riders had scratched some of the paint off, so I had a slight view of the outside world. As we drove into Raiford, my first impression was that it looked like a big university. There appeared to be round wheels and spokes. Bicycles, I thought. Rows and rows of bikes. Wow. Everyone here has his own bike to ride because the place is so big. Great.

Right, Morris! It was razor wire that I saw. If you get caught in that stuff, I later learned, it will kill you.

Raiford is huge. There are something like 2600 inmates. There are three chow halls. One seats 1000 people, while the other two seat 500 each. For those inmates who can afford it, there is a restaurant called The Patio. There is a furniture factory, a power plant, a tree nursery, a school, and recreation facilities, and—what else?— a place where they make license plates. There's even a blood bank. Guys would donate blood just so they could have contact with the women who served as nurses there.

I was brought to the transit dorm and told that I had been assigned to live in "The Rock." The Rock was Raiford's most infamous housing unit. It featured broken windows which hadn't been repaired in decades, a pigeon population that exceeded its human one, and communal toilets which hadn't been cleaned in years. Above these toilets was etched the inscription, "Ralph Loves Earl." I looked at this and thought, Well, here I am. The Rock was stocked with the meanest, baddest, most incorrigible convicts imaginable. They were said to actually enjoy living there. This was not the place for me to start life in prison.

I immediately called Strauss. He was shocked to learn that I had been processed from Lake Butler so quickly and that I was headed for the Rock. He immediately called Ron Jones of the Department of Corrections' Inmate Movement and Control section.

"How long does it normally take to process a prisoner?" Strauss asked.

"About six to eight weeks," said Jones.

"What if I told you my client was at Lake Butler on Tuesday and he's at Raiford today?"

"That's four days!" said Jones.

"That's right."

"That's impossible."

Jones made a few calls of his own. Next thing I knew, I wasn't going to the Rock after all. "Southwest Unit," they told me.

There are plenty of apartment complexes in my South Miami neighborhood that aren't as nice as the Southwest Unit. Walking from the transit dorm to the Southwest Unit was like walking from prison to the place where I'd lived in La Mesa, California, when I had played with the Chargers. The lawn was well-manicured. The buildings were new. Everything was tip-top. I thought I had accidentally wandered out of the prison yard.

It was just as nice inside. Some inmates called their living areas "cells." I called mine a "room." There were two inmates to a room. The rooms were clean, with two single beds, a toilet, a mirror, a sink, and a medicine cabinet. You had your own key, although there was a second lock so the prison could secure the rooms electronically. The dorm was air-conditioned. You could have your own radio (I did; I still have the tapes I made in prison. No warrant required!). There was a television down the hall in a common area called the Day Room.

I was in Unit C, the honor unit. Normally, to get into this unit, you have to go through a program called GOLAB—Growth Orientation Laboratory. However, I continued to do things in an unconventional manner. I went to the honor unit first, and then to GOLAB.

My first roommate in the honor unit was a big guy from the farm country named Elijah. He was serving a mandatory quarter (25 years)

217

for murder. He made license plates. He didn't say too much, but we got along fine. We played a lot of cards together—spades. "I'm the best there is at spades," he told me.

Elijah snored. His snoring was so loud and so persistent that it kept me up. I didn't know what to do. I wanted him to stop, but I didn't want to wake him up and piss him off. My best friend at Raiford, Morgan, gave me what he promised was a sure-fire solution. "Whenever he starts snoring, just reach over and kick his bed real light," Morgan advised.

I tried it and it worked. So at least once each night, I'd kick Elijah's bed. One night Elijah rolled over, sat up, and looked me straight in the eye. "Hey, man, look. You been waking me up for three weeks by kicking my bed. I'd appreciate it if you'd stop."

I said, "Hey, I'm sorry. I thought I was keeping you from snoring."

Although our accommodations were pleasant, there was no mistaking this life with life in a California apartment complex. A walk around the compound revealed that the most popular pastimes were gambling, smoking reefer, making wine, and, for some, shooting up or engaging in homosexual activities. Add scamming and outright thievery to this list. Raiford was so big that inmates weren't allowed to carry money. Despite this there were thousands and thousands of dollars on the compound at any given time, most of it for use in gambling and buying on the black market.

Instead of money, we were supposed to use coupons which came in coupon books which you could purchase. Coupons were the accepted currency at the commissary and at The Patio. I hadn't been at Raiford a week, hadn't owned my first $20 coupon book for more than a minute, when someone stole it from my bunk. I went to take a quick leak in the bathroom, hid the book under my pillow, and poof!, it vanished by the time I returned. I couldn't have been gone for more than thirty seconds. I'd waited anxiously for Bobbie to send the money; my mouth had been watering for a real meal in The Patio. Now it was gone.

Some of the guys got a real kick out of that.

"Hey, man, heard somebody beat you for your coupon book."

"Hey, man, heard you slept on that one. Yeah, you got indoctrinated, brother."

"Only thing you got to do now is put your tennis shoe on the end of a 2 by 4 and start kicking yourself in the ass, man."

I think everyone was relieved to find that I was just as vulnerable as anybody else. Fortunately, there were a few guys who also said, "Hey, man, that's okay. I'll lend you my coupons" (although this was against the rules).

So I learned an early lesson. It was essential to find a good hiding place for your coupon book and, for that matter, anything else valuable or illegal. Some of the guys showed real ingenuity in figuring out places to hide their drugs, wine, and knives—yes, knives, or "shanks," as they are called in prison. I never had one—if you were caught with one, you were in deep trouble; besides that, they were dangerous. But plenty of guys did. For some, being armed was a way of life. They made their shanks out of silverware, putty knives, anything that could be sharpened so that it could inflict bodily damage.

I tried to distance myself from all this activity as much as possible. I gambled for cigarettes or candy, drank an occasional glass of buck. But for the most part, I directed my efforts toward self-improvement. I wanted to better myself through education, enlighten myself through religion. Such an attitude was definitely against the grain.

My spiritual awakening was somewhat interrupted at Raiford. I continued to soak up the Bible and other spiritual material. The church was okay. However, I never developed a rapport with the chaplain. He was a country boy whose main claim to fame was that he had grabbed a shotgun and joined the guards in shooting at inmates during a riot in 1971. With those credentials, it was hard for me to join hands with him and seek the Lord.

Betterment through education appeared more feasible. I immediately enrolled in a course called Substance Abuse 1 and was soon taking Substance Abuse 2 at the same time (eventually I would teach these courses). I liked the approach. The program wasn't downbeat like so many programs are. I didn't like (and still do not like) the Alcoholics Anonymous type of approach that you are diseased and will be diseased your whole life even if you never take another drink or touch another drug. I know it works for some people. But in my opinion it turns many of them into beaten people who are forced to walk on egg shells for their entire lives. I went to a few AA meetings at Raiford, but only so I could eat the donuts they served!

I had been at Raiford for two weeks, was just settling into the routine and beginning to benefit from my courses when I was called in to see the prison's director of classifications. "Well, Morris, your jacket seems to be in order. When would you like to leave?" he asked.

Apparently Inmate Movement and Control's investigation had revealed some irregularities in my processing. Now the State was in a jackpot, albeit a smaller jackpot than the one I was in. One thing I was beginning to see (and would see a lot more of before I was through): the powers that be either wanted me around for the publicity or they didn't want me around for the publicity.

"I don't want to go," I said. "I'd rather stay here."

The director was surprised. I explained that I was enrolled in certain programs and wanted to stay for at least the next ten weeks until the courses ended. I was telling the truth, but there was more to it than that. I was just getting used to how Raiford worked; the prospect of learning the ropes at another institution was not terribly appealing. Equally important, some guys had been trying to get transferred from Raiford for five, even ten, years. I didn't think it would look too good if I was moved after only two weeks. People inside and outside would say I was getting special treatment (if they only knew!) and inmates might turn against me. There was a final reason for staying: I didn't want the State to think it could break me. If they wanted to throw me Raiford, fine. I'd take it and show them.

I don't like the word "rehabilitate." In order to be rehabilitated, you have to have been "habilitated" in the first place, and a lot of guys in prison weren't... ever. But semantics aside, prison doesn't in and of itself rehabilitate anyone. Even the State realizes this. The Department of Corrections was formerly called the Department of Corrections and Rehabilitation. The last two words were dropped; no sense pretending.

More than a few of the guys I met had every intention of going back to the life of crime once they got out. Case in point: Milton Wheeler. Milton was a cocaine dealer. "Yeah, man," he told me, "this is my second fall. I didn't even want to take this one to court 'cause I figured if I get a nickel (five years), I can do that with no problem. I'll go in and take this time and of that nickel I'll probably do maybe 27 months and then I'll be out and get back into that thing, 'cause that's where the money is." That "thing" was, obviously, dealing cocaine. Milton's "falls," his periodic, inevitable trips to prison, were to him nothing more than the cost of doing the kind of business he did. Prison was a time to rest and plan for the next round of deals. There was absolutely no thought given to rehabilitation.

But if prison doesn't automatically rehabilitate you, it does offer the opportunity for rehabilitation. Most inmates, like Milton, weren't interested in that opportunity. I was.

At Raiford, GOLAB was the major vehicle for betterment. As with any program, GOLAB sounded better on paper than it looked in practice. GOLAB began in about 1976, and since that time several thousand inmates have gone through the program. Not all of them have taken the program seriously, but it is there for those who don't want to languish for their entire sentence. Although my official job at Raiford was in recreation, I was asked to be a GOLAB monitor.

As a monitor, I led discussions based on standardized reading material. We discussed the five aspects of man—the spiritual man, the physical man, the social man, the emotional man, and the psychological man. I was very proud of the work I did, but the overall program itself did have flaws. First, it was only as good as its monitors, who were inmates. Sometimes it was as if a psychiatrist who is nuts is trying to help people.

When I entered GOLAB, the head monitor was an inmate named Jerry. After Jerry finished leading one of his classes, Charlie, another inmate who had previously been head monitor, came up to him and said, "I think you need to get more input on this topic because I didn't think you did it so good."

Jerry got up and said, "Hey, you sonofabitch. You don't think I did it so good. How about if I knock you through that window."

"Okay," said Charlie, "I'll kick your ass."

"Fine. Bring it on, sucker."

And here they had just finished a discussion of peace and understanding!

Besides this problem, there was a problem in the administration of the program. I was asked to be a monitor, but it seemed my superiors wanted me to be a gofer more than a discussion leader. They had me running errands for them more than they had me working in the classroom. "Here, Morris, take these papers over there," somebody told me.

"You want somebody to deliver papers instead of teach, get yourself a track star," I said. And I quit.

I went back to work in recreation, which operated out of a large hut on the compound. I enjoyed this work. I had my own key to the hut and could lose myself there whenever I wanted. There was a basketball court and weight room, a soccer field, even an area to play chess. I just handed out weights and took care of the basketballs and other equipment. I had plenty of time to pump steel and I got into that for a while. I also got into playing basketball. One on one. My opponent was Morgan, who stood about 6-foot-4. We took our games seriously. They were very competitive and very physical.

Morgan lived two doors down from me. Like Elijah, he was serving a mandatory quarter for murder—a murder he insisted he hadn't committed. As he told it, he had had every intention of killing the victim. He had donned a disguise and had taken a knife to the guy's throat in a darkened alley when a cat startled him and the guy ran away. Later the guy was found dead, and the murder was pinned on Morgan.

Like me, Morgan was from the class of 1965. This created an instant camaraderie. Besides basketball, our main activity was arguing. It didn't matter what the topic was. Every day we'd find something to argue about.

"Well, my heart was broken over that," I'd say.

"Now you know good and well the heart is for pumping blood," he'd say.

"I'm talking about the spiritual heart."

"What's that? The spiritual heart?"

We argued so much at Raiford (and at Florida City, the prison we both later ended up at) that guards would come by and say, "Hey, you guys, watch it there."

And I'd say, "Everything's all right. We're just arguing. Leave us alone."

Pretty soon other inmates or guards would come up to the guards who knew us and say, "What's wrong with those two?"

And the guards would say, "Nothing. They're just arguing. They do that all the time."

Man, we'd start arguing in front of the canteen at about 12:30 and go at it another couple of hours by the machine shop. Then we'd take a little break, and then start arguing again. I loved it, and so did Morgan.

Morgan wasn't the only character at Raiford. There was Snake, who claimed to be my cousin. Wrong! We shared Pittsburgh as a home town, but we weren't related.

There was Cadillac. "Hey, man, I'm Cadillac, and I run the prison," he told me. "Yeah, I call all the shots."

He was one of three or four guys to make such a claim. Not a minute after boasting to me he was in charge, Cadillac was called over by a guard who said, "Hey, boy, come here and clean these papers out of our area."

"Uh, yes sir, boss," Cadillac would say. And as he did it, he added, "Anything else you want me to pick up?"

"I thought you said you called the shots," I laughed.

Charlie Norman was another character. He'd been in prison about five years when I got there. He was an extremely intelligent man, who read constantly. He ran the computers for the GOLAB people and also indulged in some extracurricular activity at the terminal. At one point, he tapped into the computer system at the prison in an effort to find out if Louis Wainwright, Florida's Secretary of Prisons, was paying his own bills and filing his taxes properly—this because Wainwright seemed to have so many perks that he didn't have to pay for.

Norman wasn't the only talented inmate. There was a fellow from Michigan who was an excellent artist. Unfortunately, he directed most of his time to ranting and raving about the homosexuals at Raiford and claimed to have slit the throat of at least one.

Homosexuals. Everyone wants to know if I was ever approached. A few people even dare to ask if I ever participated. The answers are "Yes" and "No." I was approached once and turned the offer down immediately in no uncertain terms. I never participated.

Some people may consider me a judgmental person, but when it comes to homosexuality, particularly in the prisons, I'm not one to preach. I briefly had a homosexual roommate—his nickname on the compound was "Honeybuns." We got along okay, but our life-styles were so different that I moved out. I didn't condone Honeybuns's life-style, but I understood it. There are some inmates who have been in prison since they have been 14 or 15 years old, have never known a woman. That they would consummate their sexual urges with other men—the only alternative—is understandable. If they were outside of prison, they probably wouldn't act that way. Similarly, I can understand how someone who was previously a heterosexual might find another man preferable to celibacy. In fact, most of the men who take homosexual lovers do not consider themselves homosexuals; they feel they are just facilitating their own needs. I knew a kid who wrote poems about his own homosexuality. He wanted to be accepted for what he was, understood, and he wanted to be a friend. I accepted that.

223

There was another guy, Larry, who had been straight. Then rumors started to circulate. Finally, Wheeler confronted him in the chow hall. "Hey, Larry, they say you fuckin' on the compound. I ain't saying nothin' about it, because hey if you fuckin', you fuckin' and I can't do nothin' about it. I just want to know why."

"Well, it's just something I always wanted to do," Larry said quietly.

Another guy told me, "I'm 29. I've been here since I was 14. I've never driven a car, never had a date, never slept with a woman. I don't know nothing but another man's ass and calling it pussy."

There are plenty of homosexuals, or as they are called "boys," in the prison system. At Raiford, there were enough for a couple of softball teams. They called themselves "Cold Cash," and that's what they got in return for their favors. In society, homosexuals often have to go out and pay for sex; in prison it's the other way around. In fact, I'd often hear someone say, "I've got this boy I'm taking care of." That meant he was protecting him and paying him.

There was something about the homosexuality I didn't like. The exploitation factor. Some prisoners capitalized on the situation, becoming, in effect, pimps. Say a White guy or a timid Black guy came in; sensing the new man's weakness, an inmate or group of inmates might approach him and tell him they wanted his money or coupon book or they'd kick his ass. Then a cohort would come over and act as if he were protecting the newcomer. But there was a price. "Say man, I'm protecting you, so you're gonna have to do something for me if you want me to keep these guys from raping you." The "protector" may very well be grooming the kid to send him out to make money for him by screwing guys.

The guards and officers were just as bad as these conniving inmates. It seems like prison officials almost encourage homosexuality because it can be used as a lever to force inmates to cooperate or snitch—all in the name of love. I saw instances where men snitched to save their boys. Another time an officer told a prisoner, "I'm fixing to ship your boy."

"Oh, no. Don't do that."

"Well then you better bring me a shank. Bring me a shank or bring me somebody."

"Okay." The guy didn't have a knife, so he went back to the dorm and bought two. "Here, I got them. I got them."

Maybe the most amazing thing I saw was this: a guy who had

just visited with his wife was stabbed by his boy. "I'm tired of you meeting with her," the boy said, and then he took out his shank.

They rushed the guy to the hospital. He was bleeding like a pig and crying like a baby. You'd think he was crying for his wife. But he was crying for his boy. So the guards brought the boy to the hospital and the guy who'd been stabbed held his hand and said, "I'm sorry, baby. I'm sorry."

Fortunately, my meetings with Bobbie were much less eventful. It's hard to describe what a source of strength and comfort she was during this period. Without a support system like she provided, I probably would have gone crazy. I had been less of a husband and father than I should have been. That she was so forgiving and loving meant the world to me.

I was only allowed one call home a week from Raiford. Although I learned certain tricks to get around this, like calling my lawyer and then having the call transferred home, the visits were special. Bobbie came every other week. This was no small task. She had to take the bus from Miami. It left at midnight Friday and didn't get in until 8 a.m. While Maceo and Duke accompanied her periodically, Bobbie always brought Tiffany. As Tiffany was just over a year old, Bobbie would have to hold her as they rode. Thus Bobbie almost never got any sleep. When she arrived at the prison she would be frisked and searched at the gate. Then we'd visit from 10 to 3. Then she'd turn around and take the brood back on another bus which didn't get back to Miami until midnight. Not a very pleasant 24 hours.

I knew things were difficult financially for Bobbie and the kids. Strauss and his office were doing a heckuva job just delaying foreclosure proceedings so they could stay in the house, and there was little money for food and other necessities. The money from my pension had never materialized and I was still waiting for the Court of Appeal's decision on the dispute over damages in the civil lawsuit against the sanitation truck company. Only because of the kindness of our neighbors, friends like Strauss, and our church was my family able to survive. For this I am forever grateful.

Bobbie's visits kept me going. We were allowed to walk together on the compound, where there were concession stands that sold things inmates made in hobbycraft classes. The local Jaycees were there, too, taking Polaroid photographs. We talked about what Bobbie and the kids were doing and what I was doing. I kept assuring them that I would prevail on my appeal before the Third DCA.

225

Strauss and Phil Glatzer were handling the appeal, along with another lawyer I had hired, Joe Durant. Ironically, Durant had been the judge who had initially given Don Reese such a lenient sentence. When Reese violated the probation, the *Miami Herald* started calling Durant "Let 'em Go Joe." He lost his bid for reelection to an opponent who picked up on this theme and characterized him as soft on law and order.

We knew the appeal would take time. First, we had to research and file it. Then, the State had to respond. Then, we had the opportunity to reply to the State's response. Next, the court, which was extremely busy, had to schedule and hear oral arguments. Finally, the court had to research, write, and render a decision. We figured we might get an opinion in about a year, spring of 1984.

The appeal, which was filed on July 1, 1983, presented five separate points for review. These were errors which, we argued, called for the reversal of my conviction or at the least the granting of a new trial. Briefly, our points, all of which were supported by prior case law, were:

1. That Judge Gable had erred by not granting the motion to suppress in its entirety. None of the tapes should have been admitted into evidence, we argued, because they were obtained illegally and fraudulently. And further, any evidence obtained as a result of those tapes should not have been admitted under the fruit of the poisonous tree doctrine.

2. That Judge Gable had erred by not granting our post-trial motion for a new trial on the grounds that the verdicts were legally inconsistent. Our point here was that the jury had found me not guilty on two of six counts. My only defense was entrapment. So if I was not guilty on those two counts because the jury determined I had been entrapped, I should have been found not guilty on all counts. The verdicts were contradictory. Remember, while awaiting the jury's verdict, I had been momentarily buoyed when word came that they wanted to know more about the entrapment defense. Now I realized that the jury just plain hadn't understood how the defense worked.

3. That Judge Gable had erred by failing to allow us to call Eugene Gotbaum as a witness. Here Judge Gable had ruled that Gotbaum's testimony about Donaldson's drug use and his intent to set

me up was hearsay. **But**, we argued, the testimony was an exception to the hearsay rule because it demonstrated Donaldson's intent to entrap me.

4. That Judge Gable had erred by denying a mistrial based on Yoss's misleading and inflammatory statements in his closing argument.

5. That Judge Gable erred by denying an evidentiary hearing to enable me to prove that the mandatory sentence was unconstitutionally applied.

In reality, we thought the first three arguments all had a good chance of winning over the Appeals Court. The last two points weren't as strong.

I talked to Strauss quite often while the appeal was being prepared, and he periodically visited, usually in conjunction with a television interview. These interviewers, as well as the magazine and newspaper reporters, invariably asked me the same question: "How does it feel to be facing fifteen years?"

My answer was always the same: "I don't look at it that way. I can't do fifteen years before I can do fifteen minutes, and I'm not going to spend the next fifteen minutes thinking about the next fifteen years."

Strauss's first visit was in April, about five weeks after I had arrived and shortly after the first of several stabbings at Raiford which were to continue through the spring. The official story was that a guard in the Rock had just been minding his own business when an inmate stabbed him to death. The real story was that the guard had been showing off for some of his buddies who were new recruits. Showing off consisted of shoving a broom handle up a homosexual's ass.

"I'm killing you for that this afternoon," the homosexual had said.

Sure enough, later in the day his friends told several guards, including the offender, that there was an illegal moonshine operation going on in K Wing. The guards ran over there. It was a setup. When the guards arrived, the stabbing began. Several inmates—young gladiators afraid of nothing—took their shanks out on several guards. The guard who had roughed up the homosexual died, but not before he tried to run to the control room, prison's equivalent to a nurses' station, manned by a sergeant. The sergeant inside knew that if he let the guard in he'd also be letting in inmates with knives. He wouldn't open the door.

"We're gonna kill you, too," the inmates told the sergeant through the door after they took care of his fellow employee. "Every month we're gonna kill some more of you crackers."

This incident led to a prison-wide lockdown. Just being in prison, you're locked up. A "lockdown" occurs when everyone is ordered back to their rooms and electronically locked in. The officials then conduct a count. After the count, the lockdown continues until the warden determines that things have settled down enough to open the doors. So you sit and wait...and wait...and wait.

There was one other lockdown while I was at Raiford. It, too, resulted from another guard stabbing in the Rock. It took place on the evening of June 20 and continued all the next day. This seemed fitting, since June 21, the beginning of summer, is literally the longest day of the year. We were allowed out of our rooms only for controlled feeding—five at a time could go get chow.

There wasn't much to do so I took pen to paper:

Some people in the (death row) unit have no visitors or phone calls for ten to fifteen years. They come out once a day for one hour by themselves, then back to lockdown. This is the experience that has been visited on us.... Indefinite (lockdown) is a good way to describe our state of affairs. Rumor has it that we will be locked down until Monday. Today is Thursday. Well, I hope it's just a rumor.

It is now 8:45 p.m., the final minutes of a happening which comes once a year, when the sun is closest to the earth in its rotation. So in between now and the winter solstice, which marks the longest night and shortest day, I pray to God that I will be home with my family reflecting on where I've been and why! Although "why" will always be a topic of conversation.

Unfortunately, come the next winter solstice, I wasn't home. But I wasn't at Raiford either.

CHAPTER 13

DCI

The Longest Day made me ask myself if I wanted to spend too many more nights at Raiford. The stiffening of the rules that followed the incident answered the question. The place was put on the equivalent of a red alert. Extra locks, extra razor wire, and extra fences were installed. It was impossible to pass from one end of the compound to the other without going through metal detectors. The guards were understandably tense, jumpy, and hostile. So were the inmates.

Because of the "mix-up" that had sent me there so quickly to begin with, I still had a standing invitation to pack my bags whenever I wanted. I decided it was time to move on. My request for a transfer was approved, and in August, 1983, after about 23 weeks in the Devil's Triangle, I was on my way to a prison that was only 35 miles from home.

Florida City, which is also known as Dade Correctional Institute, or DCI, is a sandbox compared to Raiford. It is not nearly as regimented. At first, that seemed appealing. But as the next year unfolded, I wasn't always certain I'd made the right choice in going there. A football analogy sums it up: Even though Coach Shula and I hadn't always seen eye to eye, I had recognized that his regimented system was necessary and a key factor in the Dolphins' success and my success. In contrast, Tommy Prothro's unregimented San Diego Chargers squad was a disaster. Raiford, like the Dolphins, ran like a machine. DCI, like the Chargers, sputtered.

I had only had a few scrapes with the guards at Raiford, but at DCI the bull was back in the ring. As a result, I sank as low as I have ever been. Fortunately, God had other plans for me. I eventually overcame myself and the adversity which I was facing. In short, I grew up.

DCI was about one-fourth the size of Raiford. Shortly after I arrived, another prisoner described the population to me in the following way: "Morris," he said. "In this place you have 650 people. Five hundred fifty are snitches. Fifty are homosexual. The other fifty are good men." He proved to be pretty accurate, although he forgot to point out that DCI had been built to house only 350 inmates and was severely overcrowded.

There were seven dorms, lettered A to G. These dorms resembled the Southwest Unit at Raiford, with one exception. DCI had originally been designed as a women's prison. Therefore, there were no urinals. Unfortunately, a surprisingly large number of inmates didn't have the decency to lift up the toilet seat when they went in to the bathrooms to take a leak. The seats were always a mess. This quickly became my pet peeve. "What sonofabitch did this?" I'd bellow. "What nigger or spic? Because it can't be a man. Men don't do these things. It's gotta be an asshole."

As at Raiford, two men were assigned to a small room; again, you had your own room key. Initially, I was in F-Dorm. This was the most casual, hippest dorm in the place—the North Miami Beach, so to speak, of DCI. It was also extremely cliquish. There was the Sanford and Son group, the Archie Bunker's Place Group, and the Chico and the Man group. Translation: for the most part, the Blacks hung out with the Blacks, the rednecks hung out with the rednecks, and the Cubans hung out with the Cubans.

As was happening in greater Miami, the Cuban population at DCI was growing dramatically. This growth was a direct result of the 1980 Mariel boatlift, Fidel Castro's successful effort to send many of his country's troublemakers to the United States. DCI's superintendent was a Cuban woman who called the Mariel refugees, "my children." Most of her administrative staff was also Cuban. This led to an even greater influx of Cuban inmates and Cuban culture. Pretty soon monogrammed cabana shirts were the fashion of the day. Even though it was illegal, the Cubans started cutting their shirts, tapering the sleeves, and putting double-breasted buttons on.

We monitored the increase in the Cuban population by counting the different kinds of loaves of bread in the commissary. When I first got to DCI, the commissary bought 100 loaves of bread a week,

70 loaves of regular bread and 30 loaves of the Cuban variety, which resembles French bread. Within a short time, the figures had reversed themselves.

I had no real complaint with the shift in fashion or bread. But the Cubans brought more than their cabana shirts to the compound. They brought cocaine.

Cocaine dealing was the most nefarious of the illegal activities taking place on the compound, but there was plenty else going on. At DCI we were permitted to have money, and there was a complex black market economy. You want paint or a table to decorate your room? Fine. See the guys who work in maintenance. You want air conditioning? It can be siphoned off and directed to your room for a small fee. You want cigarettes? Fine. Go to the window where they serve coffee and instead of paying the usual fifteen cents for a cup, add a nickel if you want a generic cigarette, a dime if you want a "long." You want your clothes done every day? (A must if you worked out like I did.) Fine. That will be three dollars a week and one of the inmates in the laundry will take care of you. Wine? That's not orange juice in that orange juice carton you just picked up at the canteen window. The winemaster comes down every Wednesday with a concoction of yeast and peaches, orange juice and strawberries, bread and anything else that he can think of.

Man, of course, does not live by bread alone. The food in the prison was terrible, the portions small. Cleanliness was next to impossible. That wasn't brown sugar in the oatmeal. That was a family of maggots! This depressing state of affairs encouraged, no *necessitated*, an extensive food smuggling operation. The inmates working in the kitchen or the canteen made a living selling everything from corn flakes to sides of beef. Yes, sides of beef.

We would buy food and either cook it right in the canteen when the guards weren't looking or smuggle it back to our rooms and stick it in a crock pot. I cooked everything from my favorite—steak, green peppers, and onions—to (when the Cubans were running things) black beans and rice and plantains.

The guards knew that this was going on. Sometimes they gave us a pass; sometimes they cracked down. One time I was caught trying to sneak back to my room with a milk shake and some contraband cinnamon rolls that I had bought at the staff kitchen. A guard stopped me. "Hey, man, you're playing me too close," he said.

"What can I say? You caught me," I said.

But while he was catching me, one of my buddies went by with five or six chickens under his coat.

I was reprimanded for playing the guard "too close." The punishment could have been more severe. Once, one of my good friends at DCI, Lenny Campagno, got sent to "jail" (our term for solitary) for three weeks when he was caught cooking two chickens in his room.

My friend Morgan, who also ended up at DCI, was a master smuggler. He'd have 10 pounds of meat hanging under one arm of his overcoat, 10 pounds of chicken under the other, and he'd walk right up to the cops, "Hey, what's going on, sergeant. I know one thing: you guys are always on your job. Can't get away with nothin' around here. I'll be glad when I get a chance to go somewhere where I can at least get away with somethin'."

And the sergeant would agree, "That's right, boy. You can't get away with nothin'."

My favorite smuggling story involved a fellow who *didn't* get away with nothin'. He was sneaking back to his room with about fifty eggs under his shirt and pants when old Lazenby, a wily redneck guard, caught sight of him. "You're lookin' a little fat in the middle there," Lazenby said.

"I ain't got nothin'."

"Hey, man, you know I gotta shake you down."

Lazenby shook him down hard. Splat! An egg cracked and its insides started oozing out. Splat! Splat! Splat! Splat! By the time Lazenby was done, fifty raw eggs were streaming down the smuggler's pants. "Well, you're right. You ain't got nothin'," Lazenby laughed. But we had the last laugh. As Lazenby congratulated himself on his victory, a couple of other inmates carrying an entire side of beef from the main kitchen snuck by.

You quickly learn the tricks of the trade—the "trade" being life as an inmate. For example, you never put money in your right-hand pocket. If you're right-handed that's the pocket you're likely to put your hand in, and you don't want to bring money out in front of other inmates. Similarly, you never agree to make change for guys. They're really asking to see your bankroll. A final tip: keep your cigarettes in your socks.

Life at DCI was not all fun and games. Case in point: Suarez versus Mullin. Hector Suarez was my roommate. He was in on a drug-related armed robbery charge. Suarez was a good man, a standup guy. He had a little of that Latin temper, but he rarely displayed it. Jim Mullin was a fiery Irishman in prison for life with a minimum mandatory of three years for second-degree murder. White passion. He had killed a guy he had caught in bed with his wife.

I played backgammon with both of these guys. I could beat Suarez pretty easily, but Mullin and I usually played to a tie. It figured that Mullin could beat Suarez and he usually did. One night, however, Suarez beat Mullin best out of five games and won five dollars. Mullin refused to pay. Suarez came to me and related the conversation which had ensued:

"My brother," Suarez had said to Mullin, "if you need five dollar I give it to you. But we play for five dollar and you owe me."

"I'm not paying 'til we play more," said Mullin.

"We play more, but, my brother, you must pay."

"I'm not your brother."

"Okay, my friend."

"I'm not your friend," snarled Mullin. "You don't want to play no more, you don't get paid."

"Okay. So you don't want to pay me?"

That's right."

After Suarez told me the story, I said, "I'm sure he'll pay you tomorrow, man. He's probably just pissed that you beat him."

Suarez cut me off. "Hey, Morris. No talk anymore. My mind is made up already. I know what I have to do." His honor had been violated. In prison, you don't do what Mullin had done.

"Forget it, man," I said.

Curfew prevented any confrontation that night. The next morning, as soon as the doors opened, Suarez was up and out of the room, on his way to get his shank where he had hidden it. He got it, went to Mullin's room and knocked on the door. Mullin answered. Suarez immediately thrust the knife into his throat and abdomen. Then Suarez ran.

Mullin was a big man, 5-foot-10, 200 pounds. He was hurt bad, but he started after his attacker. Suarez was just a little guy, 5-foot-6, 140 pounds. If Mullin caught him, he could do some damage. But Mullin stopped when he realized how much blood was spewing out.

Mullin was taken to the hospital. Suarez was caught and taken to Dade County Jail to await a hearing on these "fresh charges" of attempted murder. There was no doubt that Suarez had meant to kill

Mullin. In prison, you learn that there's a particular vein that you go for if you want to take someone out; Suarez had gone for that vein.

Prison is like Mayberry RFD. Everybody knows everybody and everybody knows everybody's business. But although everyone had seen Suarez running, there were no actual witnesses to the stabbing besides Mullin. And he wasn't in shape to identify anybody. So the Cubans that hung out with Suarez came to me with a plan. "Suarez is your room partner and friend," they said. "Mullin is your friend, too. We want you to go to Mullin and tell him if he testifies against Suarez, we'll finish the job on him."

Great, I thought. Now we'll have a war between the Cubans and the rednecks.

This was my first experience as a mediator. I went to see Jimmy Carter. Not the former President, just Mullin's friend. I relayed the message from the Cubans. Instead of being angry, Carter said, "I don't blame them." Mullin had broken an unwritten code by disrespecting Suarez.

When Mullin got out of the hospital, we had another meeting. I represented the Cubans again. All of Mullin's friends were calling him an asshole and telling him he deserved what had happened. Mullin agreed not to testify against Suarez. "I got no problem with that," he said. "I don't even know who stabbed me." The prison officials were furious.

I don't think Mullin clammed up because he was afraid. There was something else going on here. The State has an obligation to protect all inmates while they are in prison. If the State is negligent in fulfilling this obligation, an inmate may claim that his civil rights were violated and sue for monetary damages. Having been stabbed, Mullin had the makings of a nice lawsuit against the Department of Corrections.

So what happened? Sometimes when the State is in the jackpot, as it was now, justice goes out the window. Although Mullin had been given a life sentence for the murder he committed, he was eligible for parole after serving the minimum three years. He had already been in for a little more than three years. Next thing we knew, he was paroled and on his way home.

As he was leaving, I came up to him and said, "I'm glad you're getting out."

He smiled. "I'll tell you something, Eugene. What you did (by trafficking) was a crime. You really messed up. *I* only killed somebody, but *you* were messing with those drugs. If you had killed somebody, you'd be going home like I am!"

How was I going to get home? I had been struck by the fact that the fence that surrounded DCI and prevented me from walking off the grounds looked similar to the fence that surrounded the Orange Bowl and kept the fans from walking in. *Looked* similar. When I was with the Dolphins, I'd sometimes walk over to that fence. Fans would come up and stick pencil and paper through in the hopes of getting my autograph. If I went too close to the fence at DCI, I was warned, I might get my head blown off. Man, look what surrounds you in a lifetime, I thought. But what is it that makes this fence so different than the Orange Bowl fence? Nothing, other than your circumstances. It's not the fence holding you in, Philbrick. It's the charges. I realized then that just as I had had to make things happen at the Orange Bowl, I now had to make things happen at DCI in order to survive and get home.

I had visited the law libraries at both Dade County Jail and Raiford. At DCI, I became a full-fledged jailhouse lawyer. In part, I have the State to thank for that. I was assigned to work in the law library as a clerk. Actually, this was my second job at DCI. My first job, which lasted only three months, involved helping to run a reading project which was part of a nationwide literacy program. It was a bureaucratic mess. I got neither the cooperation nor the materials I needed. Frustrated, I quit.

Working in the law library, I learned how to find cases that were helpful to my cause. I became somewhat of an expert on both entrapment and the rules of evidence. In light of the cases I was finding, I couldn't understand why Judge Gable had allowed any of the unauthorized tapes into evidence. Nor could I fathom why she had refused to let Gotbaum testify. Whenever I found a case, I sent it to Strauss. I knew that he probably had already seen it, but I wanted to let him know that I wasn't giving up, wanted to keep him on his toes.

Strauss visited regularly, usually to bring someone from the media down for an interview. He later explained that he felt it was important to keep my case in the newspapers, because if we ended up losing our appeal, it might be public opinion that would sway the governor to grant me a pardon.

I would describe our relationship at this time as love-hate. We had become very close. Strauss was emotionally as well as professionally involved not only with me but with my family. He and his wife had, for example, brought Bobbie and the kids a turkey on Thanksgiving. At the same time, I could get quite angry if I didn't think he was giving undivided attention to my case or any problems I might be having at the institution. "This is to drop you a line," I'd write him. Then, I'd cross that out and write, "This is to drop you off the side of a building if you don't get your ass down here to see me." He would respond that he thought his time could be better spent working for me in the office. I thought he should be doing both. When you're in prison, you tend to forget that people have other things on their minds besides your predicament, other obligations.

Actually, a surprisingly large number of people were thinking about my predicament. I received thousands of letters. Some were from school kids I had visited when I was at Dade County Jail (this would continue later, when I would leave DCI to make speeches), but most were from total strangers. In general the letters wished me well, encouraged me to hang tough, and expressed the hope that I'd be out soon. Very few were judgmental; several came from individuals who themselves had experienced difficulty with alcohol or cocaine.

My champion correspondent was a man by the name of Merlin John Schipper. He began writing me when I was first convicted, and he never stopped. Merlin John is from the class of '68, a Vietnam veteran. If you had to pick a life-style exactly the opposite of the life-style in Miami, you probably couldn't do any better than picking Merlin John's hometown, Lamar, Iowa. A typical letter from Merlin John would include a picture of his camper, the new room addition, and the bunny rabbits his two kids were raising. He worked at the Wells Blue Bunny Ice Cream Factory.

"Well, here I am tonight," he'd write. "I walked home from the factory. It's such a lovely night out. It's so great to be alive. I'm getting off at four in the morning, so as I walk home, I feel the briskness of the air and my nostrils open up as I gather in the air. It's just a beautiful night. I go home and I get in bed, and then I say, 'Wait a minute. I forgot I drove the car to work!'"

Some of his letters were less conventional. Once he sent me what he claimed was the "world's biggest letter." It was about 9 feet by 9 feet. This unorthodox correspondence caused me to get called down to the prison office. So did the "world's longest letter," which Merlin

John wrote on about 90 feet worth of rolled up adding machine paper. And so did the "picture letters" he sent me. These picture letters included mounted clippings from magazines. This was Merlin John's response to the prison's refusal to forward the complete magazines that he tried to send me. Sometimes the clippings might be about Iowa or Indians. During Black History Month he sent me literature about famous Blacks from the midwest.

Merlin John wrote me over 300 letters. I'm embarrassed to say, I wasn't very good about writing back. He didn't seem to care. He just started keeping score on the envelope. He'd write something like 213 to 7. "Well, Gene," he once wrote, "it's been 27 months that I've been in your Afro, and if you think that for any reason you're going to get me out of there, you're wrong, because I'm with you until we get through this."

We'd talk on the phone occasionally, and in 1984 he came down to Florida and visited me at DCI. I insisted he stay at our house. He couldn't believe it.

Merlin John was a big, friendly, generous man right out of the country's heartland. He drove around Miami waving at everybody he saw, shouting, "Hey, how ya doin'?"

Nobody waved back. Finally Maceo told him, "Hey, if you're waiting for the people around here to wave, you can forget it, because this is Miami. If they wave at you, they might be waving with a gun."

I don't like to wear a lot of jewelry—my wedding ring, one of my Super Bowl rings, and a watch. But since Merlin John visited I have proudly worn a simple, inexpensive religious medallion he gave me. His friendship meant so much to me that the medallion is the only thing I will ever wear around my neck.

I may have been a lousy correspondent when it came to Merlin John Schipper, but when it came to Madame Dumas, I was *tres bien*. Madame Dumas was the wife of Claude Dumas, one of my DCI roommates. Claude was a Haitian hustler serving time for dealing cocaine.

Claude wanted Madame Dumas to visit him at DCI, but they had not been speaking to each other since he had accused her of sleeping around in his absence. Still, he confessed he wished she would visit and bring their kids.

"Then write her and tell her," I counseled.

But each time he started a letter, his temper got the best of him. A typical letter might begin: "I miss you so much. I want you to visit." But it would quickly deteriorate into: "Bitch, I know you been fuckin' this guy and that guy. When I get hold of you..."

"Hold it, Dumas," I said. "You expect her to come when you've written something like that? You threatened her, man. Now you want her to come down and take a chance that you may whip her ass in the visiting park?"

He asked me to write a letter that would persuade her to come. À la Cyrano de Bergerac, I wrote six. Claude copied them over and sent them. Madame Dumas eventually came. During her stay, she asked me if I had written the letters. I confessed.

"I was wondering because I know somebody had to help Dumas with that. That was not his language," she laughed.

The good news was that Madame Dumas kept coming. The bad news was that she started smuggling in reefer which Claude started selling on the black market. "Hey, man, I got that Raw, I got that Awesome," he'd brag.

"Hey, man, you don't even smoke," I reminded him.

"Don't you be tellin' that to no one," he said.

"Well, just don't sell it out of the room," I warned him.

"Oh, no, man," he promised.

Next thing I knew there was a knock on our window. Dumas knocked back. "He wants a nickel bag," said Dumas, deciphering the code.

"Holy shit, man. Will you stop that. That could be a cop out there," I said. He finally moved the operation.

While Dumas would entertain his wife, another inmate, Rubio, was entertaining his wife...and his mistress...and his girlfriend. Three at once. Rubio got himself all dolled up for these sessions—pressed blues, shined shoes, slicked hair, shades, his gold teeth shining.

How do you handle three women at once? With great difficulty. Within a month after Rubio's release he was shot and wounded by two unhappy paramours. He wasn't the only inmate to experience violence upon his release. Dumas was killed gangland-style six weeks after he got out.

I didn't have the woman trouble that Dumas or Rubio had. Bobbie was wonderful. Now that I was closer to home, she was able to visit more often, and it was easier to bring the kids. She had a good support system at home thanks largely to our church, which continued to provide money. My grandfather and stepgrandmother also pitched in. Smitty, the man who had raised me, had actually been my mother's stepfather, my stepgrandfather. Jimmy Spencer, whom I had also been close to in Pittsburgh, was my mother's father. He and his wife, Louise, or Mama Weesie, came down to stay with Bobbie around Christmas of 1983 and stayed for several weeks. They helped with the kids and helped in the house.

Jimmy was a real character. He was somewhere in his middle seventies, but he claimed he was much younger. He'd be sitting down, then all of a sudden he'd stand up and start sparring with you or tell you he was thinking about shooting some hoops. Although he was almost legally blind, his favorite pastime was girl watching. Whenever Maceo and Duke visited me at DCI, we'd laugh about how Jimmy was always out there looking over the field. "Hey, I like them young girls," Jimmy said.

Running a close second to girl watching was cooking. Jimmy insisted on doing all the cooking. "Well, all right, Louise," he'd say to my stepgrandmother, "I want you to go out and get me some pigeon peas and some long grain rice."

Mama Weesie would do as he said. Then he'd look over the groceries. "Louise. What did I tell you to get?"

"You told me to get pigeon peas and long grain rice, Jimmy."

"That's right. And what did you get?"

"I got what you asked for, Jimmy."

"Louise, these are not pigeon peas. These are chick peas. Can't you see that?"

"I'm sorry, Jimmy. I, I didn't know." Weesie would sound truly sorry.

Jimmy would pause, then say, "Louise, with what you don' know, you could make a *new* worl'."

If I'd have had the same wonderful support from the guards on the inside that I had from family and friends on the outside, my days at DCI would have been a lot less trying. But there were several guards who had it in for me. As I was still acting like the bull in the ring, we had numerous skirmishes and more than a few battles.

To understand life in prison, it's necessary to understand the people who operate and work in the prisons. Sometimes it's hard to tell the players without a scorecard. The guards often act worse than the inmates.

I don't know what motivates a man to work as a prison guard. Maybe the idea of being able to carry a gun or nightstick or walkie-talkie appeals to a certain kind of inadequate person. Maybe the idea of being able to lord it over unfortunate inmates appeals to a certain kind of insecure person. Here's a small, but typical, example of such behavior. In order to get to my job in the law library, I had to pass through a door manned by Guard Thomas. I asked him for permission to enter. "Sure, Morris," he smiled. "All you gotta do is say, 'Hey, Boss, I gotta get to my job.'"

I bristled. "I don't say those things. I say, 'Excuse me, I'd like you to let me out so I can go to work.'"

While such an attitude was the rule rather than the exception with most guards, there were several who seemed genuinely concerned about the inmates. You couldn't take advantage of these guards, but they were willing to treat you fairly, even give you a break. The bad guards, on the other hand, contrived situations to set you up for a fall. It seemed that the older the guard, the better chance that he would be reasonable. Most of the older guards had a military background, while many of the younger guards were just punks like those serving time. Black guards were as hard to deal with as White guards, if not harder. I suspect they were trying to show their White counterparts, "Hey, I'll do a nigger worse than you." And I suspect their White counterparts' responses were, "Hey, then you're the kind of nigger we want."

The guards worked in three 8-hour shifts. Each shift as well as each guard had a special personality. This required constant adjustment on the part of the inmates. To survive, I learned to "read" my jailers. How far could you push Wallace? How close will Hamilton play you? Such deciphering was not always easy. For example, Ernie Savoya was a guard whose incarcerated son had committed suicide in prison. You might have expected Ernie to be bitter and to take things out on the inmates. On the contrary, he treated us with dignity and fairness. On the other hand, Walter Downey was a guard whose father was at Raiford (for killing Downey's mother). Young Downey directed all the hate he had for his father toward more accessible targets—the inmates at DCI.

My principal nemesis at DCI was a guard named Pitts. He was a short Black man, about 30 years old. He walked with a limp because he'd hurt himself jumping off a truck. From day 1 he was on me. Guards are in violation of Department of Corrections policy if they direct personal remarks at inmates. "You're no longer number 22, Morris," Pitts told me constantly. As if I didn't know. It had been almost ten years since I had retired. "You're number 088586.

And you ain't driving a Ferrari or BMW anymore, either. You're
not a celebrity anymore." Does that sound personal?

Violations of any number of prison regulations will land an inmate in "jail"—jail being a barren room where you are confined,
usually in solitary, and allowed out only twice a week for a shower.
My friend Lenny got 21 days in jail for smuggling those chickens
back to his room. Verbal disrespect to a guard is one of the most
popular ways to earn yourself a trip to jail. During my first few
months at DCI, I learned how far you could go in talking back to a
guard and became somewhat of a master at giving it back to taunt-
ing guards like Pitts without quite getting myself into serious trouble. I made sure I learned every rule the guards had to operate
under, and when they broke the rules I took pen to paper to let the
prison officials know.

I did get myself a few ACs—administrative confinements—for
mouthing off. This meant a couple of days under lock and key. Most
of the time, however, I managed to choose my words carefully and
be, as Pitts termed it, "in borderline disrespect."

If a guard did write you up for a violation, say verbal disrespect,
you were allowed a hearing before a prison tribunal which would
determine if you were innocent or guilty and what your punishment
was to be. Being a pretty decent jailhouse lawyer, I was confident
that if a guard *did* egg me over the borderline, I could win when I
had my day in court. (I don't know why I should have felt this way.
I hadn't won anything in court up to this point!)

Pitts and I exchanged words on a daily basis. He was always
searching my room. The beds had partially hollow poles which inmates had forever used as ashtrays. The poles were full of ashes and
cigarette butts. When Pitts searched my room for contraband—about
every other day—he'd take the poles apart and leave the ashes and
butts all over the place. He didn't have the decency to clean up.
Eventually, I started leaving him notes in all the places I thought
he'd be looking. I'd cut out the title picture from *Hustler* magazine's
"Asshole of the Month" feature. Then I'd write, "Whoever is going
through my stuff, put your face right there." I knew it was Pitts, but
I'd be careful never to put his name on the note.

I didn't have any contraband, but I was afraid Pitts might "find"
some anyway. Once he told me, "I almost found something in your
room."

"Pitts, I'm surprised you haven't put something there already."

"When I do, it's going to be something big."

"Not too big," I laughed. "Because you're not capable of thinking too big."

Pitts did write me up several times on CCs—corrective consultations. These require a talk with prison higher-ups and go into your permanent record, or "jacket." Among my violations were (allegedly) not having my hair cut and not having shaved. Failing to shave was a big deal. You were not allowed facial hairs at DCI (another way in which control was maintained over inmates). "All these CCs are going into your jacket, Morris," Pitts would tell me. "Pretty soon that's gonna stack up and you're going to look just like what's in your jacket. And I'm the man that can make that happen. I can make you look bad, or I can make you look good. That's my choice."

"If you're running this, how come you don't have any stars up on your uniform?" I asked, referring to the fact that Pitts was only a sergeant. "How come you just have those little bars on your shoulder? How come you don't have the major stuff?"

"You're a smartass, Morris, a real smartass."

"No, I'm not a smartass. What I am is a man. I was a man before I put this uniform on and a man before I put that other uniform on. If you think I'm going to buckle down to this bullshit, you have me totally confused with somebody else. I'm not intimidated by you, and I know you're not intimidated by me. I'd appreciate it if you'd leave me alone, but I know you can't do that because it's not your nature. So you'll continue to do what you're doing and I'll eventually have to go over your head to get these things taken care of. Make no mistake, I will do that. I don't claim to have a lot of power in here, but I do claim to have a whole lot of it outside of here. I've got some real big guns out there, and they don't mind taking someone to court. And you know something, I don't either."

One day Pitts apparently felt I crossed the border and wrote me up for verbal disrespect. Here's what happened. As usual, first thing in the morning Pitts came straight to my room. I was lying down. "Okay, Morris," he said. "I want you up. Time to get up."

"Hold it, Sergeant Pitts. Do you feel like it's necessary for you to come here every morning straight from your meeting and harass me?"

"It's not harassment. I'm doing my job."

"Fine. Well why don't you tell some of those other inmates who are standing around that you're *facilitating* your job right now." I always tried to talk over a guard's head. "One thing about this whole situation, Pitts: You're here every day. You trying to tell me that this isn't harassment? That you don't have something special for me? That you're not going beyond the point of duty here?"

"All right, Morris. You better take it easy now."

"Take it easy for what?"

"Because you're borderline on disrespect."

My wheels started turning. "Look, I can't *disrespect* you, because I've never established any *respect* for you in the first place. Because I respect respect, and respect has no gender and it has no rank. If you don't have any, you can't possibly get any. I'm not going to disrespect you because to disrespect you would be to disrespect myself. But I don't have any respect for you, and I don't have to have any."

Pitts wrote me up, but, in my opinion, he didn't do so honestly. His report claimed that I said something very different than I had actually said, something like, "I don't respect you. I disrespect you. The only thing you're going to get from me is disrespect."

The report also claimed that Pitts had numerous witnesses, that fifteen inmates had been standing around and could back up his statements. My response to the hearing board was: "Pitts claims he came to my room because it was his job to clear out the dorm. If that's the case, then what were fifteen inmates doing standing around. He would have had to have walked right through them to get to my room. If he was on the job like he said, he would have had them out of the dorm. But he didn't. He came right to my door, which is not facilitation but personal interpretation of his job."

Before it was time to go to the tribunal, the prison wanted to drop the charge. But I refused. I wanted the record to reflect what had happened. End result: I won.

As might be expected, the bull in the ring eventually got gored. In May of 1984, I refused to sign a corrective consultation order that Pitts had filled out on me because I thought it was a lie. This led to a confrontation with guard Downey, who frequently gave me trouble. Pitts and Downey told conflicting stories, but I was found guilty of verbal disrespect and sent to "jail" for thirty days.

When I went to jail from F-Dorm, it was a big joke on the compound. I used to say, "Hey, picture me going to jail. Picture me doing something to get to jail." I always would sing this spiritual song, "What Will You Do When the Party's Over?" Now, some of my contemporaries gathered outside my holding cell and mocked me, "Hey, picture me in jail. Picture Mercury in jail. I do. He's right there." They laughed. I laughed, too. They weren't being malicious.

I was taken to a small cell in the area of DCI called the Flattop. The Flattop housed about twenty prisoners when full, but I was alone—the equivalent of solitary confinement. I was not allowed to bring any clothes. I was given shorts, a T-shirt, and thongs. I was permitted reading material, but it had to be of a religious nature. I was allowed out of the cell twice a week to shower. Period.

I knew I had been jammed again, just as I had been jammed in Judge Gable's courtroom, but I resolved to make the best of my month. So I settled in. There's a certain monotony to solitary confinement. I'd wake up, read, do a few pushups, eat, read some more, fall asleep again, wake up for lunch, eat, read some more, etc. While this is a completely wasted time of your life, it is quiet and peaceful.

My reading material was, of all things, Charles Colson's first book, *Born Again.* I got a certain amount of solace from this. Solace from Chuck Colson! The irony was not lost on me. Here was one of President Nixon's boys who had gone to prison. In the sixties and the seventies Nixon, Colson, et al. had been my adversaries—the establishment, the makers of the war in Vietnam, the corrupters of government. Yet now I was reading Colson's book and actually seeing where he was coming from in finding it necessary to have spiritual guidance. Soon, I'd be finding it more necessary than ever.

After I finished *Born Again,* I read Colson's second book. I was beginning to find some peace, ready to ask for more religious material, when, on about my fifth or sixth day, I heard a disturbance outside my room. I periodically heard noise in the hallway. Guys in other cells would go a little crazy and kick their steel doors eighty, ninety times in succession. But this was different.

"And another damn thing, when I'm in here you better make sure that I don't see one knife that you been cuttin' meat with. I see that or I see that you been cuttin' my cheese with a knife that's touched meat, I tell you right now I'll see your ass in coat"—(that's how he pronounced "court")—"because you're supposed to respect my diet." I recognized the voice. It belonged to Bruce Simmons, DCI's ultimate jailhouse lawyer. If I was a thorn in the side of the guards, Bruce, God bless him, was an entire rose bush. "I don't eat this bullshit you all serve here," he continued. "I'm under a religious diet, and you better make sure you adhere to it."

My door opened. When Bruce came in, I saw my peace and tranquility leaving. "Hey, Merc, what's happening?" he said. Then he turned back to the guard, "Hey, you better tell that lieutenant that he better bring his ass back here every day and he better ask how I'm doin'. You better tell everyone on every shift. Because if they don't and they sign that paper that says they did, they'll see it again in coat." He was referring to a rule which required each shift lieutenant to inquire how we were doing. It was a rule the lieutenants rarely followed. They just signed a sheet saying they had talked to us. I knew they would follow the rule with Bruce. The word was out among the guards: Don't mess with Simmons. He must have had ten different lawsuits going at once. He was at odds with the guards almost every minute.

Bruce, who had been sentenced to thirty years for attempted murder, had achieved almost legendary status by taking the prison to coat (or court) over its regulations concerning facial hairs. He was part of the religious order called Coptics and had come on the compound looking like others in that order—with more hair than Don King and a moustache and goatee.

Moustaches and goatees were against the rules at DCI. Why? I think it's part of the mind game the prison system plays with inmates, a way of constantly reminding you who's in charge. It's not like a situation where you take away a guy's pocketknife; once that knife is gone, it's gone forever. But hair keeps growing back, and therefore the guards can keep coming back and telling you to shave.

Unless you're Bruce. "Two things I'm gonna do," he told the prison officials. "I'm gonna live my life and I'm gonna smoke reefer. And you ain't gonna do a damn thing about it." Reefer was also part of the Coptic tradition.

So he took them to court. The judge not only ruled that Bruce didn't have to shave, he ordered the prison to stop harassing or punishing Bruce on religious grounds. When Bruce came back to the compound after this victory, he was combing that goatee to make it as long as it could be. A guard told him he looked like a billy goat. "I know I do," he said. "And I don't care. The thing is, you ain't gonna make me not look like a billy goat if I want to look like one."

So here Bruce was making my solitary confinement very unsolitary. The lieutenants hadn't been checking in with me every day. After Bruce arrived, they did. "Simmons, you okay?" they'd ask through the door.

"You bet I'm doing okay," Bruce would yell back. "But I could be doin' better if you'd get away from the cell there so some light can come in. We ain't got nothin' but a 60-watt candle bulb in here. You know that if I file this in coat, we can have some new bulbs in here; 75 watts instead."

Once, he looked over his cheese sandwich and almost went through the roof. There was a grease spot on the cheese, indicating the cheese had probably been cut with a knife that had touched meat. Bruce started clapping his hands. "Wait a damn minute here," he yelled to the guards. "You better come on down here. You know you s'posed to have this meal right. You all bullshittin'. You better get down here right now, 'cause I'm tellin' you somethin': You cut my sandwich and you used that knife. You know my religion says I ain't got nothin' to do with meat and you all got somethin' to do with meat on my sandwich. You all is interferin' with my religion. You gonna see this sandwich again." And he put the sandwich in an envelope and sent it to the superintendent! Before a week had passed, he had me yelling at the guards just like he was. "Where's my medication, dammit," I'd yell. And Bruce would nod his approval.

Bruce was always talking about how to keep the system from beating you. He usually won. But this wasn't his first trip to "jail" and it wouldn't be his last. Not too long after we were out, a guard we called "Clint Eastwood" started bugging him. We called this guard Clint because he always wore his hat up and twirled his walkie-talkie as if it were a gun. "I'm gonna get you," he whispered to Bruce. "Somehow I'm gonna get you."

Just then some visitors passed by. Clint immediately dressed up the conversation. "So Inmate Simmons, if there's anything I can do for you, I'll be happy to do it. But you have to ask."

Bruce smiled. "What I want you all to do for me, I know you won't do." He raised his voice for emphasis as a minister does in church. "Yeah, what I want you all to do for me, I know you won't do. And that's kiss my Black ass." Bingo! Verbal disrespect. Back to jail.

On my sixteenth day in jail, I was summoned to a courtroom in Miami. Shortly before heading for the Flattop, I had agreed to settle my civil lawsuit. Instead of getting the $500,000 the jury had originally awarded me, I had reluctantly agreed to accept $300,000—the figure the trial judge, in his infinitesimal wisdom, had decided upon. Once more I felt let down by the justice system. My trip from the Flattop was for the purpose of signing the settlement papers and turning over all $300,000 to several lawyers and other creditors to whom I owed money and had previously assigned proceeds of the judgment. I was literally paying for the sins of my cocaine days. Bobbie and the kids could have used that money. They did receive a small portion of it because Strauss's firm and another lawyer kindly made contributions to the fund at our church which was helping support the family.

I was back in jail within a few hours. But a couple of days later, I was again summoned from my cell. "You're supposed to call your lawyer," a guard told me. "You can use the phone here."

I was skeptical. It was hard enough to use a phone on the main compound. I was certain that the phone in the Flattop was completely off-limits to inmates. The guard assured me that this was an exception.

Strauss wasn't in. His secretary Debbie came on the line. "The Third DCA finally handed down a decision," she said.

This was it! Knowing a decision was imminent, I had been playing the same scenario in my head for days. It was a scenario of American Justice and Poetic Justice: I would go directly from the Flattop to Bobbie and the kids because the Third DCA would rule in my favor and throw out my conviction. "What did they decide?" I asked excitedly.

"They affirmed," Debbie said.

"Affirmed!" For the briefest moment, I thought that meant I was a free man. Then I became confused. "What does that mean, Debbie?"

She explained that the DCA had upheld the jury's decision. I had lost.

My heart sank. "How could that happen?" I asked. "How could those judges go along with the horseshit I got from Judge Gable? Evidence was excluded. Justice was circumvented. Couldn't they see that?"

I had never really unpacked at DCI, never tried to make it like home. There was an inmate named Larry Cohen who had his room all fixed up with pictures and a stereo. It was very homey. He kept asking why I didn't fix my room up, and I kept telling him it was because I didn't expect to stay, that I was going to win my appeal and be back at my real home. At that point, I still had my football mentality: just give me a little daylight and I can get out of this jam.

Now my "daylight" seemed to be running out. We still had the option of appealing to the Florida Supreme Court. But unlike the DCA, that court would not have to hear the case unless it wanted to—a rare event. For the first time, I had to deal with the fact that I might actually have to serve my entire fifteen years. I was as depressed as I've ever been. To make matters worse, my headaches from the 1973 neck injury returned for the first time since the 1980 surgery.

I was released from the Flattop after twenty-four days, having received six days off for good behavior. Why, I don't know. I was feeling extremely hostile.

As I was walking down the compound after getting my clothes and property back, I almost got into a fight with an inmate named Bug Juice. One of the guys had come up to me and said, "Hey, Merc, I'm glad to see you." Another had asked, "Hey, man, how'd you like it back there?" Bug Juice was the only smartass. "Was the party over back there or what, man?" he asked.

I put my stuff down. My stare could have frozen Biscayne Bay. "Bug Juice," I said, "if you ever in your life say something smart to me again when I'm in this frame of mind, I'm gonna do something to you, man. Hear? I just got out of jail, brother, and I'm gonna stay out. But make no mistake. It ain't too bad back there, so you better watch what you're doing."

He backed off.

Now, for the first (and last) time, a "boy" approached me. "I know you've had it rough, Merc," he-she said gently. "If you ever..."

I cut him-her off before he-she could go any further. I was ready to explode—at fellow inmates, at Strauss, at the System. My head was pounding. I could hear that train coming in the distance.

It was in this state of utter physical and emotional chaos that I entered "Cambodia."

CHAPTER 14

TURNAROUND

If you go to jail at DCI, you lose your room. When you leave the Flattop, you are taken to G-Dorm, or as the inmates call it, "Cambodia." Why Cambodia? Because it's just like a war zone. There is a lot of fighting, a lot of gambling. When the cops come by, guys stick their fists in their pockets and their dice in their mouth and act like nothing is happening.

Cambodia is always filled to the brim with "refugees." Everybody is waiting for reassignment. It is an open dormitory. There are no private rooms. There is no air conditioning. There is only one television and two telephones for the seventy inhabitants.

I tried to distance myself from the action in Cambodia. Thanks to Lenny Campagno, I succeeded. Lenny arrived from the Flattop just about the time I did. I've noticed that once a lot of people reach their "golden years," they feel they have earned the right to say anything they want to and don't particularly care if it offends anybody. Lenny certainly fell into this category. To those who didn't know him well, he appeared to be the classic curmudgeon. He made no bones about the fact that he didn't like too many people at DCI—guards or inmates. "I'm not prejudiced," he'd say. "You're all dog shit." He could get away with this. Nobody wanted to hit a 65-year-old man.

Lenny didn't actually hate everybody. And if he did like you, he'd do anything in the world for you. Sharing a common interest in food and backgammon, we hit it off. He quickly became my protector—keeping the guards off my back.

One time a porno film mistakenly came on to the TV set in the day room. I hurried to get Lenny. He was in such a rush to see it that he forgot to put on his pants. Halfway down the hall, he realized he was only in his underwear. He turned around, but by the time he got back to his bunk, someone had stolen his pants, which had held his wallet. The guards immediately ordered a search of all the inmates. Two prisoners were caught red-handed. But that wasn't good enough for the guards. "Do you think Morris could have been in on this, too?" they asked Lenny.

"Don't you go trying to pin it on him," Lenny scowled. "He's the only honest person in this whole goddamn place."

After a while I started calling Lenny "Mr. Drummond," after the White father who adopts two Black children in the television series *Diff'rent Strokes*.

I was in Cambodia two months waiting for a room to open up in another dorm. I could have gone back to North Miami Beach, B-Dorm, but I really didn't want to. I didn't want to deal with Pitts again. I was tired of being the bull in the ring and I wanted a new start. This dramatic turnaround came about because of my relationship with DCI's chaplain, Joe Hunt. With his counsel, I moved from that kind of magic Christianity I had been practicing—say a prayer, take three steps backward, and turn around and everything will be okay—to a deeper, more genuine faith.

Oddly, I have my headaches to thank for all of this. After they returned, I got absolutely no comfort from the doddering old doctor in DCI's clinic. I saw him every day for two weeks. An 86-year-old former plastic surgeon, he had no idea what he was doing. "I checked your blood pressure, and it's okay," he'd tell me. Meanwhile, I could barely see. Once I passed out.

There was another prisoner, Diamond, who was suffering something similar. He couldn't get any relief from the doctor either. I told him, "Friend, here's what we have to do. We have to go to chapel because we've exhausted all medical remedies."

We prayed, and as God is my witness, the headaches went away for both of us, never to return. It was the second time God had answered my prayers. Remember, I had prayed to be released from the bondage of drugs and to get my name off the drug rolls, and this had already been achieved by the time I was sentenced. But for the last two years, I had been in the wilderness, in borderline disrespect so to speak, not in control, succumbing to every opportunity to play bull in the ring and accepting every challenge the situation brought.

The disappearance of the headaches was a pretty persuasive reason to keep on attending chapel. It was at this point I really got to know Chaplain Hunt. Actually he made the first overture. He was a big man, about tight-end size, in his fifties. He was a White southerner, but he seemed totally lacking in the traditional southern prejudice. He had taught at Black schools and preached in a Black church. He was a man of God, but he was also a no-nonsense guy. He knew when inmates were trying to take advantage of him and he wouldn't put up with that. He and I had something in common. My mother had died of cancer, and one of his sons, who was in his early thirties, was now dying of the disease. It was a difficult time for the chaplain, but he showed tremendous strength and his spiritual faith never wavered.

When Chaplain Hunt first called me in, he said he had noticed how my efforts had changed toward my "Christian walk." He told me I was allowing the things of the world to influence me. I told him that I didn't want any special treatment, but I also didn't want any special abuse like I had been getting at DCI.

"I think you have to evaluate yourself to see the rules you are making," he said. He gave me a book, *A Survival Kit for New Christians*. It's a handbook for people who want to believe in God and find spiritual direction but don't know how to go about doing it. The book offers a "Daily Walk" of anywhere from fifteen to forty-five minutes, five days a week for eleven weeks. With each walk, you learn a little more about the Scriptures.

I thought the course was great. My attitude started to change immediately as I realized my responsibility to myself was to keep the peace. Peace of mind was something I could have if I chose it.

One of the first things I did was come to an understanding with Pitts. "Well, Pitts," I told him when I saw him on the compound, "you got me. The game is over. I submit. I tried to buck you, but you're too tough for me." I offered my hand, and he took it. We got along okay after that. That was all he wanted—an acknowledgment that he was somebody. Not that he could control me, but that he was somebody.

After the first eleven weeks, I took survival kit number 2. By the time the next eleven weeks ended, I had found even greater peace

and strength. Chaplain Hunt had allowed me to see myself as I was—
reckless. And he had allowed me to see what I could be—a servant
of the Lord. He told me that I could help a lot of people by example, but that I had to *be* an example before I could *set* one. It started
to sink in. When kit number 2 ended, Chaplain Hunt asked me to
teach the class. I was happy to do so.

The Bible wasn't all I was reading. Strauss had sent me a copy of
the opinion affirming my conviction. It was, he told me, most unusual. The normal procedure for deciding a case, according to Strauss
and numerous other attorneys I have spoken with, is as follows: (1)
the District Court of Appeals reads the briefs and hears the oral arguments; (2) the three justices evaluate the case and vote; (3) a justice is selected to write the court's majority opinion. If there is a
dissent, the dissenting justice has the option to write a dissenting
opinion; (4) the opinion or opinions are published.

In my case, as usual, normal procedure was not followed. Here's
what happened: the justices voted, and I lost by a 2–1 margin. Justice Baskin wrote the majority opinion, while at the same time Justice Ferguson wrote the dissenting opinion. So far, so good. But then,
instead of publishing the opinions, something else happened. The
majority opinion was rewritten. This was so extraordinary that Judge
Ferguson felt compelled to add a "supplement to dissent." He wrote:
"The majority opinion has been revised and expanded to meet points
in the dissent."

Although it was unusual, I could understand why the majority
opinion was revised. Judge Ferguson's dissent, in which he argued
that my conviction should be overturned or, at the very least that I
should be given a new trial, was very persuasive. He wrote: "Evidence crucial to the entrapment defense (Gotbaum's testimony) was
withheld from the jury for reasons which find no support in case law
or any rational construction of the evidentiary rules. If that evidence
had been admitted, as it should have been, the jury might have concluded, as I have, that this was a textbook case of entrapment."

A textbook case of entrapment. My point exactly.

The majority opinion concluded that in Florida the only issues
material in determining whether a defendant was entrapped are the
predisposition of the defendant and whether or not he is induced to
commit the crime by the police. The intent or state of mind of the
State (through its agents such as Donaldson) was not relevant, the
majority argued. Therefore, Gotbaum's testimony that Donaldson

had intended to set me up was not relevant and Judge Gable had properly prevented Gotbaum from testifying.

By not taking into account the intent of the State, Florida was in a distinct minority. The case law in most states, I had learned through my law library readings, did take this into account. But even putting that aside, Judge Ferguson saw no predisposition on my part. "Here, the state attempted with dogged persistence, no less than a dozen times over a three-day period, to have the defendant commit the offense," he wrote. "Over half the 'houndings' came after the state's own agent (Brinson) had become convinced that defendant had no ability to arrange a drug deal, and after the defendant had failed continuously to appear or deliver cocaine. We have in this case no ready complaisance on the part of the defendant."

In his supplement to the dissent, Judge Ferguson even went so far as to criticize the State's behavior. "There is no question but that the methods employed by the state in this case fell far below standards which we can dutifully approve. Morris is a sometimes controversial football player who reached prominence during the Miami Dolphins' Super Bowl days of the 1970s. . . . Unquestionably, that high visibility accounts for the zeal which attached to the prosecutorial effort. Until the state stepped in to manufacture an offense for the purpose of prosecuting, Morris' only transgression was self-abuse by drugs—a disease which has reached epidemic proportions among professional athletes. Now he is serving a fifteen-year minimum mandatory sentence."

Interestingly, the *majority* opinion also criticized the conduct of the State, but in a different area. "Morris contends that the evidence was tainted as fruit of the poisonous tree because the state engaged in warrantless interceptions and failed to inform Judge Kogan of its activities when it sought issuance of a search warrant," wrote Justice Baskin. "Although we condemn the concealment of pertinent facts from the trial court, we believe that the trial judge was apprised of facts sufficient to establish probable cause to issue the search warrant."

Presumably, this part of the majority opinion was not rewritten, because Judge Ferguson had not touched upon that argument in his dissent. What was rewritten? Well, what was the material which, taken out of context, made me look most guilty? What was the material that George Yoss had leaked to the press at the same time he presented it to Ron Strauss? Selected excerpts from the tapes, of course. Apparently the majority thought that by gratuitously adding the profane language from my meetings with Brinson and Donaldson it could show I invited the State's participation and it could thus overcome Justice Ferguson's well-reasoned argument. But in his supplement to the dissent, Justice Ferguson had an answer to this, too. Noting that despite such tough talk in the parking lot, I still wasn't able to deliver the cocaine, Justice Ferguson concluded: "Rather than showing that Morris 'invited participation,' the added excerpt reveals only that Morris displayed a false bravado in planning a drug deal that he, at that time, could not effectuate."

Having read this opinion over and over, I was on the one hand devastated and on the other hand encouraged. It was devastating that Justice Ferguson had so clearly seen what the State had done and that the two other justices had so clearly failed to see it. Our next move was to appeal to the Florida Supreme Court. Here, I was encouraged by the fact that *for the first time* a judge, Justice Ferguson, had seen things my way. That and my renewed spiritual faith gave me strength and confidence.

Strauss wasn't as confident. The Florida Supreme Court is inundated with appeals. Unlike the Court of Appeals, it does not have to hear every appeal. In fact, unless there is a noteworthy point of law involved or a case in conflict, it turns down cases like mine. I later learned the court refuses to hear forty-nine out of every fifty cases which come to it.

We would have to go through a two-step process. First, we would have to persuade the court that it should take discretionary jurisdiction and hear the case. Second, if we were fortunate to do that (no small task), we would have to convince the court that it should overrule both Judge Gable and the District Court of Appeals. Since the DCA had wiped out my constitutional law arguments concerning the illegality of the buggings (by virtue of not addressing them), we would not be able to argue those if we got before the Supreme Court. It would come down to the entrapment issue and Gotbaum's testimony. Under any circumstances the process would take many, many months. Strauss reminded me that it still might be possible to feel out the State Attorney's office to see if they'd be interested in a deal which wouldn't require any naming of names on my part in return for dropping my appeal. He thought the State might be looking for a graceful way out of the mess it had created. My answer was the same it had been for the last twenty months: "No."

While Strauss and his partner Phil Glatzer were preparing this appeal, I settled into a more peaceful life at DCI. Turning down the chance to go back to F-Dorm, I went instead to B-Dorm. That's "B" as in brick. That's brick as in "going upside someone's head with a brick." This was not Cambodia, but it was not North Miami Beach either. It was more like the inner city.

The Cuban population was growing day by day. I found it fascinating that while all the Blacks and Anglos at DCI couldn't wait to get out, many of the Cubans were actually happy to be there. Many fine individuals arrived in the Mariel boatlift, and they have contributed greatly to society since landing in the United States. Many not-so-fine individuals also arrived. Fidel Castro opened the prison gates to let hundreds emigrate. More than a few of these quickly wound up in U.S. prisons, particularly DCI. No matter. DCI, with its three square meals a day and decent beds, was a country club for these guys compared to the Cuban prisons.

Then in 1985, as relations between the U.S. and Cuba appeared to be improving, Castro talked about taking back some of the refugees who had committed crimes in the U.S. He indicated that he would retry these refugees for those same crimes once they got back to Cuba, and he promised that justice would be swift and mercy nonexistent. While this overture met with a positive response in most circles, it scared the shit out of the Cubans.

One day a group of Mariel refugees, Marieletto, were pumping steel in recreation. "When I get out, I'm gonna open up a gym," one of them said.

Crespo, an inmate who had fled Cuba in 1960, smiled. "Where you gonna open it, man? In Havana?"

The refugees did not laugh. I have seen several men on death row awaiting execution. That's how most of the Marieletto at DCI looked, especially after officials of the U.S. Immigration Service started coming to the prison and conducting interviews. But nothing ever happened. Relations between the two countries got chilly again, and Castro never followed through on his offer until late in 1987. I suspect that, if polled, most Americans would have been disappointed. On the other hand, for the Marieletto, it was party time.

When I got to my room in B-Dorm—the room with the view of the corn field—I finally unpacked. Reconciled to the fact that I would be at DCI for a while, I decided I might as well make myself as comfortable as possible. I set up a tape player and recorded jazz off the radio. I painted the room; not with the putrid green standard issue paint, but with a mixture of green and purple smuggled out of the maintenance department. This created a cool lavender. I even put up a calendar—although I intentionally avoided crossing off the days one by one. There were many inmates who would announce each morning how many days they had left. "Thirty-five and a wake-up," one would yell. "Twenty-six and a wakeup," another would respond. That meant they had thirty-five days or twenty-six days, and then when they woke up it would be over.

I certainly wanted to wake up and find that this nightmare was over. Bobbie and the kids needed me more than ever. Maceo was beginning to get into some serious trouble. The trouble started when he was in eighth grade and continued at the beginning of ninth grade. Kids would taunt him, saying things like, "Your dad's not coming home for another fifteen years," or, "Your dad's a coke dealer." Then he'd get mad and start a fight. There wasn't much I could do. I wasn't around to provide the obvious presence of authority. I couldn't steer him in the right direction. So he was on his own, picking up his own values. He was suspended twice.

Then came the coup de grace. Maceo and a friend were taking what they called a "shortcut" to class. This involved climbing on the rafters over the girls bathroom. The rafters failed to support them and the boys came tumbling down. It sounds funny. Unfortunately, it led to Maceo's third suspension. This meant that he automatically qualified to go to an alternative school.

Maceo was told he had two choices: He could go to the alternative school for a month and then come back to his old school. If he did this, he would not only have to make up what he missed during the month, he absolutely had to repeat ninth grade the next year. His other option was to attend the alternative school for the remainder of the year. After that he would be evaluated. If he did well, turned himself around, he might not have to repeat.

Maceo is my pride and joy. I had fought all those years to win custody of him. But I was as tough with him as I was loving. During one of his visits to DCI, we talked about his choices. "You're almost in the same spot I'm in," I said. "The difference is that because you're so young, you still have an alternative. The school is not the alternative. The school is a constant. It's always there. *You*, your behavior is the alternative. You made your bed, but you don't have to lay in it. You're supposed to get up from there and learn from what the hell you've done. You've got two choices: you either go to that school and get evaluated or you continue along in the same vein. If you do that, I guarantee that you'll end up here, because you're on the road towards here now. Death row is full of people who can't make any more choices because they made all the wrong ones all the way up and nobody told them about it. But you still have choices. They're giving you an alternative. Go look that word up. It means you've got another chance. You can do what you choose to do, but I'm telling you right now, you better decide to do the wise thing."

Maceo decided to remain at the alternative school for the balance of the year. He made the honor roll. At the end of his stay, he earned the Disney Child Award. It is given to the kid who displays the most change in character and conduct throughout the entire school system in Dade County. There are some 200,000 kids in the system. I was delighted, but what made me even more delighted was this. When Maceo was interviewed by the media, someone asked him, "Don't you think you did something here that would make your dad proud?"

Maceo answered, "I wasn't really doing it to make my dad proud. I was doing it to make me proud. Because I couldn't make my dad proud until I was proud of myself."

What made *me* proud was that Maceo had been willing to accept responsibility for his own actions and then had done something about it. He understood that he deserved the punishment and that then, having accepted that punishment, he deserved the reward. I have always believed each individual is accountable for his or her actions and that shifting the blame to any other person, object, or event is just a cop-out. It was my behavior—not the headaches, not the cocaine—that had led me on my downward spiral. And it was my behavior that would have to turn things around. This seems like a pretty simple concept, but I'm amazed at the number of people who try to make excuses for themselves or for others by shifting the responsibility or blame. This is certainly the case in the way our society has approached the so-called drug problem.

Toward the end of 1984, I had the opportunity to speak to a United States Senate subcommittee in Washington, D.C., on this subject. This marked the beginning of numerous trips from prison to the world outside—trips which allowed me to share with school-

children, civic leaders, community groups, and others my experience and the philosophy I had begun to develop as I contemplated
the events of the last few years.

The trip from DCI to D.C. opened my eyes to what is in effect
an ass backward approach to the problems of drugs. Playing football
I learned a team is only as good as its front office. The same is true
in fighting drugs. Our nation's misguided effort begins with our leaders and extends all the way down to the community level. Simply
stated, the problem is that these people and institutions focus on
the drug instead of the person using the drug. Just look at how the
topic is presented: "drug abuse" or "substance abuse" or "cocaine
abuse." I can understand the term "child abuse." It is the child that
is being abused, damaged. I can understand the term "wife abuse."
It is the wife that is being abused, damaged. But how can you abuse
or damage an inanimate object like cocaine? You can't. In reality
the user is abusing himself or herself, otherwise known as "self-
abuse."

This is more than a difference in semantics. If you focus on the
drug, blame the drug, then you spend your time and money patrol-
ling borders or flying soldiers into South America to wipe out smuggling operations. These may be admirable endeavors for the moment,
but they will never be totally successful, and in the meantime you
will have avoided confronting the problem where it really lies—not
in Bolivia but within the human soul.

I think it is difficult for a person to understand this unless he or
she has gone through the process that I and others who have become involved with drugs have gone through—that need to hide
from yourself and the world. Before I left for Washington, D.C.,
Strauss handed me a speech which he had prepared for me to read.
I tore it up. It didn't say what I wanted to say. How could it? Strauss's
experience was totally different from mine.

What I told the senators was this: I hope you don't have me up
here just for the rhetoric. If you're earnest and really want to do
something, then let's do it. You have to do more than separate the
drug from the person. This is a person problem, not a drug problem. If I was running the show, I'd take all those Hollywood tinsel-
town people, all the stars who have been involved like I've been
involved and are willing to come forward and let them be a positive
influence. Develop a network of people who have survived, who can
say, "Look, man. We want to talk about survival now. Everyone

knows how this thing will kill you. We want to talk about how to keep you from dying. Because even though you've been in that spot, you've got an opportunity now to be in a better spot. And you, more than almost anybody else, will be able to appreciate life because of where you've been."

I felt that the trip was a fiasco. The people in D.C. struck me as too self-absorbed and close-minded. I didn't sense the senators really understood the point I was trying to get across—that this was a people problem. It seemed like they were more interested in public relations than public action. Before I left DCI, I was a guest on ABC television's *Good Morning, America* with host David Hartman and then-Florida Senator Paula Hawkins. I was asked to wear a three-piece suit for the interview. I refused. "I'll wear a suit to talk to Congress," I said, "but I want the American people to see where my freebasing got me." I appeared in my prison garb.

I almost didn't get to wear the suit when I got to Washington. The officials at DCI had refused to let me take a change of clothes with me. My protest that I was going to be gone for a week and would begin to smell pretty gamy without a bigger wardrobe fell on deaf ears (that I was going to be gone seven days just to make one 45-minute speech seemed crazy in itself. But that's politics).

When I told the federal marshalls in Washington about this, they were very kind. They tried to get my clothes shipped up by overnight delivery. But Strauss was one step ahead of them. My wardrobe in hand, he had already hopped a plane. He should have brought scissors along, too. The red tape was getting thicker and thicker.

I was supposed to stay in the jail in Arlington, Virginia. Instead, over my objections, I was taken to the District of Columbia jail. Dangerous felon that I was, I was transported in handcuffs and body chains. It was the weekend of the Michael Jackson concert. The D.C. police had been rounding up every questionable person in town. The jail was in a state of chaos. Old prisoners were being let out to make room for new prisoners. As I was having my mug shot taken—despite my continued protests that I wasn't even supposed to be there—the "honor" inmate taking the picture asked if he could borrow some money from me so he could buy some reefer! I told him to get lost.

This comedy of errors was eventually resolved, and I was taken across the bridge to Arlington to begin a new comedy of errors.

Strauss arrived at the jailhouse shortly after I did. He was told he couldn't see me.

"I'm his lawyer," he said impatiently.

"But you're not admitted to practice in the State of Virginia or the District of Columbia."

Strauss did all he could do to contain himself. He was finally allowed to see me through 2-inch-thick glass, but not before he was seriously questioned about whether the shaving depilatory powder he had brought me was really shaving powder and not some other substance that came in powdered form. One marshall wanted to take a sample and run a test. "Everywhere I go, they play games. Don't they?" I told him.

When it came time to go to Capitol Hill, there was a big to-do. I was whisked into a car and accompanied by what seemed like two dozen Secret Service agents. They parked the car on the sidewalk and hurried me up a special elevator into the chambers of Senator Hawkins. Former football players Calvin Hill and Rosie Grier were also there. More public relations. We posed for pictures. I talked to the committee and that was it.

After my speech, some of the marshalls asked me if I'd prefer to spend the rest of my sentence up in Virginia. During my testimony I had told the story about the inmate who had offered me coke at Dade County Jail the very day I was sentenced. "Your life may be in danger," the marshalls now told me.

"Hey, my life is in danger every second of every day," I said.

My trip to Washington generated numerous requests from other groups for me to come and speak. I was anxious to share my thoughts, but the D.C. trip made me think twice about venturing outside the prison walls. Were the powers that be always going to make it that difficult for me? If so, was it worth it? "Yes," answered Chaplain Hunt. "Yes," answered Dr. Clarence Crier, my DCI classifications officer, whom I respected as much as the chaplain. They both felt that I could teach many people by my example.

Strauss also answered "Yes." His motives were not entirely altruistic. Certainly, I could help people. But I could also help myself. He reasoned that if we lost our appeal in the Florida Supreme Court, we would have exhausted all of our judicial remedies. The next step would be approaching the governor of Florida and asking for a pardon. If I could demonstrate what a positive force in the community I was, my chances for that would be better.

I was still confident that we would win in the Florida Supreme Court. The system has to work, I kept telling myself. I remembered something I had read during my custody battle for Maceo: "The law must yield to common sense." Common sense, I thought. Forget about the law. There was Dred Scot, which denied Blacks the same rights as Whites; there were other laws that said Blacks could only testify against Blacks. The law is man's law not God's law and is subject to change. Common sense will prevail.

We had crossed the first hurdle, at odds of 50–1. The court had agreed to hear my case. For this final effort, I wanted to make a few changes on our team. I insisted that we add Robert Augustus Harper III to our cause. Harper was a lawyer who could have been mistaken for Colonel Sanders's younger brother. I wanted him because he was from Tallahassee, which happens to be where the Supreme Court sits. I didn't care if Harper did anything other than sit at our table. There is a dramatic split between northern Florida, where the court sits, and southern Florida, where I lived. The jailhouse lawyers told me to be sure the brethren saw a familiar face at my table. I also insisted that Glatzer, who had eloquently argued my case in front of the Third DCA, again argue the case instead of Strauss. This wasn't because I didn't have faith in Strauss, who was still captaining the ship. I simply felt he had become so emotionally involved with the case and with me that Glatzer, an unemotional tactician and appellate specialist, would be better.

My speaking engagements began in May of 1985. Dr. Crier coordinated them and was totally supportive. He was an example of the good things a prison can offer... seemingly in spite of itself. He was a compassionate Black man who understood the workings of the system although he didn't seem to be part of it. He was a civil rights activist with a Ph.D in education. After serving as a school administrator, he had decided he could have a greater impact working as a classifications officer in the prisons. Classifications officers work one on one with the inmates. Head and shoulders above his fellow officers, Dr. Crier was quickly offered a promotion to an administrative position. He refused, explaining that he could be much more effective in his current role.

If Chaplain Hunt was my liaison to the spiritual world, Dr. Crier was my liaison to the day-to-day world. He was my sounding board, the voice of reason and common sense. The most educated man I met in the system, he did for me what no one else could do: maintain a level of respectability between me and the State. If the State jammed me, I could count on him to make sure I was treated fairly.

Dr. Crier did all he could to make sure my journeys outside went smoothly, but the rest of the administration at DCI made these trips more difficult than they had to be. The DCI guards would either transport me to where I was speaking or turn me over to the authorities from the jurisdiction where I'd be speaking, who would then transport me. As long as I was in DCI custody, I had to be in chains. Not just handcuffs. Waist chains. Belly chains. Groin chains. Leg irons. The whole nine yards. The local authorities didn't require or even desire this. They would take the chains off as soon as I was in their custody. I couldn't understand why with the good I was trying to accomplish, DCI would want to keep its foot on my chest, but it did.

Example: In the fall of 1985, I had a speaking engagement in Tampa, a five-hour drive from DCI. I was to be transported by DCI. Handcuffed and chained, I was put in a van. It was 90 degrees outside and even hotter inside the van, which had been sitting in the sun with all its windows rolled up. We didn't take off right away. In fact, my driver just left me in the van and went back into DCI. It didn't take long for me to start sweating like a pig. Because of the handcuffs, I couldn't even wipe my brow. Thanks to my days in the NFL, I can't sit more than five or six minutes without having to stretch my legs; my knees hurt too much otherwise. The chains prevented me from stretching. A full half hour passed until someone came back to the van.

"Take me back inside," I said. "I'm not going. I don't know why I would agree to let you take me across the street much less to Tampa."

"Why don't you want to go?"

"I can't travel with my medical condition—my knees, wrist, neck."

A guard was called. I explained the situation to him. He called a sergeant. I explained the situation to him. He called a lieutenant. I explained the situation to him. Finally, they called DCI's old doctor. "Take these chains off and let me back in the compound, I'm not going," I said. And they finally agreed.

I had become more peaceful in recent months, but now I couldn't contain myself. "You know you're the only group that won't treat me like a man," I said. "The people you release me to take the chains off right in front of you. Do you know how stupid you look?"

"Morris, you're borderline verbal disrespect."

I shut up.

But I got the last laugh. Not too long after this, I had a speaking engagement in Palm Beach. The officer in whose custody I would be, Jack Maxwell, was a nice guy. I told him that the DCI people would drive me to the airport in chains. "We're not coming to get you at the airport," he said. "We're coming by helicopter."

The administration at DCI was furious. The helicopter landed on a new pad on the grounds installed with the hope it would be inaugurated by Louis Wainwright, Florida's Secretary of Prisons. (Florida is the only state with someone with that title!) Wainwright had not yet flown in. In fact, nobody had. I was the first one to use the pad! At the time the helicopter landed, the inmates were supposed to be on their way inside, but Lenny and the rest of the guys insisted on staying outside to watch. As I climbed in, they started applauding, just as the inmates did in the movie *Brubaker*.

"There goes Merc."

"Yeah, that's his private helicopter, man," said Lenny.

The guards were furious. "Re-call," they said. "Get back to the dorm."

Nobody paid them any attention.

In Palm Beach, I stayed at a minimum security work-release home. Maxwell was so relaxed that he took me out to get something to eat. Then we went to a mall. Then, believe it or not, we drove to a gun range. "Let's fire off a couple of rounds," he said. We would have, too. Except the range had just closed. What a change from November 5, 1982, I thought, when after your conviction you couldn't even have a day to close your affairs.

I found the talks, particularly those to the school kids, very rewarding. I told them the same thing I had told Maceo when he got into trouble—that they had a choice. And that a choice was a powerful thing. Even if you're going down the wrong path, you have the chance to turn around. Or you can choose to continue down the path you're on and go right into the drink if you want.

Homestead Junior High School in Dade County was one of my favorite stops. This is a middle school for about 1200 sixth, seventh, and eighth graders. The school is tri-ethnic, and the kids are on the lower end of the socioeconomic ladder. These are circumstances that might make for a bad situation, except for a terrific teacher by the name of Del Gorriz.

After I gave my talk, I signed a few autographs and suggested that if anyone wanted to write me, I would write back. I expected a few letters. What I got was a batch of twenty-five letters, followed by a batch of thirty, and so on. In all, some 300 letters. I wrote every kid back, trying to give each one some commonsense advice about the problems they were concerned with. Ms. Gorriz said that kids who normally didn't even hand in homework were now writing two- and three-page letters and copying them over before sending them so that they could show me their ability to write. "Praise God that He has allowed this to happen through you," she told me.

This got me to thinking about the Kiros, a prison organization promoting Christian retreats. There is a line: "I'm the only Jesus that some may ever know." I better understood my responsibility to these young people and the need to tell them not about me and how I overcame, but how the power of God allowed me to see. I answered every letter I received.

By the time I spoke to the Homestead School in October 1985, Glatzer had already argued my case before the Florida Supreme Court. I hadn't been there, but by all accounts it had gone quite well. The Chief Justice had apparently asked Anthony Musto, who was arguing the State's case, several tough questions. Harper later related to me dialogue that went something like this:

> CHIEF JUSTICE BOYD: Mr. Musto, in my day, my law school professor would have called this a textbook case of entrapment. Can you prove to me that it was anything different than that?
>
> MUSTO: Mr. Chief Justice, there is a difference between setting someone up and entrapping him. The State acknowledges that it was our intent to set up Mr. Morris. But that is a street term. Entrapment is a term of law.

We had come a long way since the trial, when Yoss had adamantly asserted that the State had never intended to set me up—that the State had only given me the opportunity to commit a crime which I was already predisposed to commit.

In between the time I had lost in the Third DCA and the time the Supreme Court heard my case, there had been a significant change in the way the courts in Florida looked at entrapment. In the *Cruz* decision, rendered in March of 1985, the Florida Supreme Court had joined most of the rest of the nation and said that the conduct and intent of the police *was* relevant in considering whether or not entrapment had occurred. This seemed to suggest that Judge Gable should have allowed the jury to hear Gotbaum's testimony concerning the intent of Donaldson (the State's admitted agent) to set me up. Unfortunately, since my case had occurred before the *Cruz* decision, the Supreme Court did not have to apply that decision to me. The justices could decide whether or not they wanted to make it retroactive. Despite this uncertainty, I had high hopes for a victory and release before Christmas. Interestingly, Yoss had not argued the case, but he had been in Tallahassee that day. My former co-defendant Vince Cord's parole hearing was that day. Yoss was there to recommend that the parole board *not* release Cord. It may sound a bit odd that Yoss was trying to keep behind bars a man with whom he had cut a deal and given a reduced sentence in exchange for testifying against me. One plausible explanation is that the State thought it might look bad if Cord, the dealer, got out of jail before Morris, the user.

December, 1985. Early in the month the Dolphins played the Chicago Bears on a Monday night. The Bears (who would go on to win the Super Bowl) had won all twelve of their games up to this point. The press was beginning to speculate whether they could finish the regular season undefeated and then march on to a Super Bowl victory. The only team in history to have accomplished that? The 1972 Dolphins, on which I played.

I had watched very few games this season. My mind had been concerned with more pressing matters. But this night I cheered for the Dolphins. I didn't want our team to share that spot in the record books with anyone else.

As I settled in front of the television set with hundreds of other inmates, I was again reminded how important the ritual of watching sporting events is to almost every prisoner at every institution. They reserve their seats hours in advance of the contest, take their places long before the game begins. They behave as if they are actually at the game. The action somehow has a way of carrying them beyond their rooms, beyond the walls, to the Orange Bowl. For three hours they are free.

I noticed for the first time the formalized seating system for these games. At DCI there was a balcony with a catwalk overlooking the television room. Inmates were not allowed to linger on the catwalk; the fear was that one inmate might toss another inmate over the railing. But for events such as a Dolphins game, the rules were ignored.

Déjà vu. I was back in Virginia, a quarter of a century earlier. At DCI, as in the movie theater I went to with my cousins, those of one race sat on the main floor, while the second-class citizens were forced to watch from above. There was one difference: Now it was the Blacks who ruled the roost and gathered around the screen, while the Whites meekly settled for the balcony view. (While the Blacks still had the upper hand *within* the inmate population, this was not the case with respect to the way the Department of Corrections treated us. For the most part, Blacks were given the most menial jobs on the compound. One hundred and twenty years after the Civil War, the plantation mentality was alive and well at DCI.)

The Dolphins smashed the Bears. For another year, at least, our record was safe.

Later in the month, *Time* magazine approached the Department of Corrections about taking a photograph of me for a feature called "Twenty Years of the Super Bowl." The plan was to take a current picture of a player from each winning team wearing his old jersey. The department refused to let me wear mine. If I wanted to be in the picture, I'd have to be photographed in my prisoner's outfit. You'd think that after three years they'd stop being so petty, I thought. Not surprisingly, no amount of reasoning with the department could get officials to budge. So I was photographed wearing the uniform of the Florida Department of Corrections—a "team" that expected to go undefeated from here to eternity in the games it played with inmates.

Christmas came and went with no court decision. Another cycle of corn. The one I didn't want to see.

January, 1986. More speaking engagements and more special treatment from the folks at DCI. Upon returning from a speech, I learned that a jacket that I had left in the guard's control room had been stolen. At first the administration questioned whether I even had a jacket. They finally acknowledged that the jacket had indeed

existed. Because the jacket was worth about $150, the theft consti-
tuted a felony. I wanted to call the cops.

"I wouldn't do that, Morris," prison officials told me.

"Why? Crime and punishment. Isn't that what this is all about?"

Strauss cautioned it would be unwise to make a scene. I waited
impatiently while an internal investigation was conducted. Later I
was informed that it had been determined that an officer had stolen
the jacket. He had been fired. No criminal charges were filed. I was
told I could file papers for reimbursement. I declined, indicating
that I still might take the matter to the cops. It felt nice to have the
shoe on the other foot for once.

While the people at DCI continued to give me trouble, the local
law enforcement authorities were for the most part terrific. On three
separate occasions, I was allowed to make sidetrips home from my
engagements for some R&R. My first detour took place after a speech
to a church group. Bobbie would often meet me at local engagements with a set of clothes so I could change out of prison garb and
into something more presentable. After the speech, I would change
back. This time, my two escorts—a man and a woman—told Bobbie
and me they were going to let me change at home and spend a little
time with my family. My first thought was that this was another setup, but it wasn't.

Bobbie was beaming from ear to ear when I got home. She looked
great. Hell, even the house looked great. It had been somewhat ne-
glected over the past three years, but I didn't notice that. Instead,
I saw colors, a rug, wood. What a contrast to my stark, closetlike
room at DCI.

The two other times I came home, I surprised Bobbie and the
kids. The cops would just say, "Go get your clothes at your house.
We'll be out front. You can have an hour or so." Tiffany, who was
almost 4 now, wanted to show me everything she had because she
had been a baby when I left. Maceo and Duke would show me new
dance steps they had learned. Bobbie would show me the bedroom!

February, 1986. Still no decision. We learned that one of the justices had had open heart surgery and his brethren were waiting for his
return before voting on several decisions. The wait was agonizing.

I did a public service announcement for the "Cocaine, the Big
Lie" campaign on television. I was handed a script to read. I tore it
up. Once again the message was about what drugs do to people.

Cocaine did this and that to me. Cocaine made me do this and that. Wrong. Wrong. Wrong. I refused to give a pessimistic message and I refused to transfer the blame to the drug. I wanted to give a message of life and hope, a message that we all have the ability to choose to turn our lives around. But you can't transfer responsibility to the drug anymore than you can say, "The full moon caused me to do it."

I rewrote the script to indicate that it was I who created the problems, that it was my choice to get involved, and my choice to become uninvolved and I thank God for the opportunity to be alive. "As a result of my actions, this is what happened," I said.

Many people still come up to me and tell me how moved they were by that thirty-second spot. But sadly, some people never learn. About the time I shot the spot, an inmate named Don came up to me. Don was originally from Detroit. He had been convicted of possession of cocaine with intent to distribute.

"Hey, Merc," he asked, "what do you think about the pipe?"

"What do you mean, man?"

"I mean, do you have any feelings about it?"

"Yeah," I said. "I feel like an asshole for being involved with it. Why?"

"I mean, do you ever have any yearnings for it?"

"Do I have any yearnings for the pipe? No, I don't have any yearnings. I dropped those yearnings when I got these twenty-year yearnings. Hear? They take precedent over the yearnings for the pipe. I have no desire to go back to it."

"How'd you come to that?" he asked.

"Because I'm sitting here. Because I can't see my daughter when I want to. Because I can't go home and see my wife. Because I can't lecture my boys when I want to and they need it."

Then he told me that when he had lived in Detroit a few years earlier, he and his wife had freebased all the time. One time they were freebasing in the backseat of their car while their son was driving. "Why don't you stop that shit," the son had said. So they had.

They had been off the stuff for about three months when Don said to his wife, "Honey, let's go and get ourselves about an eighth or a quarter and see if we really beat this thing." She had agreed. They had gone out, bought an ounce, cooked it up, and the whole syndrome had started again.

One night, while driving home alone after freebasing, Don had become convinced that his car was being followed. He knew what to do. He drove until he shed whomever it was tailing him. By that time he was in Florida! That's what the paranoia induced by the drug can do to you. Don had $40,000 with him when he checked into a motel in Miami. Within about five weeks, he had spent almost all of it on cocaine. Then he was arrested.

Now, some two years later, he confessed to me that he still yearned for the pipe. "I'm thinking I might go back to it when I get out," he said.

"Wait a minute," I said. "You've just described a scenario that ultimately brought you right where I am. I got the same story. But you don't know how you're gonna be when you get out?"

"No, I don't. I don't know how I'm gonna react to the stuff."

"But don't you understand? You're here because of that stuff." I said.

Don wasn't the only inmate at DCI still under the spell of cocaine. Take Jimbo. "You know, Merc, when I snort this cocaine, I feel awful smart for about twenty minutes." And then what? One night he managed to get some black-market cocaine. He snorted it in his room. Then he jacked off twice and went off and found his shank. He was cleaning the rust off of it when a guard came by. Welcome to the Flattop, Jimbo!

March, 1986. I learned that my father was dying of cancer. Like my mother he was only in his fifties. I had only recently come to grips with my mother's death. At her funeral, I had tried to hold all my emotions inside me. Her passing meant that I was now the head of the family. And it wouldn't do for the head of the family to weep or betray any sign of weakness.

I had kept those emotions bottled up for over two years. Then, in 1985, an old acquaintance named Bob Padecki visited me. Bob had been a reporter in Miami during my years with the Dolphins. Now he worked for a paper in Sacramento. He came to DCI to write an article about me. It turned out that Bob's father had recently died of cancer. The interview turned into an emotional, tear-filled session in which we each dealt with our parents' deaths. For some reason, Bob was the first person I really felt comfortable letting go with.

On hearing how sick my dad was, I started to make arrangements for another trip to Pittsburgh. Those arrangements had yet to be finalized on March 6.

I remember that day well. It was chilly. I was in my room writing letters to the kids at Homestead Junior High. I heard my name called over the loudspeaker and ignored it. I had to finish those letters. About an hour later, Dr. Crier came to my room. He told me that Strauss wanted me to call. I had no idea why Strauss had called. Somewhat irritated, I went down to Crier's office.

"We won," Strauss told me. "They've ordered a new trial." By a vote of 5–1, the court had determined that the jury should have been allowed to hear Gotbaum's testimony. Strauss's prophecy right after the conviction had been borne out. "The purpose of the government informant's conduct and communications was a proper matter to be brought before the jury and was erroneously excluded. This error cannot be considered harmless in light of the strong evidence of government involvement and persistence in this case," the court wrote.

"Praise the Lord," I told Strauss. I wasn't so much happy as I was justified. Finally the justice system agreed with me. I had to take it to the end of the line, but it agreed with me. I had always believed that as long as I got a fair trial I would win. And I had always believed that if I didn't get a fair trial I couldn't win.

I called Bobbie. She was ecstatic. When she told the kids I might be coming home soon, Tiffany said, "Oh, good, but where is Daddy gonna sleep?" She had slept in my bed with Bobbie for the last three and a half years.

All the inmates congratulated me. I think in my victory, they saw the hope for their own victories, because in prison hope is all you have.

Strauss came down to meet with me and the press. What a difference a decision makes. In the past I had met the press in a tiny room. A guard with a shotgun was always present. Now I was allowed to meet on the front steps of the prison. Security was so lax, I could have driven home with Strauss.

After meeting the media, I called my dad. He was sicker than I realized. I tried to expedite a visit to him. The Supreme Court's decision had not freed me from prison. Although the court had ordered a new trial, I was to remain at DCI until that trial took place or until some other arrangement or deal was worked out.

The State had several options: It could retry me. It could choose not to retry me and just let me go. Or it could bargain with me, agreeing not to retry me in return for something else—most likely, a plea of guilty to one of the charges. The final decision, however, would be mine. If I wanted a new trial and the opportunity for a not

I was out speaking so much, I could stay at home under the official custody of my wife instead of commuting back and forth from DCI pending either a retrial or a negotiated deal. To be honest, this was somewhat of a scam—a harmless one, but a scam nonetheless. I did have some speaking engagements, but I immediately got more so that this arrangement became a self-fulfilling prophecy.

May 8 was my last day in prison. I went out on a speaking engagement knowing I was never coming back, that I'd be living at home in Bobbie's custody until Strauss and Yoss finally did reach an agreement. This was all very hush-hush. One of the conditions of the agreement was that I didn't reveal the arrangement to the press. Even the administrators at DCI didn't know. I told them to hold my room. In fact, knowing I'd never be back, I'd call DCI every once in a while to make sure they hadn't given my room away! Small revenge.

In June Strauss and Yoss finally reached an agreement. Here is how our system of justice works: Strauss was playing in a lawyers versus judges softball game. Yoss was his coach. It was the eighth inning. The lawyers were losing. "We need a run," Yoss told Strauss. "If you knock in a run, we'll make the deal."

"If I get a hit, we'll make the deal," countered Strauss.

"If you get a hit and bring in a run, we'll make the deal," said Yoss.

Strauss doubled, knocking in a run. When the inning was over, he told Yoss, "We'll see you later tonight."

I didn't have to plead guilty to anything. I pleaded no contest to a charge of conspiracy and entered what is called a "plea of convenience." A plea of convenience is the justice system's equivalent of a draw. It reminded me of the battle between Godzilla and the Megalon Man. The two monsters faced off and hit each other with everything they had. Finally, exhausted and spent, they called it even, and that was it.

And so I was free. Free from the bondage of the cocaine lifestyle, free from the four walls which had held me for three and a half years. Thankful to God that I had been led off the path to destruction before I self-destroyed. My confidence in our system of justice—a confidence which at times had seemed pretty naive—had been justified. The system did work. The problem was it took over three years and three courts to find that out. But it was true: the higher you went, above where the biases of trial court or State Attorney's office could short-circuit the system, there were checks and balances.

Was I bitter? Not really. I would not recommend three days in jail to anyone, much less three years. But I must be honest: I needed to go through what I did to develop the character I had when I became a free man. Had I been allowed to do community service work at the beginning instead of going to jail, I don't think I would have developed that character. Maybe I had known this subconsciously when Fred Donaldson had first approached me in 1982. Maybe subconsciously I had let myself get suckered because getting caught was the only way out of that downward spiral. Maybe if I hadn't got caught in this deal where the State set me up, I would have gone on to do other deals and become someone who deserved to be behind bars. Or maybe I would have ended up in a 55-gallon drum like Frank Crawford. I don't know. I do know that the irony was that I was pushed down the hill unfairly by a bullying State. But I needed to be pushed down that hill. Thank God I had the strength to get up.

You don't go to prison to become a better person, but you have the option to become one. I did. I grew up. Unfortunately, I know a lot of young and older men in jail under circumstances not that different from mine who don't have the strength or support systems to climb the hill.

CHAPTER 15

FREE

After entering my plea of convenience, I thought it might be convenient to take a few months off to get reacquainted with my family and to try and straighten up a tangled web of financial affairs. We were still in debt up to our ears, still in danger of losing the house.

The best-laid plans often go astray. One week after I had entered the plea, Len Bias, the promising young basketball player from the University of Maryland, died of a cocaine overdose the day after he was drafted by the Boston Celtics. Much of the media proclaimed that this would be the tragedy that would persuade our children not to get involved with drugs, but within a week, Don Rogers, the promising young football player for the Cleveland Browns, was also dead from an overdose—this on the eve of his wedding.

Having already developed a philosophy or approach to this subject, I was very much in demand to appear on the national talk shows, all of which became instantly interested in the "drug problem." At the same time, the requests for me to speak to young people poured in. I realized that for the time being at least, this would be my calling.

When I speak to young people, I never tell them what to do, just as I didn't tell Maceo what to do when he had trouble. I tell them they have choices and that they must get as much information as possible so they can make an educated choice based on wisdom— wisdom being something you practice. The "Say 'No!' to Drugs" campaign is fine for kids Tiffany's age. But it's not enough for kids in high school or college. They have to know why they should say, "No!" I prefer a different emphasis, "Say 'Yes!' to Life."

I tell these kids that sometimes it is difficult for them to get accurate information because the government leaders are themselves misinformed. I have heard President and Mrs. Reagan speak about the "drug problem" and the "alcohol problem." Their intentions may be honorable, but I believe their information isn't always accurate and their approach is counterproductive. First, alcohol *is* a drug. It is the Number 1 killer among drugs, involved in some 90,000 deaths a year. Cocaine, on the other hand, is involved in less than 1000. Are those 90,000 lives no less important, no less noteworthy than the cocaine deaths? My point is we have to put alcohol and cocaine on the same page.

Equally disturbing is that phrase they use along with almost everybody else: "drug problem." Only when this is viewed as a *people problem* will we begin to make true progress. When I speak, I ask three volunteers from the audience to join me on stage. I ask one to pretend he has an ounce of pure cocaine, the second to pretend he has a fifth of Jack Daniel's, and the third to pretend he's holding a ballpeen hammer. Then I ask the first to snort, the second to drink, and the third to hit himself on the head. Again and again and again. I point out that if each volunteer did this all night long, each would wake up in about the same shape in the morning. And each would have abused himself. Put any of those objects on a table and they are harmless. They can't do anything until a person—you—pick them up.

If you do pick them up, I tell them, you may survive. But there's a chance you may not. It's like the lottery. Maybe the odds of dying are 1000 to 1, maybe the odds are 1,000,000 to 1. But there's still the 1. Len Bias was that 1; so was Don Rogers. If you're going to play this lottery, you owe it to yourself to know what's involved. And the only way you can know that is by listening to someone who has already played. How can a young person be expected to base his or her behavior on the fact that someone like Ronald or Nancy Reagan tells them to say, "No."

"I have been there," I say. "If Len Bias took six times the lethal dose, I've probably had 6000 times the lethal dose. I'm here to tell you about it." And I do tell them about it—the danger and stupidity of the life-style in general and of my life in particular until I got wise. "You can't blame cocaine for the deaths of Len Bias and Don Rogers," I say. And perhaps some in the audience think I'm being unkind to the memory of these young men. But the fact is that these athletes chose to adopt a life-style, chose to play the lottery. Don Rogers overdosed in late June. You're supposed to be in shape for the up-coming football season by then, have your mind on your profession. What was he thinking when he took that cocaine? By all accounts, he was a fine person. The Cleveland Browns, under my friend Paul Warfield, had one of the best in-house programs for counseling play-ers. But you can't be in the house all the time. There were two Don Rogerses. The Don Rogers of the day and the Don Rogers of the night. We all have those two personalities in us. We have to recog-nize that and make the decision who's in control.

"You have a choice," I say. "None of us makes the right decision every time. We can go all the way back to the first man on Earth to see that. Adam screwed things up for all of us by making a bad de-cision! But the wonder of the world is that even if you make the wrong choice, you have the power to change course and make the right choice. You learn from your mistakes and move forward. But you have to acknowledge that they are your mistakes."

I often end my talk by telling those in my audience that if you break a bone in your body, something miraculous happens. If the bone is set properly and the cast is put on properly, when the heal-ing process is done, the place of the break, once your most vulner-able spot, will now be the strongest. So it is with the human spirit. I have never felt stronger.

One of the places I spoke during the summer of 1986 was my un-cle's church in Farrell, Pennsylvania. After I finished, I went back to Ben Avon. I stopped my car and took a walk in the Hollow. It was the first time I had the freedom to do this in years. I soon found myself on Spruce Street, where I'd grown up.

Trees now stand where the house I lived in once stood. It was never rebuilt after the fire in 1964. The trees are already large, well on their way to adulthood. The lot looks so small. It is hard to imag-ine my grandfather's house, which always seemed to have so much room. The street seems narrower, and the nearby creek where I once played is no more.

This is new, I said to myself. Then I thought about it. No, this is the way it was long ago. Nature has returned. The more things change the more they remain the same.

Before I left the Hollow, I stopped by and saw Doss Russell. When I was a little kid, Doss had worked on my grandfather's trucks.

Now, thirty years later, he was still working on a truck. This time it belonged to my uncle. Doss thought I was a bad kid because I'd do things like open his lunchbox and take a bite out of his sandwich and then put it back in. One day when I was in sixth grade, I asked him for a ride to the baseball field. He said he was too busy.

"Okay, then I'm just gonna run on the hood of your truck," I said. And I did, giving it an awful pounding.

Doss came after me. I took off. I can still picture the scene: I'm laughing at Doss and looking back and he's still coming. All of a sudden I turn around and it's not so funny, because I've gone about half a mile and he's still behind me. What am I going to do? I run through the woods to my mom's place and hide under the porch. I watch Doss while he runs by.

Doss later said that he ran all the way to the river trying to find me, and that if he had found me he would have torn up my rear end.

For most of my life I was able to run just fast enough, shift gears just quick enough, so that my rear end didn't get torn up. It was kind of fun, but there was always that breathless question: *What am I going to do?*

Only by slowing down did I find the answer.